planning & management in
DISTANCE
EDUCATION

Open and Distance Learning Series

Series Editor: Fred Lockwood

Activities in Self-Instructional Texts, Fred Lockwood
Assessing Open and Distance Learners, Chris Morgan and Meg O'Reilly
Changing University Teaching, Terry Evans and Daryl Nation
The Costs and Economies of Open and Distance Learning, Greville Rumble
Delivering Digitally, Alistair Inglis, Peter Ling and Vera Joosten
Delivering Learning on the Net, Martin Weller
The Design and Production of Self-Instructional Materials, Fred Lockwood
Developing Innovation in Online Learning, Maggie McPherson and Miguel Baptista
    Nunes (forthcoming)
E-Moderating, Gilly Salmon
Exploring Open and Distance Learning, Derek Rowntree
Flexible Learning in a Digital World, Betty Collis and Jef Moonen
Improving Your Students' Learning, Alistair Morgan
Innovation in Open and Distance Learning, Fred Lockwood and Anne Gooley
Integrated E-Learning, Vim Jochems, Jeroen van Merriënboer and Rob Koper
    (forthcoming)
Key Terms and Issues in Open and Distance Learning, Barbara Hodgson
The Knowledge Web: Learning and Collaborating on the Net, Marc Eisenstadt and Tom
    Vincent
Learning and Teaching in Distance Education, Otto Peters
Learning and Teaching with Technology, Som Naidu
Making Materials-Based Learning Work, Derek Rowntree
Managing Open Systems, Richard Freedman
Mega-Universities and Knowledge Media, John S Daniel
Objectives, Competencies and Learning Outcomes, Reginald F Melton
Open and Distance Learning: Case Studies from Education, Industry and Commerce,
    Stephen Brown
Open and Flexible Learning in Vocational Education and Training, Judith Calder and Ann
    McCollum
The Open Classroom, Jo Bradley
Planning and Management in Distance Education, Santosh Panda
Preparing Materials for Open, Distance and Flexible Learning, Derek Rowntree
Programme Evaluation and Quality, Judith Calder
Reforming Open and Distance Learning, Terry Evans and Daryl Nation
Reusing Online Resources, Allison Littlejohn
Student Retention in Online, Open and Distance Learning, Ormond Simpson
Supporting Students in Open and Distance Learning, Ormond Simpson
Teaching with Audio in Open and Distance Learning, Derek Rowntree
Teaching Through Projects, Jane Henry
Towards More Effective Open and Distance Learning, Perc Marland
Understanding Learners in Open and Distance Education, Terry Evans
Using Communications Media In Open and Flexible Learning, Robin Mason
The Virtual University, Steve Ryan, Bernard Scott, Howard Freeman and Daxa Patel

open &
flexible
learning
series

planning & management in
DISTANCE EDUCATION

edited by
santosh panda

KOGAN
PAGE

London and Sterling, VA

First published in Great Britain and the United States in 2003 by Kogan Page Limited

120 Pentonville Road
London N1 9JN
UK
www.kogan-page.co.uk

22883 Quicksilver Drive
Sterling VA 20166-2012
USA

© Individual contributors, 2003

ISBN 0 7494 4037 6 (hardback)
    0 7494 4068 6 (paperback)

British Library Cataloguing-in-Publication Data

A CIP record for this book is available from the British Library.

Library of Congress Cataloging-in-Publication Data

Planning and management in open and distance education / edited by
Santosh Panda.
    p. cm.
Includes index.
  ISBN 0-7494-4037-6 -- ISBN 0-7494-4068-6 (pbk.)
  1. Distance education--Planning. 2. Distance
education--Administration. 3. Open learning. I. Panda, Santosh K.
(Santosh Kumar), 1959-
  LC5803.P5P53 2003
  371.3'5--dc21

                              2003010390

Typeset by JS Typesetting Ltd, Wellingborough, Northants
Printed and bound in Great Britain by Clays Ltd, St Ives plc

Contents

Contributors

Professor Dele Braimoh, Professor of Adult Education, Institute of Extra Mural Studies, National University of Lesotho, P.O. Roma 180, Lesotho, Southern Africa. E-mail: ad.braimoh@nul.ls.

Professor Sohanvir Chaudhary, Director, School of Education, Indira Gandhi National Open University, New Delhi 110068, India. E-mail: chaudhary38@ hotmail.com.

Professor Terry Evans, Associate Dean of Research, School of Education, Deakin University, Geelong, Victoria 3217, Australia. E-mail: tevans@deakin.edu.au.

Dr Glen Farrell, Former President, British Columbia Open University; presently Senior Consultant, The Commonwealth of Learning, Suite 600-1285, West Broadway, Vancouver, British Columbia, Canada V6H 3X8. E-mail: glenf@col.org.

Professor Suresh Garg, Pro-Vice Chancellor, Indira Gandhi National Open University, New Delhi 110068, India. E-mail: scgarg@ignou.ac.in.

Professor Charlotte Gunawardena, Organizational Learning & Instructional Technology Program, College of Education, University of New Mexico, Albuquerque NM 87131, USA. E-mail: lani@unm.edu.

Professor James Hall, Chancellor, Antioch University, 150 E, South College, Yellow Springs, Ohio 45387-1697, USA. E-mail: jhall@antioch.edu.

Professor Margaret Haughey, Associate Chair, Educational Policy Studies, University of Alberta, Edmonton, AB, Canada T6G 2G5. E-mail: margaret.haughey @ualberta.ca.

Dr Alistair Inglis, Senior Lecturer, Learning Technology Services, Bundoora Campus, RMIT University, Plenty Road, Bundoora, Victoria 3083, Australia. E-mail: alistair.inglis@rmit.edu.au.

Professor Olugbemiro Jegede, Director General, The National Open University of Nigeria, 15/16 Ahmadu Bello Way, Victoria Island, Lagos, Nigeria. E-mail: jegede@oliv1.ouhk.edu.hk.

Professor David Kember, Centre for Learning Enhancement and Research (CLEAR), Chinese University of Hong Kong, Room 427 Esther Lee Bldg, Shatin, Hong Kong. E-mail: david.kember@cuhk.edu.hk.

Professor A R Khan, School of Social Sciences, Indira Gandhi National Open University, New Delhi 110068, India. E-mail: arkhan@ignou.ac.in.

Deborah LaPointe, Albuquerque TVI, 525, Buena Vista SE, Albuquerque NM 87106, USA. E-mail: debla@tvi.edu.

Professor Colin Latchem, Distance Education Consultant, 11, Reeve Street, Swanbourne, Perth 6010, Western Australia. E-mail: clatchem@iinet.net.au.

Professor Fred Lockwood, Director, Learning and Teaching Unit, Manchester Metropolitan University, All Saints, Manchester M15 6BH, UK; and Series Editor of Kogan Page OFL Series. E-mail: f.g.lockwood@mmu.ac.uk.

Dr Don Olcott, Jr, Executive Director, Division of Extended Studies, Western Oregon University, 345 N. Monmouth Avenue, Monmouth OR 97361, USA. E-mail: olcottd@wou.edu.

Professor Santosh Panda, Professor of Distance Education (and former Director), Staff Training & Research Institute of Distance Education, Indira Gandhi National Open University, New Delhi 110068, India. Currently Fulbright Visiting Scholar, OLIT, College of Education, University of New Mexico, Albuquerque, NM 87131, USA. E-mail: spanda@ignou.ac.in.

Professor Ross Paul, President, University of Windsor, 401, Sunset Avenue, Windsor, Canada N9B 3P4. E-mail: rpaul@uwindsor.ca.

Dr Hilary Perraton, Senior Research Fellow (and former Director), International Research Foundation for Open Learning, The Michael Young Centre, Purbeck Road, Cambridge CB2 2PG, UK. E-mail: hperraton@irfol.ac.uk.

Professor Otto Peters, former Vice-Chancellor, and presently Professor Emeritus, ZIFF, FernUniversitat, D–58084, Hagen, Germany. E–mail: otto.peters@ fernuni-hagen-de.

Professor K B Powar, former Secretary General, Association of Indian Universities, 16 Kotla Marg, New Delhi 110002, India. E–mail: aiu@del2.vsnl.net.in.

Professor Greville Rumble, Professor of Distance Education Management, The Open University, Walton Hall, Milton Keynes MK7 6AA, UK. E–mail: g.rumble@ open.ac.uk.

Dr Douglas Shale, Academic Analyst, Office of Institutional Analysis, University of Calgary, 1617 Education Tower, 2500 University Drive N.W., Calgary, Alberta, Canada T2N 1N4. E–mail: dgshale@ucalgary.ca.

Alan Tait, Sub-Dean, Faculty of Education and Language Studies, The Open University, Milton Keynes MK7 6AA, UK. E–mail: a.w.tait@open.ac.uk.

Professor Mary Thorpe, Director, Institute of Educational Technology, The Open University, Walton Hall, Milton Keynes MK7 6AA, UK E–mail: m.s.thorpe@ open.ac.uk.

Professor Graham Webb, Director, Centre for Higher Education Quality, Monash University, Clayton, Victoria 3168, Australia. E–mail: graham.webb@ adm.monash.au.

Acknowledgements

I would like to express my sincere thanks to all the contributing authors for their valuable contributions. It has been a pleasure and a significant learning experience in working with you all and in going through the long process it has taken. My apologies that the book took so long to appear. I am also grateful to Professor Fred Lockwood, the Series Editor, for his constructive editorial suggestions, and to Stephen Jones, Commissioning Editor, Kogan Page for his valuable guidance and suggestions and for seeing it through the process of publication.

Series editor's foreword

There are times when I wonder if I have been promoted to a 'level of incompetence'; times when I realize that the bulk of my experience is as a practitioner in distance education and training and not as a planner or manager. However, I find myself in that role and acknowledge that successful management and planning are vital not only for the day-to-day functioning of the university, provision of quality materials and support to our learners etc, but to its future development if not survival. This is increasing the case as Communications and Information Technology is embraced, the division between conventional and distance teaching institutions is blurred, and pressure increases to expand provision.

I also acknowledge that practitioners need more than a mere awareness of planning and management issues if they are to make a significant contribution to learning and teaching – just as planners and managers need more than an awareness of the issues facing teachers and trainers. *Planning and Management in Distance Education*, edited by Santosh Panda, is a book that can span the needs of this wide audience at a time of major change. It brings together acknowledged experts in distance education and training; almost a *Who's Who* in the field. They provide both an overview and an insight for those of us involved in not only the planning and management of distance education and training but also its reform. The book will be invaluable to all involved in learning and teaching – regardless of our particular contributions – since it identifies the important areas of:

● distance education policy;
● core organizational planning;
● organizational leadership, management and change;
● staff development, research and development;

- financial and human resources;
- multimedia material development and delivery;
- learner support, networked learning and telelearning;
- programme evaluation, quality assurance and accreditation;
- internationalization of distance education and training.

Planning and Management in Distance Education offers critical reflections on these important core and functional areas of distance education; it draws upon and presents the evidence needed to inform decision making. The ideas and arguments presented are applicable to both large and small organizations – those that wish to transform themselves so as to meet changing needs. The book does not identify simple solutions, rather it recognizes that like most endeavours planning and management is an ongoing challenge that needs to respond to local, national and international pressures. However, I believe the book will be invaluable to educators and trainers in general, and distance educators and training managers in particular; to those in colleges and universities, training and business enterprises, government and non-government organizations. It will help you reform your distance education and training provision.

Fred Lockwood
Manchester, April 2003

Introduction

Santosh Panda

The context

Distance education has evolved from traditional correspondence courses to online and networked learning – from the first generation to the fifth (Taylor, 2001, 2002). Today, a host of educational and training forms and processes are presented under the banner term 'distance education'. It is practised through single-mode distance teaching institutions, distance learning/educational development/flexible learning centres of higher and further education institutions and business enterprises, individual courses of academic programmes and schools of studies, and national/regional/international alliances and consortia. Not all mega universities (Daniel, 1996) are single mode, and as Harry and Perraton (1999) remark, both open universities and dual-mode institutions are now major players. Distance education today includes an array of organizational and delivery structures. This book takes the position that distance, open, flexible, distributed and online learning are all major forms in the emerging scenario, and therefore addresses planning and management issues and imperatives within this framework.

The management of distance education operations is as much the responsibility of organizational leaders as that of the staff, with staff responsibility varying across organizational types. For example, in the single-mode institutions the course team may include dozens of staff; an electronically delivered course in a conventional university may involve one staff member who is responsible for all aspects of production and delivery. Irrespective of variations in provision and organization, both government and institutional policies on placing distance education at either centre stage or the periphery of educational planning are heavily influencing distance education practices and reforms.

At the organizational level, distance education and distance training represent two elements in the significant growth of this form of non-classroom communication. For the first, it is worth quoting Sir John Daniel: 'Those of us who work in universities have a personal commitment to the academic mode of thinking' (Daniel, 2002: 2). The second is more mundane, practical and application-oriented (see Berge, 1998). In a recent work, Keegan (2000: i) 'challenges the premise that distance training lacks academic excellence and status'. Many distance education institutions experience conflict between the two within their educational provisions, while it has been smooth sailing for business enterprises and private concerns. An organizational development chart represents reforms in both these elements, and a significant management challenge is to maintain a judicious balance between the two in their theory, practice and research.

Further, the dividing line between distance learning and campus-based learning is gradually blurring, and convergence through the mechanisms of ICT, networked flexible learning and credit transfer/accreditation is taking place (see Tait and Mills, 1999). Shale (1989) appropriately remarks that the 'morphological differences' between distance education and mainstream education are 'falling', with technology facilitating simulation of the usual exchange between teacher and student. Moreover, as the need to shift from independent learning to collaborative learning models and practitioner networks increases (Thorpe, 2002), the shift in planning and management imperatives is inevitable. In the process, the variety of forms and models of distance education have become interwoven into a cohesive whole providing variety and flexibility to learners. Daniel appropriately remarked that 'the study of distance learning is rather like overcooked spaghetti; once you pull on one strand you find you are engaged with the whole tangled mass' (2002: 3). It is a core management challenge to address the dynamics of flexibility and the tangled mass. Also, it is imperative to successfully plan and manage the organization and its operations such that it not only initiates reform and change, but also sustains them for organizational growth and greater learner satisfaction.

Through the critical analyses, presentations and reflections of the various authors of the chapters, this book attempts to address the following questions:

- How to work towards a progressive, changing and effective management of distance education?
- How to initiate and sustain management reforms contributing to overall reforms in education and training?
- How to help integrate ICT in teaching–learning, faculty role and holistic organization-wide development?
- How to balance external pressure and internal organic changes to the advantage of the organization?
- And, overall, what does it take for effective networking, collaboration, accreditation and internationalization of distance education?

Though the book does not purport to provide ready-made answers to the above questions, it brings together the experiences and critical reflections of internationally acclaimed distance educators, leaders and researchers and aids our own critical reflection. It is acknowledged that those involved in policy planning, management and implementation of distance, flexible and online learning constantly face the challenges of established educational discourse, rapid developments in ICT and pressures of innovation and change. While the traditional distance education institutions and programmes are struggling hard to cope with the demand for access and quality, those heavily using the new educational technologies are hard pressed to reform, change and converge. The critical discussions in various chapters of the book will contribute to the debate between academic demands and management imperatives, and the question of how to initiate and sustain reforms and manage change.

Outlines of the book

The 22 chapters explore a wide range of areas and issues confronting the management of distance education and training. The chapters are organized into six parts or thematic areas associated with planning and management. The major outcomes, from the critical analysis and reflection by the authors of the chapters, suggest the following:

Distance education, openness and flexibility

In the only chapter in Part 1 of the book, Peters reviews several models of distance education in respect of their openness and flexibility. It may be noted that over the years distance education theorization has come a long way: from independent learning (Charles Wedemeyer), through the industrialized system of education (Otto Peters), guided didactic conversation (Borje Holmberg), two-way communication (John Baath), transactional distance (Michel Moore), human support (David Sewart) and communication loop (Garrison and Shale), to the constructivist interaction analysis model of online learning (Gunawardena, Lowe and Anderson). From a planning and management perspective, a variety of models – ranging from the hierarchical model of a business-oriented form of distance education (Rumble, 1986) to the collaborative model of online learning – coexist today and are visible in many organizational planning and management initiatives. Peters argues that despite the use of different terminology (with varying openness and flexibility), distance education still represents the umbrella concept in the field, and concludes that 'distance education is by far the most open and flexible form of learning and teaching'.

Policy and planning

The three chapters in Part 2 of the book focus on policy and planning issues in education in general, and distance education in particular, in developed and developing countries. Governments in many parts of the world have undertaken policy initiatives in the field of adult and lifelong learning such that these opportunities are provided with openness and flexibility. However, such initiatives are not value-free, and also they are heavily influenced by the general national educational policy and planning (see Harry, 1999; Perraton and Lentell, 2003). In Chapter 2, Evans contends that distance education (especially when offered virtually) is heavily influenced by government policies *per se* and by educational policy and policy changes within education. He regards a 'developed country' as a 'compulsively developing' one ('one that values change and progress as central to its national character'), and notes that most of these countries are using distance education in the process of developing into developed nations. In terms of access and equity, distance education is facing the challenges of competition and globalization, and in doing so is meeting their economic and business needs. The trend has been towards reduced government funding and increases in cost recovery from students. He suggests that those involved in distance education need to be critically aware of policy and development issues within their organization, and contribute to it through their active participation. In the developing countries, remarks Perraton in Chapter 3, while commissions appointed by international agencies for national and institutional developments may bring international experience to the projects, most of the national policies are framed by national governments themselves. In this context, non-governmental organizations (NGOs) have played a crucial role in shaping distance education, especially at the level of open schooling and open basic education. While open universities have benefited from considerable autonomy, dual-mode distance education institutions have been subservient to the policy of the conventional university. It is suggested that governments would be advised to determine the comparative merits and limitations of single-mode and dual-mode distance education before undertaking policy initiatives.

In Chapter 4, Haughey extends the debate further, and observes that postsecondary institutions, the world over, are facing competition from other providers of distance education and training. She notes that under such pressure they may join the broader alliance of a knowledge system. Failure to respond to this challenge, she argues, may result in corporate bodies entering the postsecondary sector and instituting corporate practices of outsourcing, collaboration, privatization, re-engineering and restructuring, rather than collegial decision making, scholarship and research. She suggests that while strategic planning has remained the main focus of postsecondary institutions, contextual planning models have been advocated that ensure the repositioning and reshaping of the institution in the changing environment. Contextual planning involving the faculty in delineating change, provision of opportunities to initiate experimentation based on existing faculty and organizational strengths, and addressing organizational and academic cultures are important prerequisites to successful planning and management. In other words, it calls for *holistic planning* for open and flexible learning.

Institutional management

The five chapters in Part 3 are concerned with various aspects of institutional management: decision making, leadership, academic development, R&D, and resources management. Managing people forms a major part of institutional management, and though a separate chapter is not devoted to this area, this is reflected in the discussions in many of the chapters of this section (for further discussion, see Panda, 2003). Powar in Chapter 5 notes that at the institutional level, management of (distance) education requires 'detailed planning, timely and appropriate decision making, and skilful coordination of activities'. The chief executive of the institution needs to have not only a holistic view, detailed knowledge about the institutional operation, and willingness for innovation and change, but also the ability to take timely decisions, and to facilitate, motivate and communicate effectively. Distance education institutions generally have a bureaucratic model for decision making for the central administration, and a collegial model for the schools and academic units. The most successful strategy for managing such institutions is likely to include: delegation of authority, monitoring the progress, assessment of performance, and coordination of activities of various subsystems through a strong Management Information System (MIS). In an earlier work, Paul (1990) had noted that leadership with a clear vision, openness, integrity, humanism and humour can make a difference in the institution, and how things are done is as important as what is done (also see Hall, 1998). In Chapter 6, he extends the discussion further and notes that though new providers of education and training, for-profit universities and corporate providers are making an impact in distance education, it is likely that postsecondary education and training will continue to be provided by existing institutions, and in doing so they will need to adapt to new information technologies. In an institution, there will always be some who resist change – especially technology-oriented change – and, therefore, the real challenge for managers and leaders is to encourage debate and choose from the newly emerging alternatives. Involvement of staff and customers in the change process may slow down the pace of development, but it ensures real and permanent change, and involvement of almost all in the change process. To make a difference and for successful management, he suggests, institutions require strong, open and sensitive leadership.

Alongside institutional/organizational change, academic development and human resource development assume considerable importance in that people need the understanding and skills to facilitate an effective learning experiences for the students. Webb, in Chapter 7, notes that reflective practice in the cycle of course planning, development, delivery, evaluation and quality assurance is central to these activities. They need to be seen as integrated rather than separate tasks undertaken by separate groups of people, and staff development strategies should reflect this situation. Institutions need to have a staff development policy which acknowledges the dual importance of teaching and research and which aligns university policy, academic development and flexible learning. He contends that staff who have developed understanding and skills through the process of 'grounding in the discourse of university teaching and learning' will be in a better position to adapt to flexible learning and new educational technology.

A crucial aspect of a management function is research and development (R&D) and its integration into decision making for the organization as a whole and for its subsystems. In Chapter 8, Kember posits that the process of organizational placement and management of R&D is challenged in times of expansion and when concerns for quality increase. Management of R&D in the form of action research is one of the frameworks available to an organization for such an exercise, with the sole intention of improving the practice. The framework developed by Kember and colleagues over a considerable period of time illustrates that Action Learning may be helpful in the management of 'a wide variety of research and development initiatives' in open and flexible learning. Many colleagues involved in distance teaching do not possess the skills needed to undertake research to inform practice. There is, therefore, a need to provide research training at various levels, and thus contribute to their continuing professional development (Panda, 2000). While the dynamics of course teams are well researched, the dynamics of collaborative research teams and collaborative online research need further investigation.

The management of resources, especially financial resources, is of prime importance irrespective of where money comes from – public subsidy, student fees, self-generation, and so on. Rumble, in Chapter 9, argues that in order to maintain cost-effectiveness, institutions have to ensure a judicious balance between the expected student population, the media choice and media mix, life of the course and its revision. He argues that within a given budget and educational need, frequent course revision is possible provided the rate of academic productivity is high. He suggests that 'productivity rates are a useful way of modelling and controlling the size of the establishment'. In this context, the dual-mode distance education systems may have the cost advantages since the same materials can be used for both on-campus and external (distance) students. For example, the cost of course development can be reduced by using single-author courses, wraparound courses etc. He further suggests that irrespective of the strategies adopted for achieving economy of scale, distance teaching institutions need to have a balance between cost and customer satisfaction; emphasis on the latter leads to greater investment on training, and vice versa.

Process management

Part 4 of the book contains seven chapters that explore the management of various processes concerning distance teaching–learning. Readers may like to study a previous work by Freeman (1997) on this area. The process of distance education may include such subsystems as material design and development, their production and distribution, operations management, learner support services, telelearning and networked learning, assessment and evaluation. The structure and organization of these subsystems differ considerably for different models of distance education and training described in Chapter 1. Central to teaching and learning at a distance is instructional design and development. Successful management can contribute to a reduction in the cost and time required for their production and can increase the quality of learning materials. In Chapter 10, Jegede explains that instructional systems design functions within a systems approach, an approach that brings together learning theories associated with the design of printed materials, audio and video programmes, audio, video and computer conferencing, interactive multimedia, online learning, and face-to-face interaction. Crucial decision making involves a selection from behaviourist, cognitivist and constructivist models in order to enable both the tutor/trainer and the learner to engage actively in the process and achieve the instructional goals. Successful instructional design is a result of successful management of its various phases of design, development, implementation and evaluation. Effective management of the team involved in the process is via the various bodies that are involved in approving the process and assuring the quality of the products. In Chapter 11, Panda and Chaudhary analyse the management of media selection, instructional design for electronic media, and their production and distribution. The analysis also includes issues concerning media comparison, the need for instructional design, academic–producer conflict, in-house production versus outsourcing, collaborative production and training.

Certain policy decisions concern the production and distribution of materials; in particular, in-house production versus outsourcing, availability of infrastructure, and staff role in the process of production and distribution. Khan and Garg in Chapter 12 discuss various aspects of production and distribution of print materials, and related operations management. The authors' view is that while designing and copy editing can be carried out in-house, printing is cheaper if outsourced, provided there is strict benchmarking for quality production. With the availability of newer production technologies, they argue that contract printing is economical, requires less storage space, and that developments in computer software facilitate successful inventory management. As a word of caution, the authors point out that the mechanism of distribution of materials should be such that the onus does not fall on the students.

As a part of instructional delivery, learner support is assuming critical importance and is an area of debate in most distance teaching institutions. In Chapter 13, Tait emphasizes that less autocratic and more learner-centred approaches to learner support (either as individuals or as groups) is emerging as more note is taken of student needs. In a decentralized and more localized system of learner support, a large part of services remain invisible to those charged with management responsibilities and, therefore, management of both staff and systems assumes greater importance. Tait contends that while the bottom-up approach involves induction and mentoring, the top-down approach should involve a managerial responsibility of commitment, trust and conversation. This requires professional management of systems where those with academic responsibilities work in close collaboration with those with management responsibilities for learner support services.

Information and communication technology (ICT) plays an important role in the provision of both individualized and networked learning. Inglis in Chapter 14 analyses the planning and management issues concerning networked learning at both institutional and project level. At the institutional level the planning responsibility for ICT may lie with a central unit, and the individual teacher or course team concerned may be responsible for course-level planning and management. Irrespective of technology enthusiasts or idea leaders, organization-wide adoption of networked learning necessitates an organizational change strategy. This may be read in relation to the suggestions for holistic planning discussed by Haughey in Chapter 4. Inglis further suggests that at the institutional level, the best way to introduce sustainable networked learning successfully is to examine existing organization strengths; fund projects based on individual interests and strengths, and those that contribute to organizational strategic goals; and build the results with incremental project funding and organization-wide implementation. At the project level, the planning of learning activities, student induction, and management of online group interaction require significant change in the approach of the course teams for networked learning. Planners and managers may like to consider a decentralized version of ICT-based learning, ie a multi-purpose and community-based telelearning centre. In many parts of the globe, such centres address the issue of provision of education and training for disadvantaged communities, irrespective of their location either in remote rural areas or in metropolises (Latchem and Walker, 2001). In Chapter 15, Latchem describes three kinds of telelearning centres – single-client, multi-client and multipurpose community telelearning centres or telecottages. Access, training, accommodation, networks, management and evaluation are important considerations in establishing such centres. For their successful management, it is essential that there is a commitment by those involved, a realistic proposition on what exactly they can achieve and what they can't, significant continuing training for those involved, proactive management, continuous evaluation and R&D, and working towards their sustainability.

Learner assessment is the last theme of the section on process management. Such assessment, especially in contexts of distance learning using interactive technologies, is a challenging task. Gunawardena and LaPointe critically analyse in Chapter 16 various assessment types and techniques in technology-based learning contexts. They point out that, increasingly, there is a convergence of the assessment methods of Web-based and interactive television courses. Irrespective of the type of educational method used, learner assessment must be based upon theories of learning with pre-stipulated learning outcomes. Ideally, there should be some flexibility in assessment strategies, in choice of assignments, and in the nature of feedback provided. It is important to ensure student anonymity, speed of feedback, and trust of students in the instructor. Both online and proctored testing are useful in distance education, though the latter is increasingly being replaced by online discussion, peer review and e-portfolios. They further posit that course design and assessment based on contructivist theories are difficult to handle; and, besides questionnaire and interview, it is useful to consider the interaction analysis model based on social construction for judging the quality of the content of the message (see Gunawardena, Lowe and Anderson, 1997; Gunawardena, 2001).

Quality assurance and accreditation

The five chapters in Part 5 deal with programme evaluation, performance indicators, quality assurance, and accreditation. In Chapter 17, Braimoh draws attention to the fact that programme evaluation, at periodic intervals, is essential to monitor the process of programme delivery and learners' reactions to various components of the education or training programme. Similarly, external institutional evaluation through independent experts, or internally assembled teams, can aid institutional decision making. It can provide valuable information to funding agencies, to learners, to the general public, and can be judged against the mission of the institution. Thorpe in Chapter 18 suggests that wide variations exist in quality control/assurance mechanisms across institutions associated with distance teaching and learning, as also the agencies responsible for quality assessment and accreditation. In some, the agencies responsible for formal education and training regulate distance education, in others there are designated agencies for the purpose; some regulate courses while others do so for institutions. She points out that preference of approach is often dependent on national practices and cultures; invariably, the university providers face more regulatory checks than the private providers, and external control leads to the tendency of compliance to external assessors rather than adherence to quality practice. Irrespective of the locus of control, institutions themselves should develop quality assurance systems and procedures that are acceptable to them and the stakeholders. Shale in Chapter 19 explores a related aspect, performance indicators, which he says are useful tools for institutional and subsystems evaluation, but they need to be used carefully, with clarity in intention of their application and utilization. He argues that performance measures are not value-free and that system-level performance indicators are influenced by wider societal contexts and policy decisions – standardization across the board has been possible, as in the case of the Quality Assurance Agency in the UK. In this context Shale and Gomes (1998), in an earlier comparative study on a conventional and an open university in Canada, found wide variations and concluded that standardization of performance indicators is not possible in the face of inter-institutional differences and uniqueness of institutions. Performance measurement and quality assessment are inextricably related to each other. For deriving practical benefits from such exercises, Shale suggests the following: those involved in measurement, assessment and suggesting implications should have knowledge about the processes of the units assessed; indicators should be kept to a minimum; should relate to organization's missions; should be as simple as possible; and there should be clear specification as to who will use them and for what.

As noted earlier, considerable blurring of on-campus (residential) and distance (outreach) education and technology is taking place, and therefore accreditation has assumed all the more importance to assure quality. In Chapter 20, Olcott, Jr analyses accreditation of distance education in the United States, and much of what he has argued is applicable to other institutions across the globe. He points out that the expansion of Internet technologies has furthered the process of more institutions adopting distance education. Institutional and programme accreditation are common to most of the institutions of higher learning – these are granted for a few years to be renewed continually after rigorous assessment. The criteria usually used for assessment and accreditation include: clearly stated institutional mission and purposes; effective organization of resources, meeting its educational and other purposes, and continuous meeting of this criterion; demonstration of integrity in practices and relationships. He suggests that while multimedia-based distance education has been easy to deal with, programmes delivered digitally require new guidelines and protocols for evaluation and accreditation; and draws attention to the 'integrated convergent model' which recognizes not only the need for similar outcomes irrespective of differences in means, but also the differences in the processes of various educational delivery modes. The regulatory agencies, therefore, need to re-examine their policies, criteria and procedures of programme and institutional assessment and accreditation.

Hall, in Chapter 21, extends the discussion on convergence and accreditation. He notes that although the two established institutional frameworks for exclusive distance education delivery – the mega universities like UKOU and IGNOU, and the new organizations like the Western Governors University in the western United States – are still growing, a new framework with convergence between distance education and campus-based education towards networked education emerged during the latter part of the 20th century. The networking capabilities of new information and communication technologies have blurred the distinctiveness of campus-based and distance education. This development has allowed some new players to challenge the existing organizations. These new ventures, including corporate training and the conventional continuing education programmes of universities, have adopted the assembly-line industrial course model of the 1960s to deliver materials at a relatively low cost. The problem is not the speed of delivery, rather the vision of what constitutes good and effective education and training. Hall contends that the national and trans-regional accrediting bodies find it difficult to address the issue of accreditation of the new and emerging networked learning, and suggests three guiding principles – curriculum/full programme, learner support, and learner assessment and programme evaluation – that provide the framework to address the issue. To meet the international standard of quality of education with fuller accommodation of national, cultural and institutional expectations, he proposes that there is a need for a global body to examine not only the validity of national or regional accreditation, but more importantly that of the networked learning through transnational and trans-regional institutions and organizations.

Internationalization

Part 6 contains only one chapter by Farrell as a conclusion to the book. Farrell echoes similar sentiments that the advent of the WWW and the growing power and expansion of ICT have brought more international collaboration and greater convergence between conventional and distance education and training. There are both push and pull factors to globalization and convergence. ICT, desire for change, extending overseas campuses, partnership, internationalization of curricula, and the need for a global presence act as push factors to globalization. The pull factors include: lack of access to ICT, strong belief in teacher-directed classroom learning, governmental regulatory constraints, cultural invasion, attitudinal constraints of teachers, the problem of credit transfer and accreditation, and lack of skills to use and benefit from the new ways of learning from ICT. Farrell suggests that one has to make a judicious balance between these factors to the organization's advantage. Further, the very dynamic nature of the international context of distance education opens up mechanisms and possibilities for its quality planning and management.

In conclusion

This book is as much for policymakers and institutional leaders as for practitioners of distance education, working in either single-mode or dual-mode institutions, or open and flexible learning centres/programmes, or even in industrial houses and business organizations. The experiences, analyses and discussions contained in this book should equip the planners, managers and staff engaged in traditional distance education to plan carefully for reform to a more modern distance education. It should also aid those engaged in the newer generations of distance education to manage successfully those reforms and innovations in education and training taking place in this digital world. This collection may also induce management-driven reforms. The analyses and presentations, it is hoped, should lead to further critical reflection on the theory, practice and research for successful management of this form of 21st-century learning (Latchem and Hanna, 2001).

References

Berge, Z L (1998) 'Conceptual frameworks in distance training and education', in *Distance Training: How innovative organizations are using technology to maximize learning and meet business objectives*, eds D A Schreiber and Z L Berge, Jossey-Bass, San Francisco

Daniel, J (1996) *Mega-Universities and Knowledge Media: Technology strategies for higher education*, Kogan Page, London

Daniel, J (2002) 'Why research distance learning?', conference keynote address at the 2nd Conference of Research in Distance and Adult Learning in Asia 2002, 5–7 June, Hong Kong

Freeman, R (1997) *Managing Open Systems*, Kogan Page (and the OU), London

Gunawardena, C N (2001) 'Reflections on evaluating online learning and teaching', in *Using Learning Technologies: International perspectives on practice*, eds E J Berge and M Haughey, RoutledgeFalmer, London and New York

Gunawardena, C N, Lowe, C A and Anderson, T (1997) Analysis of a global online debate and the development of an interaction analysis model for examining social construction of knowledge in computer conferencing, *Journal of Educational Computing Research,* **17** (4), pp 397–431

Hall, J (1998) Leadership in accreditation and networked learning, *The American Journal of Distance Education,* **12** (2), pp 5–15

Harry, K (ed) (1999) *Higher Education Through Open and Distance Learning,* Routledge, London

Harry, K and Perraton, H (1999) 'Open and distance learning for the new society', in *Higher Education Through Open and Distance Learning,* ed K Harry, Routledge, London

Keegan, D (2000) *Distance Training: Taking stock at a time of change,* RoutledgeFalmer, London

Latchem, C and Hanna, D (2001) *Leadership for 21st Century Learning: Global perspectives from educational innovators,* Kogan Page, London

Latchem, C and Walker, D (eds) (2001) *Telecentres,* The Commonwealth of Learning, Vancouver

Panda, S (2000) 'Mentoring, rewards and incentives in research as professional development', sub-theme keynote address at the 1st Conference of Research in Distance and Adult Learning in Asia 2000, 21–24 June, Hong Kong

Panda, S (2003) 'People: Staffing, development and management', in *Policy for Open and Distance Learning,* eds H Perraton and H Lentell, RoutledgeFalmer, London and New York (forthcoming)

Paul, R (1990) *Open Learning and Open Management: Leadership and integrity in distance education,* Kogan Page and Nichols Publishing, London and New York

Perraton, H and Lentell, H (eds) (2003) *Policy for Open and Distance Learning,* RoutledgeFalmer, London and New York (forthcoming)

Rumble, G (1986) *The Planning and Management of Distance Education,* Croom Helm, London and Sydney

Shale, D (1989) 'Foreword', in *Understanding Distance Education,* D R Garrison, Routledge, London and New York

Shale, D and Gomes, J (1998) Performance indicators and university distance education providers, *Journal of Distance Education,* **13** (1), pp 1–20

Tait, A and Mills, R (eds) (1999) *The Convergence of Distance and Conventional Education: Patterns of flexibility for the individual learner,* RoutledgeFalmer, London and New York

Taylor, J C (2001) 5th generation distance education, *DETYA's Higher Education Series, Report No. 40.* http://www.detya.gov.au/highered/hes.htm

Taylor, J C (2002) 'Teaching and learning online: The workers, the lurkers and the shirkers', sub-theme keynote address at the 2nd Conference of Research in Distance and Adult Learning in Asia 2002, 5–7 June, Hong Kong

Thorpe, M (2002) 'From independent learning to collaborative learning', in *Distributed Learning: Social and cultural approaches to practice,* eds M R Lea and K Nicoll, RoutledgeFalmer (and the OU), London and New York

Part 1

Open and distance education models

Chapter 1

Models of open and flexible learning in distance education

Otto Peters

Introduction

Experts in charge of planning, developing and managing open and flexible learning realize very soon that there are inherent similarities and relations between the concepts of *distance education* and *open* and *flexible* learning. Therefore, it might be appropriate to begin with a description and analysis of some of the more typical models of this particular form of learning and teaching.

Before this can be done, let me describe what is meant by using the terms *open learning* and *flexible learning* in a *pedagogical* context in order to avoid misunderstandings.

Open learning

In the literature 'distance education' is often linked with concepts of 'open learning'. The impulse for this came from the establishment of the British *Open University*. Its phenomenal success prepared the ground for the rapid acceptance of this particular designation, and we can see that these two terms have fused with one another. In spite of this, express reference will be made here to openness as this concept has now assumed new importance: 'Put simply, educational institutions are being required to 'open' their structures and practices to the needs of (...) new students, their employers and governments in ways that are shaking the traditions of these institutions' (Evans and Nation, 1996: 3). How can this openness be achieved?

- Firstly, by extending access to universities to all who are able to study by removing traditional educational barriers.
- Secondly, by designing learning programmes which are open in the sense that they are not completely developed and determined beforehand in an empirical-scientific manner, but are 'open' for unforeseen developments in the build-up of individual ability to act (ie open curriculum).
- Finally, this type of learning does not take place in relatively enclosed institutions that are defined (and often paralysed) by bureaucratic organization, but is to be opened up by keeping to the practices of everyday life.

The special term 'open university' can also be explained by the motives that policymakers have when they establish these institutions. Governments, for instance, may find and support them as they hope to establish less expensive systems of education, to relieve overcrowded traditional universities, to establish new groups of students in the realm of higher education, to realize and support lifelong learning activities, to enable more people to take part in cultural life and to further the democratization of society (Boom and Schlusmans, 1989: 6).

These requirements are not, as might be thought, utopian, because technological progress enables us to fulfil them. The virtual learning environments and the World Wide Web (WWW) also add important new dimensions to the term 'open learning'.

Flexible learning

Recently, the term *flexible learning* has often been associated with 'distance learning' or with 'distance and open learning'. It has become almost proverbial to speak of 'open and flexible learning' when, in fact, the reference is to distance education.

Experienced distance educators might be surprised at the great emphasis presently laid on this obvious feature of distance education. What do we refer to when we speak of *flexible* learning? *Theoretically* speaking, there are several dimensions of flexibility. Institutions, administrative structures, curricula, and strategies and methods of learning can be either rigid and fixed or flexible and easily adaptable. While the very *goals* of education are reconsidered and quite often changed, we are in a transformation process even with regard to our values. *In practice*, however, flexibility has assumed special meanings which have become instrumental in university reform: 1) there is a focus on increased accessibility – universities should be flexible enough to attract and enrol more and new groups of students; 2) there is a focus on the individual learners in order to allow them to learn when they want, what they want and how they want.

The urge to make our universities more flexible has increased so considerably that one can speak of a campaign towards more flexibility at many universities. In Australia, for instance, Murdoch University has developed a master plan for a 'flexible teaching and learning policy' in which students should be allowed 'to have a choice of teaching modes, assessment modes, accesses to teachers, peers and learning resources which suit the style and circumstances of the learner' (Atkinson, 1997). A similar plan has been developed by Macquarie University, in which individual need is met by providing for choices offered in time and place of study, learning styles, access, pace, progression and learning pathways (Gosper, 2000: 1).

The gap between theory and practice

This description shows clearly that the two terms partly overlap, especially in the area of access and teaching methods. Flexibility seems to be the more powerful and influential concept. The subsequent analysis of eight models of distance education will show an inherent relationship between the terms *openness, flexibility* and *distance education*. Seemingly, these terms are in the process of merging. However, if we have a closer look we can see that the current juxtaposition of the terms distance, open and flexible learning does not always mirror the reality of distance education. Keegan (1993: 290) rejected the equation of other terms with 'distance education' with the sarcastic argument that 'open and flexible learning systems seldom work with distance education and distance education systems are often neither flexible nor open'. However, it is useful to continue emphasizing these two dimensions of distance education, as they signify new perspectives of pedagogical reform.

Models of distance education – in retrospect

Consciously or subconsciously, every distance teaching institution is shaped by certain theoretical notions and ideas about distance education. These can be transformed into concepts. If these concepts are strong and convincing they can be developed into models. The models we are going to refer to are pragmatic ones in the sense that they can be tested in experiments as well as in practice. But not only this, most of these models have already become fixed or even 'petrified' as they are institutionalized; so, references will be made also to corresponding institutions. The focus will be on their different conceptual underpinnings and their inherent qualities of openness and flexibility.

Historically speaking, it might be useful to select and refer to the:

- examination preparation model;
- correspondence education model;
- group distance education model;
- learner-centred model;
- multiple mass media model.

The origin: examination preparation model

A prerequisite for this model is a university that limits itself to holding examinations and conferring degrees. This means that it *abstains* from teaching. Consequently, the students study recommended literature, and discuss it with partners and others. The institution provides information about the examination regulations and special reading lists.

This model was designed and institutionalized when the University of London was founded in 1825 for the benefit of those who could not afford to be enrolled at the University of Oxford or Cambridge or who could not attend these universities as they lived far away in the colonies of the British Empire. Presently, this model is still practised by the University College of the University of London, and also by the Regents of the University of New York. Recently the Chinese government has established a great system of self-study after the same model. More than 1.8 million people, most of them adults working for a living, have already earned their diplomas and certificates in this way (Song, 1999: 1).

This model is not discussed in the literature, and many practitioners even deny that it exists. However, it plays a certain role in distance education, and has the following characteristics:

- *Openness*: It is remarkable that this early model of distance education was developed in order to facilitate and open *access* to university for those who could not afford to study at Oxford or Cambridge. It was designed to provide education for the class between the 'mechanics' and the 'enormously rich' (Encyclopedia Britannica, 1999). This humanitarian goal mirrors liberal ideas of the time about education in a very distinct way. We recognize an early approach to what was to be labelled much later 'equality of opportunity' in the second half of the 20th century.
- *Flexibility*: In a way it is possible to maintain that this model of learning and teaching is the most flexible one we can imagine. There are no fixed curricula, no fixed times and places, no fixed age groups, no fixed external impediments. It is entirely up to the students themselves to adapt the learning process to their very personal needs and circumstances.
- *Features characteristic of distance education*: This form of self-study is *distance education* as the students learn at their homes and follow the reading instructions given by the faculty of the university where they are enrolled and where they take their examination. It is an early form of distributed learning. If we refer to the beginnings of the University of London, it was a model of distance education for several additional reasons. For the first time, higher education was to be extended to adults who had to work for a living; the university was opened for new and alternative groups of students; university reform was suggested as it required independent and autonomous learning in its purest form; and the protagonists of this model were motivated by liberal, religious and humanitarian ideas. Seen under these aspects, this model can certainly be considered a forerunner of the next model developed 10 to 20 years later.

A longstanding convention: correspondence education model

This model is more than 150 years old and is the most widely used, as it was and still is applied in many countries all over the world. It is, so to speak, the 'examination preparation model' plus the teaching activities of presenting written or printed teaching texts, assignments, correction of assignments, regular and ad hoc correspondence between teachers and students, and examinations.

Correspondence schools and correspondence colleges started using this model in the second part of the 19th century; for example, Toussiant-Langenscheid in Germany, Denmark's Brevskole, Wolsey Hall in England, Ecole Universelle in France, and PBNA in the Netherlands. The University of South Africa used this model in the second part of the last century. In principle, it is also used to a great extent by distance teaching universities, even by those that take pride in informing us that they are 'multiple media and open universities'. Everyone who wants to understand fully the methodology of teaching at a distance today must study this first-generation model of distance education, which reveals the following characteristics:

- *Openness*: This model provides access to all those who cannot attend regular schools for quite a number of reasons. Schools patterned after this model tend to enrol as many of these students as possible – be it for humanitarian or profit reasons or both. In particular, they are open to adults.
- *Flexibility*: By using the technology of the time – printing press, railways, post – the correspondence schools developed a new system of teaching and learning mainly based on written instruction with a certain degree of inter-activity by means of self-tests and tutor-marked assignments. This is the reason for its incomparable flexibility. Not only could the students decide when, where, for how long and how they wished to engage in their studies, the system could also offer tuition to students living in many different places.
- *Features characteristic of distance education*: This is a model of fully developed distance education. Its structure is patterned on principles of the industrialization process (division of labour, use of technical means, quality control etc). Important elements are: planning, design, production and delivery of pre-prepared and mass-produced printed courses, and written communication between teacher and taught. The model is used for commercial as well as humanitarian reasons. Quite often it helps to overcome emergency situations (eg in times of war and depression).

We should see and acknowledge that over a period of 150 years this model has developed a considerable number of specific pedagogical approaches typical of distance education, which are not necessary and hence unknown in other forms of academic instruction. Even today's virtual instruction has its roots in these correspondence schools and colleges. There is the danger that the special pedagogical strategy of the correspondence model will be neglected, ignored or even shunned by enthusiastic technology protagonists and will eventually be lost.

The Asian version: group distance education model

This model is similar to the multiple mass media model as radio and television are used permanently as teaching media. However, lectures through these media are not received by individual students but rather by *groups* of students attending obligatory classes where they follow the explanations of an instructor, discuss what they have heard and watched on TV, do their assignments and take their tests. No special printed teaching materials are developed and distributed, with the exception of the customary 'lecture notes'. Because of the continuous use of radio and television (cable and satellite) and recently also of videoconferencing systems, this is also a model of the open university.

The Chinese Central Radio and Television University (CRTVU) is the most prominent example of this model. But similar models are also used by the University of the Air in Japan and by the Korean National Open University. They display the following characteristics:

- *Openness*: This model is open not only to degree students, but also to secondary school students, school leavers, and 'independent viewers and listeners'. This type of open university leaps over the boundaries of traditional educational institutions, and opens its door to great numbers of students.
- *Flexibility*: The flexibility of this model is impressive as it overcomes the limitations of time and space, age, occupations, subjects, and traditional institutions. It is astounding how easily techniques of distance education and regular face-to-face instruction can be combined.
- *Features characteristic of distance education*: This is a model of distance education based on the transmission of lectures by radio and television, listened to by registered students in classes. However, the methods of teaching and learning are not adapted to the special needs of the distant learners. This means that we can interpret this model as a form of technically extended campus-based education.

In quest of autonomy: learner-centred model of distance education

This model envisages a college with the mission to reach out to students who choose to pursue college learning through *alternative means* to campus-based instruction with fixed schedule, place, programme and structure. These students study independently at home, meeting the assigned tutor individually about once a month for counselling, mentoring and guidance. The students' discussion with their tutors on their plan, what and how to study are written down in form of a *contract* between the student, the tutor and the university (contract learning). The students study the agreed-upon literature, sometimes attend a course in local educational institutions, and use learning resources offered by their college, eg small group meetings, online courses, learning packages and special courses for distance learning.

The Empire State College of the State University of New York has the longest and most successful experience with this particular model. Within 26 years, it had produced 30,000 graduates by teaching students in this way. The model shows the following characteristics:

- *Openness*: The college has been successful in providing access to higher education from the State of New York to those (including minority learners, persons with handicaps, and senior citizens) who are under-served by campus-based universities.
- *Flexibility*: Because of the departure from the traditional academic structure (like set courses, time, residential obligations) and because of its alternative techniques and learning modes, this college shows the highest degree of flexibility in many ways, including the adaptation of the learning–teaching system to the learning needs of the *individual* students, and cooperation with many educational institutions everywhere in the state in order to provide additional support for the students.
- *Features characteristic of distance education:* This model is a further example of learning at a distance as the students live and learn in locations distributed all over the state. While special programmes are developed for lifelong learning, it also contributes to continuing education and university reform, and to the creation of a *learner-centred* approach and *autonomous self-regulated learners*. The Empire State College can serve as a structural model for the emerging 'virtual university'.

A big thrust forward: multiple mass media model

This model was developed in the 1970s and 1980s. Roughly speaking, it combines elements of the earlier two models, namely 'independent self-study' and 'correspondence education', along with use of radio and television and provision of learner support at study centres. The necessary faculty has to be employed; many specialists in instructional design, media pedagogy, testing and institutional research have to be integrated into the academic structure; and cooperation with radio and television corporations has to be ensured. This model became very important as it helped to shape the structure of many distance teaching universities all over the world. The British Open University has developed this particular model of multiple (mass) media distance education to perfection. More than 40 open universities all over the world have been influenced by its outstanding achievements. This model shows the following characteristics:

- *Openness*: Providing access for new groups of students is an important feature of this model. It was used for initiating and supporting the movement towards 'open learning' and 'open universities'. These universities are open because of not only the use of broadcasts for wider coverage, but also the provision of opportunity to those without any formal university entrance qualification.

- *Flexibility*: The singular flexibility of this model can be traced back to the fact that the flexibility of the correspondence education model is increased still further by the possibility of using the five distinct instructional elements with different weightage and in different ways: printed course material (plus audiovisuals), set books, radio broadcasts, TV broadcasts and various activities in study centres. Secondly, it can be adapted to new target groups who have to be trained in a special way and only for a limited period of time. Thirdly, the distance universities lend themselves much more easily to continuing higher education than traditional universities, at least in Europe. Fourthly, operation with industry is easily planned and implemented in order to provide academic continuing education to employees.
- *Features characteristic of distance education:* This model is significant because it has developed 'features' and 'standards' which can only be found in distance education:
  - It is carefully planned and developed by professional designers.
  - In principle, the best scholars available in the given discipline are engaged in order to produce really first-rate and authentic material (quality courses), and with low prices.
  - Cooperation between subject matter specialist, instructional designers and media experts is required for the development of courses and learning packages.
  - The product – the teaching – is objectified and mass-produced.
  - Technical media (eg radio, television, computers) are used in order to target the greatest possible number of students.
  - The instruction is developed to cater to the disadvantaged: the protagonists of this model are motivated by an abiding concern for equity of educational access.

Current models of distance education

Two recently developed models include: 1) the network-based distance education model; and 2) the technologically extended classroom teaching model.

Digitization: network-based distance education model

This model is currently emerging as part of the digital transformation of our world. It makes it possible to work in a 'digitized learning environment' that profits from a combination and integration of several advanced information and communication technologies, the most important ones being computer technology, multimedia technology, network technology and telecommunication technologies. Students may work offline or online; use CD-ROMs with distance education courses in hypertext form, data-file courses or just databases; and may take part in virtual seminars, workshops, tutorial and counselling meetings, tuition or project groups, and chat with their fellow students.

The greatest pedagogical advantage, however, is that the students are challenged to develop new forms of learning by 'searching for, finding, acquiring, evaluating, judging, changing, storing, managing and retrieving information' when needed. They have the chance to learn by discovery and to be introduced to learning by doing research and becoming autonomous and self-regulated learners. Models of this kind have already been realized at the UK Open University, Maryland University College, SUNY Empire State College, FernUniversität and the Universitat Oberta de Catalunya (Spain), to name just a few. The following characterize this model:

- *Openness*: The degree of openness is highest here, and the distance teaching system can be used by students everywhere in the world at the same time.
- *Flexibility*: The most impressive and convincing form of flexibility can be observed in the pedagogical structure. This is due to the emergence of at least 10 virtual learning spaces, each of which challenges the student to develop and practise distinct learning behaviours: learning by searching for information, with multimedia, increased communication, collaboration, documentation, exploration, representing learning results, simulation and in virtual reality (Peters, 2000a). By combining two, three or more of these learning behaviours an unprecedented flexibility can be achieved. Bates (1997: 183) has indicated a further dimension of this format of distance education, namely the move 'to more and more flexible interfaces between the human user and the computer, through voice command, voice recognition, pointing and hand gestures to control programming, and artificial intelligence to enable computers to better interpret human commands and requirements'.

The impact of communications industry: technologically extended classroom teaching model

This model was developed in the United States and has become important there over the past 10 years. We should like to include it here as it also runs under the label of 'distance education'. And, in fact, this model provides instruction at a distance: one teacher usually teaches a college class (or a studio class), and his or her presentation or instruction is transmitted to two or more other classes by cable or satellite TV or with the help of a videoconference system. Keegan (1995: 108) refers to this form of teleconferencing as 'face-to-face teaching at a distance'. Rubin (1997), who is familiar with distance education systems within the Maryland University College and outside the US, admits the disadvantages of this model. It is not as efficient as is normally expected of distance teaching because the size of the classes that can be connected, and their number, is limited. The students in the connected classrooms often have the feeling that they are alienated from the main classroom.

Owing to the commercial success of companies like Sony, Picture Tel, Vtel and others, most universities in the United States and elsewhere in the world are at present using their teleconferencing technologies. Experiments with this model are being conducted, and it is also integrated into regular courses at many universities.

The following represent the characteristics of this model:

- *Openness*: This system is not open as classes are accessible for regular students only, and, in addition, the number of students is limited.
- *Flexibility*: The teaching behaviour is not as flexible as in the models described so far, as the teachers have to use strategies of classroom teaching. However, there are possibilities for transcultural, global initiatives when two or three classes on different continents are instructed at the same time.
- *Features characteristic of distance education*: Since this model does not extend the accessibility of higher learning, does not reach out especially to adults with vocational and family obligations, does not contribute to the establishment and support of lifelong education, does not offer a second chance to work towards a degree and is not an industrialized form of education, it cannot be considered a form of distance education. However, its worldwide diffusion cannot be ignored. There are thousands of successful and pedagogically useful projects not because they merely imitate classroom teaching as exactly as possible, but because they deliberately carry out individual and particular functions in overall systems of regular classroom teaching or of distance teaching.

Prospective model of distance education: virtual distance teaching university

If the required software and hardware are developed further it will be possible to combine digital learning and teaching techniques with one another, and to integrate them. Students can then develop more learning activities in their digital learning environments than in any other learning location. Not only will they use interactive multimedia distance teaching courses on CD-ROM, on the Internet or via ISDN, and talk to other students and attend virtual seminars and practical courses in the form of teleconferencing, they will also profit from other functions, such as those offered by a university on a real campus. Here we can see the initial outlines of a 'virtual university'. The example of the FernUniversität can be used to illustrate these efforts. Its 'user interface' (Schlageter, 1996: 13) provides students with the following services:

- *teaching*: access to virtual teaching;
- *research*: both teachers and students can acquire information on the state of research in individual fields;
- *topnews*: contains information found on noticeboards;
- *shop*: above all, for buying additional learning and teaching programmes;
- *cafeteria*: for informal contacts with other students, not necessarily to do with studies;
- *office*: carries out all administrative procedures;
- *library*: for ordering books, examining digital books and magazines, bibliographical research;

- *information*: answers all questions on the FernUniversität, shows the university to potential students, ie virtual visitors, and is used for talks with tutors.

So far, there is not yet a real virtual distance teaching university. The term 'virtual university' is quite often used when a single course or part of a teaching programme is presented via the Internet by campus-based universities for experimental reasons or as part of the regular teaching. The following characteristics explain this prospective model:

- *Openness*: This model provides for at least as much openness as the model of open universities, although virtual distance teaching universities will not be accessible to students who cannot afford the required digitized learning environment.
- *Flexibility*: The virtual distance teaching university will probably become the most flexible institution of higher learning ever seen in the history of education. This will be true with regard to the administrative and academic structure, but especially to the pedagogical structure. 'Teaching' can be innovated by combining and integrating activities in at least seven new teaching spaces, namely the virtual spaces for collaboration, exploration, documentation, multimedia, digitized word processing, simulation, and virtual reality. 'Learning' will undergo far-reaching changes because of rapid access to desired information, teaching programmes with different origins, and simplified access to joint talks, or group discussions. A radically new situation has been created in which everything that is required for reading, looking up, studying, training, revising, constructing, arranging, informing, saving and reminding, browsing and navigating is available at the click of a mouse (Peters, 2000b).
- *Features characteristic of distance education*: 1) educational mission: adults in full employment will remain the main target group; scientific continuing education will be a substantial part of the teaching programme; lifelong learning will remain the overall goal; 2) pedagogical goal: the tradition of carefully and professionally developed pre-prepared courses will be sustained, continued and enhanced by multimedia and hypertext methodology; the already consolidated support systems will be further developed by the integration of many forms of digitized communication and face-to-face dialogues and academic discourses with teachers, tutors, mentors and fellow students in study centres; the system of self-test assignments will be developed by a sophisticated system of computerized self-evaluation; 3) humanitarian goal: the virtual distance teaching university will expand access to postsecondary education and thus contribute to greater equality of educational opportunity; it will be especially successful in catering for groups of persons who are under-served in higher education. Daniel (1998: 11) has scornfully rejected those virtual universities that deliver course materials only by saying: 'Much of the commercial hype and hope about distance learning is based on a very unidirectional conception of instruction, where teaching is mainly presentation and learning is merely absorption.'

Conclusion

Reconsidering the institutions which stand for the eight models of teaching at a distance, it is easy to see that seven of them show the following marked features:

- They have been pioneers in making education available to persons who are normally denied it. They *facilitate* and *open* secondary and higher education for 'alternative' learners. Broadcast distance education is even open for great numbers of interested learners who are not enrolled in the respective institutions.
- They have always been extraordinarily *responsive* to new *technical information and communication media*. This started 160 years ago when correspondence education relied on the printing press, the railway and the penny post (De Volder, 1996). Later, every advance in printing techniques and transportation means was used. In the 1970s radio, television, the first computers, a variety of audiovisual media, telephone and the facilities of study centres became constitutive elements of the teaching–learning process. And, at present, this development is culminating as digitization permeates the pedagogical structure of distance education.
- These models of distance education have also been very *responsive to changes in society*. The first ones were developed as a reaction to the process of industrialization. Times of war or depression usually caused increased scope and activity of correspondence colleges. Net-based distance education and the envisaged virtual distance university stand as models of transition in a time of rapid and far-reaching societal changes.

The focus of this chapter has been on 'openness' and 'flexibility'. The relevance of these two qualities increased and became more differentiated from model to model, partly due to the new technical media employed. Three dimensions mainly catch the eye: *access* was increasingly extended and facilitated, *autonomous learning* developed from model to model, and *individualized curriculum structures* could be provided to more and more students. They individualized mass learning. If we evaluate these dimensions together with the great number of pedagogical formats and approaches referred to, we are justified in maintaining that 'distance education is by far the most open and flexible form of learning and teaching'. It is no small wonder that it is at a premium these days.

This comprehensive analysis of the models provides a strong background to the analysis of policies of open distance education in the developed and developing worlds, and the management of its various aspects, within the chapters that follow.

References

Atkinson, R (1997) 'Flexible teaching and learning', Discussion Paper, Teaching and Learning Centre, Murdoch University, Australia

Bates, A W (1997) The impact of technological change on open and distance education, *Distance Education*, **18** (1), pp 93–109

Boom, W J G van den and Schlusmans, K H L A (1989) *The Didactics of Open Education*, The Open Universiteit, Herleen

Daniel, J (1998) In *American Association for Higher Education: AAHE Bulletin*, May, Washington, DC

De Volder, M (ed) (1996) *From Penny Post to Information Super-Highway: Open and distance learning in close-up*, Acco, Leuven

Evans, T and Nation, D (1996) *Opening Education: Policies and practices from open and distance education*, Routledge, London

Gosper, M (2000) 'Flexible learning – educational services', Working Paper, Macquarie University

Keegan, D (1995) 'Teaching and learning by satellite in a virtual European classroom', in *Open and Distance Learning Today*, ed F Lockwood, Routledge, London

Keegan, D (1993) 'Introduction' to Chapter 4 of K Harry, *Distance Education: New perspectives*, eds J Magnus and D Keegan, Routledge, London

Peters, O (2000a) 'A pedagogical model for virtual learning spaces', paper presented to the Conference *Distance learning – global trends*, The Danish Institute for Educational Training of Vocational Teachers, Copenhagen

Peters, O (2000b) 'The transformation of the university into an institution of independent learning', in *Changing University Teaching: Reflections on creating educational technologies*, eds T Evans and D Nation, Kogan Page, London

Rubin, E (1997) Intervention in the 'Virtual Seminar Professional Development in Distance Education', 30 Jan, in *Final Report and Documentation of the Virtual Seminar for Professional Development in Distance Education*, eds U Bernath and E Rubin, pp 161–62, 1999, A Project within the AT&T Global Distance Learning Initiative sponsored by the AT&T Foundation and the International Council for Open and Distance Education Education (ICDE), BIS-Verlag, Oldenburg

Schlageter, G (1996) Gespräch mit Professor Dr. Gunter Schlageter, in *Contacte*, Fernuniversität, Hagen, pp 10–13

Song, Y (1999) 'Das Selbststudium als Vorbereitung auf eine akademische Prüfung', in *Grundlagen der Weiterbildung: Praxishilfen*, Chapter 9, Neuwied: Luchterhand, pp 1–14

Part 2

Policy and planning

Chapter 2

Policy and planning in the developed countries: coping with compulsive development cultures

Terry Evans

Introduction

The term 'developed countries' seems to be somewhat misleading. It conveys a sense that the 'developing' is over and that the countries in question have reached a stage of being developed: there is no further room to improve. However, a fundamental characteristic of a 'developed country' is that it is speeding simultaneously along various lines of development. Hence, what might have seemed a well-developed feature of a country in the past – be it a policy, programme, building or organization – is ripped apart, cast aside, torn asunder or demolished and something new planned, implemented, erected or restructured, all in the name of progress. Sometimes, on reflection, the feature demolished will be subsequently sadly missed, regrets will be held and maybe something of the past will be restored – usually with various modernizations; but for purists only the original will do.

It could be said that developed countries are anything but developed, and that they are, on present indications at least, never likely to be so. Their national cultures

value change and progress to such an extent that even the most daunting circumstances and the most worrying precursors of change are spoken of as 'challenges'
and 'opportunities'. If systems are running well, or products are proving satisfactory,
then it is seen that there is a danger of complacency setting in. Systems must always
be re-evaluated and enhanced; products improved and repackaged. Therefore, the
so-called 'developed country' is actually a *compulsively developing* one; one that values
change and progress as central to its national culture.

This chapter contextualizes current management issues in open and distance
education in developed nations in terms of their broad changes. Its argument is that
to a greater or lesser degree, everyone involved in open and distance education, not
just those involved in management, needs to understand the broad issues that
surround the policy and planning of their organization. In effect, everyone has a
responsibility towards the good management of their work and their institution. A
critical awareness of the policy and development issues surrounding and pervading
open and distance education institutions, it is argued, helps people to perform
actively within their roles and to contribute constructively to their own career
management and to the shape and performance of their organizations. The
arguments here are particularly focused on the tertiary education sector, although
some reference is made to primary and secondary education.

National policy and local effects

Policy and planning are important features of the compulsive development cultures
in developed nations. At the national level, policies are the tools used by governments to enact the changes they wish to make. Often, the policies are shaped by
appeals to mass interests, or by trade-offs and compromises to keep party factions
or potential coalition partners 'on side'. Therefore, the normal conditions of
democratic developed nations require the regular and frequent development of
policies, which are often tinged with political expediency and glossed by elec-
tioneering. The majority of these policies will not be implemented, as the losing
parties either scrap them or file them away, maybe to be brushed-off and re-jigged
for another election. Those policies that survive rest within the government
(parties) and are implemented as best they can within the practical circumstances
of the day.

These national policies are further complicated if the government rules over a
federal system with state or provincial governments. In these circumstances there
is usually, except in clear cases of national interest such as defence or foreign policy,
some sharing of responsibilities between national and state or provincial governments. In the case of education, federal nations such as Australia, Canada and the
United States of America have different mixes of responsibilities for education. In
Australia, for example, the state and territory governments have major responsibility for schooling and the training sector of tertiary education, whereas higher
education (universities) is the principal responsibility of the national government

(although most universities are established under state acts of parliament). In Canada and the United States, the responsibilities for most aspects of education rest with the state or provincial governments. However, these lines of demarcation are not clear, uncrossed and unchanging. In particular, national governments control budget allocations to the states and provinces and will often use these as 'levers' to influence educational policy and practice in the states or provinces.

Educational policy is one of the major areas in which national governments seek to make policy. Typically, along with health and defence, education is one of the largest consumers of government expenditure. Education is also often seen as the means to implement change within the nation. Therefore, national governments, by 'pulling the policy levers', can effect and affect change to matters such as school retention rates, second language policy, science and technology education, the education of minorities, etc. There is a sense in which national governments see themselves (rather than the taxpayers) as the paymasters who can use their control over budgets to shape educational policy throughout the nation.

Another feature of contemporary developed nations is that educational policy and its implementation has to be interpreted against the backdrop of other government policies. There are both direct and indirect reasons for this. In terms of direct influences, it is often the case that governments use education as a means to address, ameliorate or solve other non-educational problems. Typically these are of a social, welfare or economic kind, but they may also range into almost any sphere of government influence, such as transport, the environment or defence. The indirect effects on education are perhaps best exemplified in the past decade or more by the intense pressures in developed nations for governments to reduce spending and to balance their budgets. These policy 'drivers' require that education, along with most other government funded or supported ventures, 'does more with less'. There are other examples too, such as government policies on telecommunications and information technology, which can have profound, if unintended, consequences for education.

Therefore, wise and forward-thinking managers and other members of educational organizations need to be aware of the broad policy environment in which their institution is placed, not just the educational policy environment itself, although they might well expect to focus their most critical scrutiny here. In some respects, the 'traditional' face-to-face educational institutions may be slightly less vulnerable to the vicissitudes of government policies, in that they tend to be more firmly fixed in both the landscape and the community. That is, their buildings and grounds, and the people who attend from the locality, provide a powerful, if conservative, consistency to their operations. An open or distance education organization, especially those that operate in the most locally disconnected, flexible and virtual ways, arguably is more vulnerable to changes in government policy. However, what is their vulnerability in one sense is also their strength in another, in that they can exploit their more fluid circumstances to respond to demands, needs and opportunities with more freedom than their traditional counterparts.

Open and distance education policy contexts

Educational history over the past century shows that national governments – and state or provincial governments where they apply – have often directed the origin, nature, structures and practices of distance education in developed nations. Indeed, for nations such as Australia, Canada and New Zealand, distance education has been an important element of them *developing* into *developed nations*. Drawing on the argument above, it is necessary to recognize that, although these policies may seem to be about open and distance education, in effect they are really about what open and distance education can contribute to fixing, solving or addressing some social, economic or educational problem or need (see, for example, Haughey and Roberts, 1996; Jakupec, 1996; Johnson, 1996). Governments are rarely intrinsically interested in open and distance education structures, institutions and practices themselves, rather it is the costs, control and outcomes of open and distance education that are their concern. This is not intended as a negative criticism, but rather it is intended to emphasize that those who have to deal with government policy and relate it to their own institutions and contexts need to be mindful of the overt (and sometimes covert) purposes of governments. It is arguable that this is generally the case for most educational policy, but it is particularly the case for open and distance education. In effect, this is because open and distance education are forms of education that have been developed to deal with aspects of educational provision that 'traditional' face-to-face institutions find difficult or impossible to provide.

For about two decades from the mid-1960s, an important policy element of open and distance education provision in developed nations was focused on the access and equity concerns of governments. A paradigm case is the policy debate leading to the establishment of the Open University in the United Kingdom (UK) and the 'open access' provisions of its operations (Harris, 1987). Here the government of the day was keen to provide a 'university of the air' as a 'second chance' for people who missed, or were unable to access, university education earlier in their lives. The problem in the UK was not one of developing a new nation in a geographically large and demographically dispersed nation, such as Australia and Canada. Rather it was more a matter of access and equity. However, even in Australia and Canada, which already had well-established distance education provision from school through to university levels, the access and equity imperatives emerged. Existing institutions, together with the new and emerging providers (Moodie and Nation, 1993), were required to address the access and equity outcomes of their policies and practices. From the late 1980s, these requirements have receded, although not disappeared, as developed nation governments have become more concerned with economic and business prosperity, international competitiveness and the globalization of financial, media and telecommunications structures. The interplay between these elements, together with the global influence of transnational corporations, has led to significant challenges not only to education (Evans, 1997; Marginson, 1997), but also to the nature of government in developed nations (Giddens, 1994, 1998).

Contemporary open and distance education in developed nations at the higher/ tertiary education level is now increasingly being expected to provide courses that serve the needs of commerce, industry and the professions, especially at the postgraduate levels. These courses are often related to the 'compulsive development cultures' in developed nations. Changes are expected to be of such a significance, and of such a pace, as to mean that not only do people have to learn how to cope with, and plan for, change in their organizations and work, but also they may expect to have to change their occupations during their working lifetimes. For both of these situations it is assumed that further (even 'lifelong') education is required and that institutions need to adapt their provision to suit these ever-changing needs.

This provision is no longer likely to be funded by government, although there may be some subsidy. The prevailing trend is towards charging fees for professional development courses and for those fees to constitute at least full cost recovery, if not a profit. The advantages of forms of distance education in the provision of such courses, especially when enhanced by Internet-based educational technology, have created some sizeable 'markets' for the institutions involved. Institutions relying on face-to-face provision in the form of scheduled classes, even if during the evening and/or at weekends, find it difficult to compete with the distance education providers who can make their courses and support systems available 'anytime, anywhere'. They can also do so on a much larger scale than the 'traditional' face-to-face providers and, therefore, reap whatever economies of scale are possible in their circumstances. Alongside these changes has been the rise of 'flexible learning/ flexible delivery'. In the new 'compulsive development cultures' flexibility is the touchstone. Flexibility is required in the provision of goods and services, in the workforce and labour market and, axiomatically, in education and training. However, the terms 'flexible learning/flexible delivery' are actually quite *flexible* in their meaning too (Evans and Smith, 1999). The conceptual cloudiness which results is not a good condition for those involved in policy and planning in the field. However, most seem to cope by working within the practices of open and distance education, and using 'flexible learning/flexible delivery' as a slogan to attach to their policies and marketing (see also Edwards, 1997; Nicoll, 1997).

The expansion in postgraduate coursework and professional development courses in the 1990s has also contributed to a demand for the highest levels of postgraduate education: the doctorate. This demand has spawned a growth and development in doctoral education. This has not just been in the traditional on-campus PhD, but rather it has led to new forms of doctorate offered part-time and off-campus (Evans and Pearson, 1999; Evans, 2000). We are now in a position where virtually every aspect of tertiary education has been affected by, and is expected to contribute towards, the compulsive development culture. Therefore, virtually every aspect of institutional policy and planning has to cope with, and adapt to, these conditions.

Institutional policy and planning

Open and distance education institutions' managers and staff need to look to the national and international scenes, not just for direct educational policy, but also for those policies that indirectly relate to their work. There are some delicate balancing acts to be performed. Most obviously, the political and business interests that drive the compulsive development culture of developed nations are so powerful that to ignore their demands would be fatal for an institution. It may be possible to do so if the institution is funded by benefactors, religious bodies and the like, but for most institutions that depend on provisions from the government purse and/or have budgets dependent on business, this is not an option. So, on the one hand, it is necessary to be incorporated within the compulsive development culture. However, on the other hand, universities especially, but other forms of education as well, are expected to provide and foster a critical awareness of the world in which we live and this must logically include adopting a critical stance in relation to the compulsive development culture itself.

It is important, therefore, to understand the 'core business' of one's educational institution, not just in terms of the provision of educational services to the economy, but also in relation to the sustenance of a democratic society which is critically aware and reflexively enabled. These may, or may not, be difficult things to balance. For example, a previous state government in Australia – the Liberal and National Party 'conservative' government led by Jeff Kennett in Victoria until late 1999 – forbade its employees, including teachers in the education sector, from commenting on government policy and its implementation. In 'corporate' Victoria all staff were expected to believe, or at least follow unquestioningly, the 'company line'. However, a democratic society is not a company, and a government is not a board of directors answerable to a number of shareholders. A democratic society is an aggregation of people with a diversity of goals, interests, needs, values and understandings. A government is elected by almost all the adult members of society to act in all members' interests. Arguably, in order to function effectively, it is necessary to have members of the society well educated and able to communicate their goals, interests, needs, values and understandings, irrespective of whether they are employed by the government or not. It is this necessity that educational policy-makers and planners need to keep in mind as a fundamental function of their organization.

One of the major areas in which institutions have been severely affected by the compulsive development culture is in the broad area of information and communications technologies. At least since the early 1980s, the challenge to purchase computer hardware and software has been issued to policymakers and planners. Evans and Nation (2000: 173) observe:

> In most cases, the institutional policies around new technology reflect the global push into new technologies in education and universities in particular. It is seen as inevitable that a 'competitive' university will need to keep pace

with technological change, even if, as Katz muses of US university presidents, many would like to put the 'genie back in the bottle.'(Katz and associates, 1999: xiii)

Katz and his colleagues' (Katz and associates, 1999) concerns are framed by Evans and Nation in the context of the global challenge to jump on to the new technology bandwagon. The changes that have been brought about have been quite profound, but not always for the good, and not always in the ways predicted by the boosters of new technology. For example, library catalogue systems have shifted from card indexes which need to be manually browsed to computer databases which can be searched electronically and remotely, and both speedily and intuitively. However, university offices have not become the oft-predicted paperless offices; indeed the new technology has encouraged and enabled the production of more elegant and colourful text, tables and figures on paper.

A major contemporary challenge for educational policymakers and planners is the best strategy to adopt in terms of the 'online' provision of courses. The online boosters argue that the future *is* online learning and that institutions that are educational minnows will be swallowed by a school(!) of sharks in the form of cartels of universities established to compete for dominance in the global educational marketplace. The online Luddites (see Evans and Nation, 2000: 161) argue that the classroom is king and will never be dethroned. Policymakers and planners in open and distance education need to take a careful, critical stance in shaping their policies in this regard. In a sense, their institutions – as distance teaching institutions – have always had to work against the Luddite view; but the boosters may well need to be worked against as consistently too. What is required is: a good understanding of the institution's history, strengths and weaknesses; a clear assessment of the current circumstances; and a rational and careful analysis of what options are available for the future. What is also required is an understanding of the foundations and roots of the organization and where its previous 'investments' lay, and whether they are, and will continue, paying. An analysis of the future options can then be based on what is already established and can be built upon, and what new things are required. After the policy position is adopted, a strategy plan can be developed which shows exactly how the institution will get to where it has decided to move.

Peters (2000) argues that universities, in dealing with the challenges of the new technologies, need to be guided by educational principles, especially those that lead to creating the university of the future as one of independent learning and lifelong learning. He values the 'social intercourse' of the traditional university, but argues that this should not be used for presentational purposes, such as the lecture, but rather for interaction and dialogue. He has a vision of the future university which uses the new technologies to 'destructure' and 'delimit' its traditional presentational forms and encourage 'self-learning' in its students, but which retains and intensifies the strengths of the educational technology of the seminar and tutorial for the purposes of interaction and dialogue.

In short, it is a new balance that Peters proposes. It can be seen that institutional policy and planning is about estimating the right balance for the future and setting a strategic course towards it. It cannot be slavishly following the compulsive development dictates of government or business, but about considering institutional interests in the light of those dictates, setting the policy and developing and implementing the best possible plans.

Conclusion

Giddens (1988) has articulated what he sees as a new way for social democracy in developed nations. His focus was particularly on Britain where its (then aspiring) prime minister, Tony Blair, argued for a 'third way' in contemporary democratic politics: a way between the old Marxist socialism and the then declining Thatcherite free market, individualism. Giddens notes that '[e]ducation and training have become the new mantra for social democratic politicians' (1998: 109). However, the notion that following the mantra will somehow remove social inequalities, as Giddens notes, is not without its problems. Education is as good, if not better, at producing inequalities as removing them. The new demands on modern democratic developed nations in terms of sustaining their compulsive development cultures are both founded on, and rooted in, education and training. Not only does each rising generation have to be equipped to 'compete' in the new 'hi-tech' world, but they also have to be instilled with the values of compulsive development so that they are always seeking, or at least compliant with, change and development.

In this context it is argued that everyone involved in open and distance education, not just those involved in management, needs to understand the broad policy issues that surround the management of their organization. Everyone has responsibility for the good management of their work and their institution. A critical awareness of the policy and development issues surrounding and pervading open and distance education institutions, it is argued, helps people to perform actively within their roles and to contribute constructively to their own career management and to the shape and performance of their organizations. A fundamental aspect of this is the compulsive development values of modern developed societies. It is important that a critical understanding of the political and economic 'drivers' of such values is not lost in the good exercise of educational management and policy, and that educational institutions work towards providing courses that not only reflect government policies, but also critically reflect upon them too.

References

Edwards, R (1997) *Changing Places? Flexibility, lifelong learning and a learning society*, Routledge, London

Evans, T D (1997) '(En)Countering globalization: issues for open and distance educators', in *Shifting Borders: Globalization, localization and open and distance education*, eds L Rowan, L Bartlett and T D Evans, pp 11–22, Deakin University Press, Geelong

Evans, T D (2000) 'Meeting what ends?: challenges to doctoral education in Australia', *Proceedings of the Quality in Postgraduate Research National Conference*, Adelaide

Evans, T D and Nation, D E (2000) 'Understanding changes to university teaching', in *Changing University Teaching: Reflections on creating educational technologies*, eds T D Evans and D E Nation, pp 160–175, Kogan Page, London

Evans, T D and Pearson, M (1999) 'Off-campus doctoral research in Australia: emerging issues and practices', in *Supervision of Postgraduate Research in Education*, eds A Holbrook and S Johnson, pp 185–206, Coldstream, Victoria, Australian Association for Research in Education

Evans, T D and Smith, P J (1999) Flexible delivery in Australia: origins and conceptualizations, *Federation for Information and Documentation Journal*, **1** (2/3), pp 116–120

Giddens, A (1994) *Beyond Left and Right: The future of radical politics*, Polity Press, Cambridge

Giddens, A (1998) *The Third Way: The renewal of social democracy*, Polity Press, Cambridge

Harris, D (1987) *Openness and Closure in Distance Education*, Falmer Press, London

Haughey, M and Roberts, J (1996) 'Canadian policy and practice on open and distance schooling', in *Opening Education: Policies and practices from open and distance education*, eds T D Evans and D E Nation, pp 63–76, Routledge, London

Jakupec, V (1996) 'Reforming distance education through economic rationalism: a critical analysis of reforms to Australia higher education', in *Opening Education: Policies and practices from open and distance education*, eds T D Evans and D E Nation, pp 77–89, Routledge, London

Johnson, R (1996) 'To wish and to will: reflections on policy formation and implementation', in *Opening Education: Policies and practices from distance education*, eds T D Evans and D E Nation, pp 90–102, Routledge, London

Katz, R N and associates (1999) *Dancing with the Devil: Information technology and the new competition in higher education*, Jossey-Bass, San Francisco

Marginson, S (1997) *Markets in Education*, Allen and Unwin, Sydney

Moodie, G and Nation, D E (1993) 'Reforming a system of distance education', in *Reforming Open and Distance Education*, eds T D Evans and D E Nation, pp 130–49, Kogan Page, London

Nicoll, K (1997) Flexible learning – unsettling practices, *Studies in Continuing Education*, **19** (2), pp 100–11

Peters, O (2000) 'The transformation of the university into an institution of independent learning', in *Changing University Teaching: Reflections on creating educational technologies*, eds T D Evans and D E Nation, pp 10–23, Kogan Page, London

Chapter 3

Policy and planning in the developing world

Hilary Perraton

Introduction

Planning is seldom the detached and rational process we might expect. When Rabindranath Tagore and Leonard Elmhirst were planning Santiniketan, 'with terms of reference that would flummox any Education Authority, the poet and the agriculturist sat down together to draw up a scheme for the new school' (Young, 1982: 83). Much more recently, as Britain was planning its Open University, one member of the planning group suggested they should consider the level at which the University should operate and whether undergraduate degrees were the top priority. Jennie Lee, the minister responsible, immediately responded that anyone with an open mind on that issue should not be on the committee. It was to be a university and nothing less.

So we start with a caution: that an analysis of policymaking will make the process look cooler, more detached, and more rational than is really the case; and with a worry that planning ought to leave room for the poet as well as the educator. Given those concerns, this chapter seeks to analyse who is making policy for open and distance learning, and what they are trying to do. It may illuminate how far planning for open and distance learning is different from that for other forms of education.[1] And it tries to look at the role of policymaking in strengthening educational service and quality.

Levels of policymaking

Policy for open and distance learning in the public sector may be framed at four or more levels: international, regional, national and institutional, and is increasingly influenced by decisions and activities of the private sector. The University of the West Indies, for example, reshaped its programme of distance education in the light of a commission set up by an international agency, the Commonwealth of Learning, and funded some of its new work with a loan and grant from an international development bank. As a regional institution, its policy is shaped by the 14 governments of the region which own the university. At the same time the national policies of the governments it serves affect its work, while the day-to-day running of its courses depends on decisions made within the same institution. When the university wanted to update its teleconference network, it needed technical advice which was available only from the private sector, and it relies on a telecommunications system run by the multinational company Cable and Wireless. Decisions at these four levels, and the differing interests of the private and public sectors, all interweave as policy is developed and implemented.

In Table 3.1 we identify a set of questions whose answers illuminate the process of policy development and suggest both the level at which the question is likely to be answered and how the issues may be addressed at each. We begin with four basic questions: Who designs policy and how? What is it trying to do? What are the critical options? What criteria are used to choose between them? We can pose the questions at each level – international, regional, national and institutional – always recognizing that the world is untidier than the planner's toolkit. Answers will spill over from one level to another; decisions to be taken in one case at an institutional level (say, how should this course be accredited?) might be taken internationally in another; policies at one level are always likely to conflict with, or subtly differ from, those at other levels.

Who decides policy and how?

Policy for open and distance learning is being shaped at all four levels. Some international agencies have developed formal policy documents. Examples come from UNESCO and, for the European Union's activities within Europe, from the European Commission. International conferences have made reference to the significance of open and distance learning, and of the application of communication technologies to education, often more in terms of promise than of achievement. Perhaps more significant, the major funding agencies have begun to develop both policy and practice for distance education. The World Bank, for example, has expressed some interest in distance education since the 1970s, and from time to time made loans for distance education programmes (Perraton, 2000: 154–56). Its interest has, however, effectively been limited to the use of distance teaching methods in higher education and, even here, has been edged with caution.

Table 3.1 *Some critical planning issues*

	International	Regional	National	Institutional
Who designs policy and how?	Multilateral and bilateral funding agencies Specialist agencies (eg COL, CIFFAD) Professional associations Extensive use of commissions and development of formal policy documents	Regional universities (eg UWI) Regional professional associations (eg AAOU)	Ministries of education University funding councils	Senior management
What is it trying to do?	Influence national policy? Enhance regional competitiveness	Meet regional needs	Probably balance between issues of equity, expansion, quality, economy	Develop effective teaching and management system Compete successfully with other institutions for resources
What are the critical options?	Funding agencies: investment choices Specialist institutions: balance between technical assistance and international cooperative activities	All national issues may be addressed regionally	Governance, institutional structure, regulation and relations with rest of educational system Sources of funding Audience and purpose	May also address all national issues Teaching methodology and choice of technology Staffing Accreditation
What criteria are used to choose between them?	Cost effectiveness Institution's perception of comparative advantage	May overlap with international or national	Cost effectiveness Political prestige and influence of various institutions	Educational effectiveness Response to demand Student recruitment Budgetary constraints

The two international agencies, the Commonwealth of Learning (COL) and its French-language equivalent, the Consortium International Francophone de Formation à Distance (CIFFAD), came into existence to support the use of distance education and international cooperation to support it. Perhaps their single greatest achievement in policy development is to assist its processes regionally and nationally. COL commissions, like that to the University of the West Indies, have helped the development of national policies and plans for distance education.

Despite globalization, the most significant policymakers are still national. Leaving aside the corporate sector, by far the largest number of bona fide distance-teaching institutions are set up by governments, funded at least initially and in part by governments, and regulated by bodies which derive their authority directly or indirectly from governments. Policy is not always made directly by governments. At university level, for example, funding councils may play a key role in determining how tertiary-level distance education is developed. In India, the Indira Gandhi National Open University (IGNOU) has a national planning and funding responsibility that takes it into considerable policymaking for the other open universities. When starting new institutions, many governments have kept planning at arm's length by setting up planning commissions to prepare detailed proposals. In an analysis of plans for open universities set up in the 1970s and 1980s, Dodd and Rumble (1984: 240) found that many were drafted in this way and that there were perceived advantages in using a commission that was 'isolated from the normal (and potentially hostile) bureaucracy of government'.

At other levels of education, national planning is critical, both within government and outside. Institutions offering alternative forms of secondary education, including open schools in Asia, large broadcast-based projects in Latin America and correspondence study centres in central Africa, all depend on ministry of education policy. Outside government, many non-governmental organizations (NGOs) are national rather than international organizations. In many countries of Latin America, for example, there are national radio schools, offering non-formal and secondary equivalence courses, with policy determined nationally although outside government.

There is no clear dividing line between national and institutional policymaking. As institutions become established, so policy is more likely to be developed at an institutional than at a national level, and to be shaped by negotiation between staff members at both levels. In Taiwan, for example, the decision to allow the open university to offer full degrees was a national decision but one that followed experiment by the university and, we may assume, was influenced by the university's own wishes (Hung-Ju, 1999).

Policy is thus being developed at all four levels. There has been a tendency for international actors to play a significant role as new institutions or programmes are developed, either through funding decisions or through the international exchange of experience. As time goes on, actors at national and institutional level tend to take more of the critical decisions.

What is it trying to do?

The aims of educational policy are in large measure a function of the location and standing of the policymaker. International and regional agencies may both have a particular interest in influencing national policy. At regional level, agencies may be concerned with enhancing regional competitiveness – a stated concern, for example, of such different institutions as the University of the West Indies and the European Commission – as well as of meeting needs that are common across their regions. At the level of national policy for education, government action is likely to be in one of four areas: financing education, providing it, administering it or regulating it. Some of these functions may be devolved to a lower tier of government, or left to the private sector, or handed over to a specialist agency (Hallak, 1990: 79).

In considering the purpose of open and distance learning, as of other forms of education, governments have had to make choices between the demands of educational equity, of expanding the educational service in response to demand, of raising its quality, and of meeting the demands of the economy. Within higher education, all four tasks have been quoted as among the functions of open universities (Perraton, 2000: 90–91). Within policy documents there has been less recognition of the tensions between different aims: equity is ill-served if the quality of distance teaching programmes is so low that the more deprived learners get the worst service; teaching the specialists needed for one sector of the economy may involve carefully planned expansion in particular disciplines that are not the ones sought by large numbers seeking educational opportunities. Some of these conflicts also influence policymaking at the institutional level but, for the most part, decisions here are likely to be concerned with the development of an efficient teaching and management system and, increasingly, with competition for resources with other institutions.

Decisions about the broad aims of policy provide a framework within which agencies, governments and institutions can examine critical options as they develop open and distance learning.

What are the critical options and what criteria are used in making choices?

We have enough experience of the use of open and distance learning within the south, at all levels of education, to go on and identify the critical options available to policymakers at each of our four levels. In doing so we can also identify the criteria that are used, or might be used, in choosing between alternative policies.

The international funding agencies face the simplest and starkest choice: to invest, or not to invest, in a programme or institution. Their criteria look as simple: to estimate the return on the loan or grant. In practice, things are much less simple. While UNESCO, as an agency with little to spend, has developed a policy document on open and distance learning (UNESCO, 1997), the World Bank, as the most significant source of funds for development, has not done so. Its more recent documents appear to see distance education as relevant only to higher education and to teacher training (World Bank, 1995; Perraton, 2000: 154–55). Funding decisions appear, in practice, to be more eclectic than formal statements of policy. A recent analysis of the work of the World Bank, USAID and the British Department for International Development (previously the Overseas Development Administration) concluded that:

> the funding agencies have played only a minor role in shaping the development of open and distance learning. The World Bank's policy agenda has driven its lending – although its actual portfolio of loans is more diverse than that might suggest – and it has rarely been convinced of the value of distance education. The British have eschewed policy. If they have influenced distance education it has been as a result of pressure from the invisible colleges of consultants whom they employed than a consequence of government policy. The Americans have had policies, of promoting technological solutions to educational problems, but have had difficulty in ensuring that their demonstration projects are sustainable. (Perraton, 2000: 160)

At regional and national level, governments, NGOs, and to a lesser extent institutions, have been framing the policies that determine the day-to-day activities of distance teaching institutions. Critical policy decisions fall into three broad areas. First are issues of governance and institutional structure, of regulation, and of relationships with the rest of the educational system. Next are questions about funding. Last, but it might properly be first, are questions about the audience for open and distance learning and the purposes for which it is being used or considered. This categorization assumes that questions about how an institution works, and about its choices of teaching method, fall to the institution.

In determining how a distance teaching institution should be governed, perhaps the most difficult questions concern the extent of its autonomy. The difficulties spring partly from the fact that these institutions are different from conventional schools or colleges and the usual structures do not easily fit. Often institutions have a national remit, rather than a local one, while their funding needs are always likely to be of a different order. As a result, even where institutions are working at secondary level, for example, governments have tended to give them more autonomy than an ordinary school. The Indian National Open School was established initially as a project of the Central Board of Secondary Education but later was granted autonomous status by the government of India. The Thailand Department of Nonformal Education enjoys a considerable measure of autonomy which contributes to its record of success (Edirisingha, forthcoming). Central Africa provides interesting and contrasting experience. In Malawi, Zambia and Zimbabwe, government correspondence departments have been under the control of their ministries of education, with quite limited autonomy. Despite their consequent organizational closeness to government they have been starved of funds and, over years, operated at limited effectiveness (Curran and Murphy, 1992). Botswana established a Botswana Extension College in 1973 which was answerable to the ministry of education but enjoyed a considerable measure of autonomy. Within 10 years, and following the advice of an external consultant (beware of them, always), it was moved inside the ministry where it languished for another decade. By 1998, policy and language had shifted and the Botswana College of Distance and Open Learning was re-established as a parastatal agency.

We can discern two different dominant patterns in higher education. First, open universities have generally been established under a different procedure from conventional universities. Most have then enjoyed a measure of autonomy which is probably comparable to that of conventional universities.[2] Second, and especially in small and medium-population states, distance-education departments have been established within conventional universities where their governance and structure has been controlled by the parent university. One consequence is that their structures and methods of working tend to shadow those of conventional university arrangements. A key planning issue for any government considering launching distance education, or expanding its use, is therefore to compare the advantages of a single-mode or dual-mode approach. Scale may be the most important criterion here: it is easy to justify the establishment of an open university in a country with a population of over 100 million, more difficult if the population is below a million. Rumble (1992) has argued that dual-mode institutions are at a competitive advantage as compared with open universities in part because of the opportunities they offer for sharing resources. On the other hand, as universities are moving from being single to dual mode, many face difficulties in their staffing policies, illustrated by practical problems of getting course material written, which are a severe constraint on their development (cf. Perraton and Creed, 1999).

The choice of organizational model has implications for the relationship between open and distance learning and conventional education. Students at dual-mode universities in India, for example, can move between studying on-campus and studying at a distance, while open university students have not generally been able to switch modes. In Indonesia, the Open School structure means that conventional schools act as centres that provide support also to the out-of-school students studying mainly through open and distance learning. Here, too, the policymaker may need to resolve a tension between the wish to give a measure of autonomy to distance-teaching institutions and a concern to develop an integrated system of education.

In his analysis of educational planning, Hallak (1990) suggested that, even where government did not itself provide some part of the educational service, it retained responsibility for regulating it. The expansion of open and distance learning raises questions about appropriate procedures for its regulation. Governments need therefore to decide where responsibility for regulation should lie and the extent to which open and distance learning requires different procedures from those of conventional education (see Chapter 20). Institutions are likely to need a code of practice that covers areas irrelevant to conventional education.

Governments have adopted a range of different policies towards the funding of open and distance learning. In some cases either government funding or overseas aid has been used for initial capital development. Beyond that, public funding has sometimes been available for the greater part of the costs of distance education programmes. Many programmes of teacher education, for example, have charged no fees. In China, employers and central government have been meeting about 95 per cent of fees for radio and television university students. At secondary level the government of Mexico meets a higher proportion of the costs of *Telesecundaria* than it does of conventional schools. But these are exceptions: far more often students are themselves expected to meet the greater part of the costs of their education at a distance, either at secondary or at tertiary level (Perraton, 2000: 185–89). Hong Kong, where students must fund all their costs, provides a contrast with mainland China: 'Adult higher education [in Hong Kong] is not seen as a government responsibility – it is regarded as an individual responsibility and government's role is only to provide an environment in which an adult educational enterprise can function through its own efforts' (Hope and Dhanarajan, 1994: 44). Where they have been articulated, policies have assumed that, as distance education learners study part-time, they are likely also to have a job and income from which they can meet the cost of fees.

Framing a coherent policy requires the decision maker to take a view about the balance between individual and social benefits flowing from enrolling on a course and about equity between students following different modes of education. Decisions here are, therefore, likely to be influenced by perceptions about the value of distance teaching institutions – perhaps mainly in terms of their contribution to workforce development – and about their political strength and influence. If they demonstrate not just that they have recruited large numbers of hopeful students over a decade but that they have awarded qualifications comparable with those of the conventional sector at a similar or lower unit cost, then they are in a powerful position to argue for sympathetic funding treatment by governments. Further, they need to address the issues of the nature of the audience, their needs, circumstances and background.

The institutional policymaker is likely to revisit all the issues addressed at national level, both in order to implement them within the institution and to bring pressure on a government or parent institution as policies develop or evolve. At this level, too, decisions are required, for the institution as a whole and for individual programmes or courses, on the choice of technology, on appropriate staffing structure, and on accreditation.

The criteria used for determining policy are, then, likely to be a function of decisions about governance, funding and educational purpose. Decision makers are likely to seek trade-offs of various kinds. Increased autonomy will give greater freedom to plan open and distance learning outside the, sometimes inappropriate, assumptions of conventional education. But the price for this may be decreased opportunity to get guarantees of public funding. Again, where an institution is running courses seen as of major economic or social significance for government, funding is likely to be assured, but autonomy may be diminished. All decisions in these areas are, at the time of writing, influenced by public-sector stakeholders of various kinds, by students, and by the staff of open and distance learning institutions themselves. The criteria by which decisions are taken may change if corporate universities, and a new wave of activity by the private sector, begin seriously to affect the shape of open and distance learning.

What is the new agenda?

The practice of open and distance learning and literature about it have grown so rapidly that some answers to many of the policy questions are available for the policymaker from experience. (If there had been as much good research as there is tedious literature the policymaker's job would be lighter still.) Changing politics, globalization and new communication technologies are, however, putting new issues on the agenda. While it is difficult to see how far these changes will affect day-to-day education, or decide whether discussion of virtual universities and Web-based learning is hype or sober forecast of a revolution in learning, we can illustrate by reference to some of the new issues. One of these, which bristles with difficulty, concerns the international business of education and issues that flow from cross-border enrolment.

When the Commonwealth of Learning was being planned, the Briggs group noted that distance education lent itself to cross-border enrolment and that the 'new communication technologies make it possible for learners to have access to the world's knowledge no matter where they live'. At the same time they warned that 'there could be an even further widening of the gap between rich countries and poor in their access to information' (Briggs *et al*, 1987: 8). Since that time, alongside the much-publicized growth in communication technology has gone a rapid and aggressive expansion of international education.

There is, today, a widespread assumption that education can properly go beyond national boundaries and that there are roles within it for both the public and the private sector. Taking matters even further, proposals were prepared for the aborted World Trade Organization meeting in Seattle in 1999 to liberalize education generally, so that commercial agencies, at any level and in any country, would be able to compete with state systems of education. These changes in assumption about education and its practice put new issues on the policy agenda at the intersection between national interest and consumer protection:

- How should governments regulate cross-border enrolment in order to safeguard the interests of their own citizens?
- Given the disparity in costs between the north and the south of a labour-intensive activity like education, how can we reconcile a desire for free mobility of learning and ideas with a concern that education should be socially progressive rather than regressive?
- How can the individual student distinguish a bona fide course from a foreign country from one offered by a snake-oil merchant?

There are major difficulties for nation states, and especially for small states, in setting up systems to monitor, advise or control, and, in doing so, to pursue legitimate national interests without restricting individual choice. There may, then, be a vitally important role for the international specialist agencies, not to enforce codes of practice (they can't) but to develop, publicize and encourage the use of protocols of good practice.

One final issue for the new agenda is to ask who can afford which kind of technology. Open and distance learning has thrived and grown because it promised to use technology to widen educational opportunities. Many of those working in it, and many of its institutions – from the radio schools of Latin America to the open universities of the north and the south – have been motivated by a desire to equalize educational opportunities. There is a sad irony in the possibility that the new technologies, which tend to be both absolutely and relatively cheaper in the north than the south, may end up by increasing educational disparity rather than reducing it.

Notes

1. I use the term 'distance education' for 'an educational process in which a significant proportion of the teaching is conducted by someone removed in space and/or time from the learner', and 'open learning' as 'an organized educational activity, based on the use of teaching materials, in which constraints on study are minimized either in terms of access, or of time and place, pace, methods of study, or any combination of these'. As an umbrella term I have used 'open and distance learning' (cf. Perraton, 2000: 13–14).
2. I am not aware of any comparative study of the governance of conventional and open universities.

References

Briggs, A *et al* (1987) *Towards a Commonwealth of Learning: Commonwealth cooperation in distance education and open learning*, Commonwealth Secretariat, London

Curran, C and Murphy, P (1992) 'Distance education at the second level and for teacher education in six countries', in *Distance Education in Anglophone Africa: Experience with secondary education and teacher training*, eds P Murphy and A Zhiri, World Bank, Washington DC

Dodd, J and Rumble, G (1984) Planning new distance teaching universities, *Higher Education*, **13**, pp 231–54

Edirisingha, P (forthcoming) *New Approaches to Basic Education: International experience of open and distance learning*, IRFOL, Cambridge

Hallak, J (1990) *Investing in the Future: Setting educational priorities in the developing world*, International Institute for Educational Planning, Paris

Hope, A and Dhanarajan, G (1994) 'Adult learning and the self-funding imperative – funding the Open Learning Institute of Hong Kong', in *The Funding of Open Universities*, ed I Mugridge, Commonwealth of Learning, Vancouver

Hung-Ju, Chung (1999) 'Contemporary distance education in Taiwan', in *Higher Education Through Open and Distance Learning*, ed K Harry, Routledge, London

Mitford, J L (1970) Let us now appraise famous writers, *Atlantic Monthly*, **226** (1), pp 45–54

Perraton, H (2000) *Open and Distance Learning in the Developing World*, Routledge, London

Perraton, H and Creed, C (2000) *Applying New Technologies and Cost-effective Delivery Systems in Basic Education* (Thematic study for World Education Forum, Dakar), UNESCO, Paris

Rumble, G (1992) The comparative vulnerability of distance teaching universities, *Open Learning*, **7** (2), pp 31–45

UNESCO (1997) *Open and Distance Learning: Prospects and policy considerations*, UNESCO, Paris

World Bank (1995) *Priorities and Strategies for Education: A World Bank review*, Washington DC

Young, M (1982) *The Elmhirsts of Dartington: The creation of an utopian community*, Routledge and Kegan Paul, London

Chapter 4

Planning for open and flexible learning

Margaret Haughey

Introduction

Universities have been social institutions since the 12th century, but today the notion of postsecondary institutions as the repositories and creators of knowledge, the society's knowledge memory, is being replaced with the expectation that they consider themselves to be an industry and part of the knowledge sector. This is one of three major trends putting pressure on postsecondary institutions to reconsider their vision for the future. A second trend is the influence of telecommunications and digital technologies on the administrative and research capacities of institutions; and the third is the growing interest in new curriculum and learning models for postsecondary education based on models of learning that connect brain research, psychological studies of active involvement, pedagogical developments and epistemological theories of meaning-making. In addition, postsecondary institutions, including institutes of open and distance education (as have been analysed in Chapters 2 and 3), have to respond to demands from government and the public to contribute more directly to national growth and economic development, to help speed the technology transfer from laboratories to new investment, to meet the demands from groups who previously have not had access to postsecondary education, and to provide increased opportunities for continuing professional education.

The enormous pressure for postsecondary institutions to think like corporations and adopt strategies from business and industry comes at a time when burgeoning demands for places cannot be accommodated because of economic restraints. Under these pressures it is not surprising that the target of the arguments for the adoption of telecommunications and computer-mediated technologies is the transformation of the instructional function of postsecondary institutions, in particular the present configuration of classroom-based, contact-hour specific, semestered instruction. This chapter reviews the pressures facing postsecondary institutions and examines the need to undertake a planning exercise to address this challenge. It discusses the move from *strategic* to a more *holistic* form of planning and what that would involve, and outlines the different planning actions that institutions might undertake in their efforts to plan for open and flexible learning.

Pressures facing postsecondary institutions

Postsecondary institutions have not been impervious to the pressures of our postmodern world. The development of a knowledge-based economy, the rapid expansion of the telecommunications industries and the globalization of business and industry (Haughey, 2000) have all brought pressures for change. Universities have traditionally been on the fringe of societal movements, somewhat impervious to change and more interested in knowledge creation and dissemination than in its subsequent utility to other sectors of the economy. Now, governments and the public are looking to postsecondary institutions to provide more research to support the transfer from resource-based to information industries, and to produce science and technology graduates who would be equipped to work in such a sector. Globalization has also brought pressures to improve the linkages between industry and postsecondary education through programmes designed to better serve the professional and training needs of these employees and to provide them with greater flexibility in when and where they can access courses and programmes (Tait and Mills, 1999). The imperative to be able to study and work also comes from students. In a time of declining public support for postsecondary institutions, students need to be able to work while attending school, and once employed need to be able to continue to upgrade their qualifications while remaining on the job.

Traditionally, postsecondary institutions have adapted to pressures from industry and from their clientele in an incremental fashion, but to do so assumes that the changes being demanded fit within a fairly stable understanding of society. Today's institutions have to look beyond internal adaptive measures to reconsider their position within society. Knowledge, its creation and dissemination, is no longer the sole purview of the postsecondary sector; business and industry have set up their own research laboratories and in some cases their own education programmes. Private organizations have also provided competition for students and the ubiquity of the Internet has put the decision of when and where to study much more firmly in the hand of the learner. In addition, besides the growth of research parks and new partnership forms among postsecondary institutions and industry, the communications industry has also sought to respond to the market for information through developing itself as a knowledge broker. What this means for postsecondary institutions is that they need to do careful planning to ensure they have a place in this new economy which is less willing to accord them the position traditionally reserved for them.

Peterson and Dill (1997) contend that the reason postsecondary institutions need to re-examine their position is that the postsecondary education sector is no longer different and separate from other business sectors. They propose that in North America these organizations can no longer think of themselves as members of a network of somewhat similar postsecondary institutions but instead should see themselves as one contributor in a comprehensive postsecondary knowledge industry. They argue that while we have traditionally confined our comparisons to the activities of our competitors (ie other postsecondary institutions), we now need to pay more attention to the general as well as local societal context and the positions adopted by new players in this sector.

Peterson and Dill predict that given the forces shaping the nature of the postsecondary network it will come to involve many different providers whose activities will form a knowledge system able to provide access to knowledge and information using a wide array of teaching and learning options. This would mean the involvement of many other types of providers beyond those traditionally involved in postsecondary education. They suggest that if the postsecondary sector refuses to accept itself as a member of a global industry, other corporate entities will move forward to fill the gap (see also Daniel, 1999). The postsecondary system, they contend, needs to give greater consideration to issues associated with being an industry member. These include: Who are the new alternate providers? How well are we meeting our clients' needs? How are we reacting to the desires of funders? What are the demands of employers who are not only our suppliers and receivers of our students but who can also become providers of substitute services? How can we adopt technological advances to make our work more effective and cost-efficient? What is our level of competition with other institutions?

Much of the writing about postsecondary education proclaims the need for the postsecondary system to change in the face of all these issues. The response demanded is systemic change that will 'break the traditional higher education paradigm' (Van Dusen, 1997: 9). What is called for is for a complete rethinking of postsecondary education. In a review of trends in writings in higher education between 1997 and 1999, Kezar (2000: 1) listed the most recurrent themes as 'outsourcing, privatization, mergers, re-engineering, collaboration, technology and equity' and noted the principles underlying them as 'a concern with saving and containing costs, institutional structure, and best practices rather than research'.

Academic restructuring is framed in terms of 're-engineering', 'restructuring', or 'transforming'. Embedded in these terms is the belief that it is no longer possible to respond to contemporary pressures by improving the administrative capabilities of institutions. The concept of postsecondary institutions as bureaucracies needs to be discarded and replaced with an electronic analogy, the institution as a loosely connected network of interdependent work processes (Gumport and Pusser, 1997).

Some of these will involve partnerships and outsourcing, possibly credentialing. Unlike previous models of institutional change, this envisioning requires that not only the administrative but the instructional and research functions – the core operations of the institution – be redesigned. Such a move calls for a redefinition of academic work life.

Re-engineering is predicated on the integration of communications technologies into the instructional work of the organization. Gumport and Pusser (1997: 463) support this view, noting that 'Re-engineering academic work will involve rethinking the educational process itself, the way faculty work, and the standards of educational technology.' Some of the assumptions on which this orientation is based include the belief that technology will help lower costs and increase efficiencies by providing Internet-based courses to greater numbers of students. Kennedy (1993) has suggested that it will also affect research and some evidence of this trend is already available. Funding organizations are showing a preference for funding research teams who come from different organizations and from different disciplines, one indication of a network of scholars who are expected to be able to work collaboratively using telecommunications technologies.

Restructuring, a facet of re-engineering, is similarly focused on enhancing efficiencies and increasing the flexibility and response of the organization. It stems from a strong corporate emphasis on the university as a multi-product organization. Like the corporate press for privatization, which supports outsourcing of services, restructuring looks at developing corporate forms within the institutional structure. This trend is most evident in the new partnerships with industry funders where for immediacy and flexibility the research profit centres are more likely to follow corporate procedures that would not be accepted in the instructional part of the institution.

Transforming, the third trend, speaks most directly to the redesign of instructional processes. Driven by a desire to ensure increased efficiencies, it also reflects a trend in knowledge management, the use of teams for product design and implementation, also evident in the restructuring of research initiatives.

Much of the pressure facing institutions stems from the rapid developments in the telecommunications industry and, as many analysts point out, these cannot be separated from the other challenges facing the postsecondary sector. Technology is seen as the linchpin for addressing these issues but the literature is replete with reports of technologies, from radio and television to videoconferencing and computer-assisted instruction, which were supposed to bring fundamental change to the instructional process and failed. These innovations were generally seen as additions to enhance the prevailing instructional system. With communications technologies, the need is to consider how they can transform these processes. Their effectiveness will depend on how they are integrated into the academic processes of the institution.

Need for a more holistic form of planning and what that would involve

Planning in postsecondary institutions has largely been in response to changing resource environments. Peterson (1986) noted how the explosion of enrolments in institutions in the 1960s, which led to the planning for new campuses, was followed by fiscal and resource planning in response to external constraints in the 70s. He argued that comprehensive planning only gained emphasis as the need for broader institutional responses to continued fiscal restraints became more evident. It took two forms. One was long-term managerial-level planning undertaken to achieve better information for decision making, and the other, market analysis, came from a market-driven orientation with a focus on attracting and retaining students. As the emphasis shifted in the 1980s to a concern with quality and outcome measures of effectiveness and efficiency, organizations sought to find areas where they could ensure a market for quality students from specific programmes, and strategic planning became the focus. Today, while the numbers seeking further education are again increasing, the context for postsecondary education is very different from that of half a century ago. Changing patterns of diversity, globalization, the telecommunications industry, the emphasis on lifelong learning in a knowledge society, the demand for greater contributions to the nation's productivity, all have renewed implications for postsecondary institutions.

Most educational organizations have initiated some form of institutional analysis, most often in the form of long-range planning, in order to assist with their decision making. While long-range planning assumes internal and external predictability and seeks to respond to the external environment, strategic planning is adaptive in orientation. Its focus is to scan the environment, assess current and future environmental opportunities and threats, assess competitors' strengths and weaknesses, and identify the appropriate strategic niche (Mintzberg, 1994; Watson, 2000). Strategic planning's strength lies in the thoroughness of its environmental scanning, but it considers this environment to be external to the core work of the organization and hence there is a greater focus on identifying the institution's comparative advantage and positioning relative to others in the environment. Internally, strategic planning calls for units to be more 'loosely coupled' (Weick, 1976) but the flexibility of operation is coupled first to more specific goal setting and then to review processes for measurement of results.

In examining planning and managing for a changing environment, Peterson *et al* (1997) propose that the planning model that best responds to our contemporary challenges is a contextual model (Chaffee, 1985). They argue that while aspects of long-range and strategic planning are very useful and should be retained, the extent of the challenges facing postsecondary education are such that planners need to assume an orientation different from those of these earlier planning models. In this environment, they contend, it is important to consider the possibilities of the environment that can be managed, identify realistic new roles and potential partnerships for the institution and then attempt to shape both the environment and the institution so as to be a strong competitor in this new environment. In simplest terms, contextual planning seeks to know how the environment is changing and how we can reposition aspects of our institution within that environment and then what we need to do to reshape our institution to ensure our continued viability.

Many organizations operate from a population ecology perspective which focuses on fitting with the environment (Hall, 1994). In contrast, the resource-dependence model (Pfeffer and Salancik, 1978) proposes that rather than being passive recipients of environmental forces, organizations make strategic decisions about adapting the environment to its advantage. From a contingency theory perspective (Lawrence and Lorsch, 1967), decisions made depend on the nature of the environment, and the more turbulent the environment, the more differentiated the organization. Scott (1995) has proposed a neo-institutional theory which conceptualizes institutions as consisting of 'cognitive, normative and regulative' structures and activities that provide stability and meaning and are transported by cultures, structures and routines. Chaffee's contextual model reflects aspects of these orientations. The environmental adaptation of the resource-dependence model, the need for differentiation in a turbulent environment from contingency theory and Scott's notion of organization as a collection of processes embedded in routines provide useful perspectives for planners.

In implementing a contextual planning process, the focus would shift from the postsecondary sector to the nexus of that sector and others such as the bio-chemical, telecommunications and entertainment sectors. Questions derived from the pressures facing postsecondary institutions such as the provision of substitute services by suppliers of learners and employers of graduates need to be explored. Others include how the institution relates to its competitors and whether that pattern is and should change and in what ways. The insights gained should help planners who have assessed the strengths and weaknesses of the institution to identify selected initiatives that will position or reconfirm the institution's part in this trend. The initial focus is on identifying these broad directions.

Unlike strategic planning, which depends on clear objectives to direct the process, implementation of these broad initiatives requires the provision of an infrastructure to support the direction but acknowledgement of the variety of possibilities that the faculty may undertake which would help support this direction. The investment is a visible indication of long-term support that encourages movement towards the initiative, and of institutional commitment.

One of the biggest dangers of this form of incentive is that the work of the early few who immediately adopt the initiative is considered to be sufficient evidence to ensure widespread acceptance. The opposite is unfortunately the case. Many initiatives flounder after the pilot stage. Therefore, it is important to provide broad-based opportunities for involvement, recognized incentives that reach across the institution and to embed these within the traditional policies involving recognition and reward. At the same time, barriers to effective implementation of initiatives, whether lack of adequate training or more general policy issues, need to be identified and rectified.

The development of incentive planning is more inclusive and open than the clearly delineated objectives of the strategic planning process. It is important, therefore, to periodically review the progress of specific projects and determine which have run their course and which need to be disseminated more broadly and integrated into the ongoing management of the institution. It may well take several years before the institution fully implements the initiative. Often, excellent initiatives are not adopted because others lack information about the initiative and its accomplishments. Hence frequent and significant communications both within and to external stakeholders is important in positioning the revised 'image' of the organization among its competitors, in providing recognition for those involved and as another indication of the institution's commitment to the process.

Planning for the implementation of open and flexible learning

There are three aspects to the change process: the realization of the need for change; the mobilization of internal and external support for the change; and the actual implementation of the change and its integration into the ongoing operations of the organization. Often, plans focus on the first two of these, but most falter on the third. As indicated in the second and third chapters, many postsecondary organizations already recognize that the most critical issue facing them arises from the rapid developments in the telecommunications industry and they have responded by implementing a technology plan. These comprehensive planning efforts were designed to provide campus students and personnel with institutional infrastructures for the use of digital telecommunications. The rush to 'wire' campuses often occurred even before there was a coherent institutional plan about potential uses.

Today, most institutions have Web sites which act as portals to their institutional services. However, the influence of information technologies on everyday life has brought about other pressures – a desire for relevancy and demand for flexibility. New institutions, without the traditional manifestations of campus classrooms and pre-designed programmes for selected learners, may use a similar telecommunications infrastructure to offer courses and programmes that have more relevant and flexible designs. It is therefore not sufficient for existing institutions to consider the addition of telecommunications technologies as yet another administrative communications system. Many institutions have begun to grapple with the costs of transferring and redesigning their administrative procedures for an electronic environment which students can access. This is important but much of the potential of the new technologies will be lost, if institutions do not also consider how to redesign their instructional core to take advantage of this infrastructure.

What is called for is not a simple convergence process. Other reforms have cut, reduced and realigned departments and units but few have tackled the tasks at the core of postsecondary education – instruction and scholarship. Instruction is at the heart of faculty culture and hence any change means a transformation in the academic culture. It depends for its success on the willingness of faculty to embrace its potential. In such situations, the contextual model may have more to offer than the strategic planning model. It acknowledges the fundamental importance of culture and it provides opportunities for the contributions of academics in the delineation of the change. It suggests that providing opportunity for experimentation may be more positive and creative than establishing a set of objectives and then focusing on implementation. If academics view the move to transformation of the instructional system as the imposition of technology they are unlikely to support the venture. Instead, since there is no single best blueprint, faculty should be encouraged to develop a number of different projects to address the issues of student flexibility, enhanced learning options, and institutional responsiveness. Bates (2000: 16) enumerated six of the most frequently cited reasons for using technology in teaching: improving the quality of learning, giving students opportunities to develop skills they will need in their professional lives, widening access to the services of the institution, responding to the 'technical imperative', reducing costs, and improving cost-effectiveness.

It is important to know who on campus has already begun to work in this area, to acknowledge their efforts and consult them for advice. But while small-scale innovation can be accomplished by enthusiasts, large-scale change requires:

- addressing infrastructure issues;
- developing a critical mass of activity;
- encouraging a shift in organizational and academic cultures;
- creating a reward culture for open and flexible learning;
- ensuring ongoing funding, for while short-term funds can provide monies for pilot projects, a sustained change needs to be built into the institution's budget.

Infrastructure refers not only to the technology infrastructure, which has usually been addressed in an independent plan, but also to the provision of faculty support in the design and implementation of open and flexible learning. Both networks are necessary and need to work in tandem. For example, the technology team needs to be able to provide software options that provide the greatest flexibility to instructors and students and proposed pedagogical designs need to be reviewed by the technology team in order to ensure ongoing compatibility.

All alternative instructional options are based on a combination of synchronous and asynchronous learning experiences. The movement from a teacher-centred to a learner-centred approach, recognition of students' increasing need for flexibility in place and time as well as institutional pressure for spaces, and increasing requirements for faculty to devote more time to research encourage the exploration of asynchronicity. This is the question that faculty need to address. Open and flexible learning provides for different combinations of asynchronous and synchronous options. The latter may be classroom specific or, using computer conferencing, need only be time specific. Redesigning instructional patterns may well result in restructuring the workflow of the unit and changing the traditional power structure and communications patterns. This is where a project management model provides for faculty support while encouraging creativity. Integrating technology into instruction is much more complex than wiring the campus, but those who choose not to get involved are likely to see potential students move to competitors who provide them with greater flexibility and more inclusive learning options.

Bates (2000) provides a list of tasks that an institution contemplating integration of technology into its instructional system needs to undertake. More importantly, he also confirms that since such changes are fundamentally to the culture of the institution it is essential that senior management share a common sense of purpose about the integration of technology and work to publicly facilitate and support its integration throughout the campus. No one suggests that it will be easy to implement a strategy that affects one of the core cultures of the institution but the common advice would be to:

- involve faculty early and broadly;
- start from strengths rather than addressing new needs;
- allow for differentiation and innovation;
- provide ongoing, realistic and sufficient support;
- ensure that the financial system supports the proposed technological developments;
- require that the links to other administrative systems such as faculty evaluation and programme design do not work against the strategy;
- publicize the change and celebrate the successes.

As Lynch (1997: 146) concludes:

> The efforts of traditional universities to reconcile the idea of flexible learning with traditional values should be a healthy activity resulting in improvements in [postsecondary] education. It will stimulate examination of assumptions, policies and practices that will make it possible to reinvent a more useful, competitive and vibrant university.

References

Bates, A W (2000) *Managing Technological Change: Strategies for college and university leaders,* Jossey-Bass, San Francisco

Chaffee, E E (1985) 'The concept of strategy: From business to higher education', in *Higher Education: Handbook of theory and research,* ed J C Smart, Agathon, New York

Daniel, J S (1999) *Mega-Universities and Knowledge Media: Technology strategies for higher education* (rev edn), Kogan Page, London

Gumport, P and Pusser, B (1997) 'Restructuring the academic environment', in *Planning and Management for a Changing Environment: A handbook on redesigning postsecondary institutions,* eds M Peterson, D Dill, L Mets and associates, pp 453–78, Jossey-Bass, San Francisco

Hall, R H (1994) *Organizations: Structures, processes and outcomes* (7th edn), Prentice Hall, Englewood Cliffs

Haughey, M (2000) 'A global society needs flexible learning', in *Flexible Learning, Human Resource and Organizational Development: Putting theory to work*, eds V Jakupec and J Garrick, pp 11–29, Routledge, London

Kennedy, D (1993) Making choices in the research university, *Daedalus*, **122** (4), pp 127–56

Kezar, A J (2000) Higher education trends (1997–1999) (Administration), ERIC Clearing House on Higher Education, http://www.eriche.org/library/admin.html (obtained 4/11/00)

Lawrence, P R and Lorsch, J W (1967) *Organization and Environment*, Harvard, Cambridge, MA

Lynch, W (1997) 'Flexible learning: Is it as good for the university as it is for the students?', in *Flexible Learning in Action*, eds R Hudson, S Maslin-Prothero and L Oates, pp 142–46, Kogan Page, London

Mintzberg, H (1994) *The Rise and Fall of Strategic Planning: Reconceiving roles for planning, plans, planners*, Free Press, New York

Peterson, M (1986) Continuity, challenge, and change: An organizational perspective on planning, past and future, *Planning for Higher Education*, **14** (3), pp 7–15

Peterson, M and Dill, D (1997) 'Understanding the competitive environment of the postsecondary knowledge industry', in *Planning and Management for a Changing Environment: A handbook on redesigning postsecondary institutions*, eds M Peterson, D Dill, L Mets and associates, pp 3–29, Jossey-Bass, San Francisco

Peterson, M, Dill, D, Mets, L and associates (eds) (1997) *Planning and Management for a Changing Environment: A handbook on redesigning postsecondary institutions*, Jossey-Bass, San Francisco

Pfeffer, J and Salancik, G R (1978) *The External Control of Organizations: A resource dependence perspective*, Harper & Row, New York

Scott, W R (1995) *Institutions and Organizations*, Sage, Thousand Oaks, CA

Tait, A and Mills, R (eds) (1999) *The Convergence of Distance and Conventional Education: Patterns of flexibility for the individual learner*, Routledge, London

Van Dusen, G C (1997) *The Virtual Campus: Technology and reform in higher education*, ASHE-ERIC Higher Education Report Vol. 25, No. 5, The George Washington University, Graduate School of Education and Human Development, Washington DC

Watson, D (2000) *Managing Strategy*, Open University Press, Buckingham

Weick, K (1976) Educational organizations as loosely coupled systems, *Administrative Science Quarterly*, **21**, pp 1–19

Part 3

Institutional management

Chapter 5

Management of institutions

K B Powar

Introduction

The successful management of academic institutions requires detailed planning, timely and appropriate decision making, and skilful coordination of activities. The organizational structure of the institution is often a determinative factor. Distance education generally is imparted through three types of institutions: the purpose-built distance education institutions (open universities), the mixed-mode (or dual-mode) institutions and the consortia (Rumble, 1986). In the case of mixed-mode institutions, the department or school of distance education is only one of the academic units of the parent institution and, therefore, the managerial responsibilities relating to it are limited. The consortia are essentially materials development and distribution agencies with management stressing the commercial aspects. Hence, the ensuing discussion is focused on the management of open universities, though much of what will be stated could also be applicable to the two other institutional types. It may also be mentioned that the management of distance education institutions is rendered difficult by the facts that these have a number of subsystems with different functions and responsibilities, and that their different administrative and academic units are spatially separated.

Management and the role of the manager

Before considering the management of distance education institutions *per se* it may, perhaps, be desirable to understand what is generally meant by the term 'management' and define the role of a manager. Broadly, management is the art of guiding actions and controlling situations in a manner that yields results that best meet the objectives of the institution. By implication, it means that a manager's basic task is to continuously strive to improve the situation and take it as close as possible to the ideal. As Checkland and Scholes (1990) put it: 'The "Manager" tries to improve situations which are seen to be problematical – or at least as less than perfect – and the job is never done . . . because as the situation develops new aspects calling for attention emerge, and yesterday's solution may be seen as today's problems.'

It has to be remembered that effective managerial performance depends upon the successful interplay of a number of factors, including the personal competence (in terms of skills, knowledge and aptitude) of the chief executive and his/her senior colleagues; and the existence of a stable institutional framework in the form of policies, rules, guidelines, conventions and information. It can be enhanced by provision of opportunities (say, to experiment or to innovate) and extension of support (in the form of appreciation, reward or promotion) to subordinates (Davies, 1996: Fig. 2).

The leadership provided to the institution is a crucial factor in management. The chief executive needs to have, among other things, a clear perception about the goals and objectives of the institution, a yearning for success but also the willingness to accept setbacks with stoicism, a confidence in colleagues and subordinates but not over-dependence on them, equanimity coupled with a sensitivity to the feelings of co-workers, an understanding of the strengths and weaknesses of the institution, a full knowledge of the functioning of all divisions and units in the institution, the (inborn) capability of having a holistic overview, the ability to take timely (and sometimes unpleasant) decisions, an appreciation of the need to change and the willingness to adopt new and innovative strategies, a commitment towards quality, and the ability to listen patiently and communicate effectively. The chief executive has to be not only a leader but also a motivator, coordinator and facilitator.

Organizational models and working cultures

The successful governance of an academic institution is dependent, to a considerable extent, on its organizational structure. Paul (1990) has recognized four major operational models for universities and other academic institutions:

- the *bureaucratic model* which has a well-established hierarchy – from the vice chancellor down to teachers and support staff – and is governed by laid-down rules and procedures;

- the *collegiate model* which has a collection of specialized professionals who try for consensus in decision making in an attempt to protect the autonomy of the individual professional;
- the *political model* in which due recognition is given to power groups and the need to protect their interests in decision making;
- the *anarchic model* in which the institution is considered to be 'an organized anarchy' where goals are vague and diffuse, technology unclear and participation fluid.

Each of these models results in different working cultures that determine the style and effectiveness of management. Following Davies (1996), we recognize four types of working cultures:

- the *corporate culture* where the emphasis is on the leadership provided by the senior management personnel, top-down planning and monitoring through performance indicators;
- the *enterprise culture* where there is a strong quality framework but considerable freedom for the individual to interact with external agencies, and results are expected;
- the *bureaucratic culture* where there is a dominance of administration and committees, with emphasis on rules and precedent, and a desire for uniformity and stability;
- the *collegial culture* where there is a respect for individual autonomy, considerable devolution of authority, the dominance of academic committees and a tendency to be loose regarding procedures.

Specific to the distance education institutions, Mugridge (n.d.) recognizes:

- an *educational culture* which focuses on fostering freedom of expression, critical thinking, respect for individuality, independence, and emphasis on process;
- an *industrial culture* which is characterized by hierarchies, division of labour, standardized mass production and line management.

By and large, the open universities are organized on the 'bureaucratic model' but have a culture that is a mix of bureaucratic, collegial/educational and industrial cultures. Thus, while the officials in the central administration may act in a bureaucratic manner, the academic units like the schools and resource centres may be decidedly collegial in their approach. The fact that distance education institutes have to mass-produce considerable amounts of learning materials adds a touch of Mugridge's industrial culture. The bureaucratic approach of a chief executive and the immediate subordinates is understandable, so also the working of the academics at their own pace, to attain scholarly objectives, without being unduly bothered by procedures or even rules. Even this assessment of a mixed model and culture may, in the view of some, be simplistic. A few decades back, Cohen and March (1974) considered the modern university to be an 'organized anarchy' because its goals are vague, technology unclear, issues ill-defined and approaches (of individuals) self-defined and, therefore, multi-directional. Hence, getting the best out of the professionals (teachers, researchers, technical experts) becomes a skill or even an art. Paul (1990) has drawn attention to this inherent conflict between the orientation of the professionals and the norms of bureaucracy. The silver lining is provided by the fact that most chief executives of academic institutions, as also their senior officers, are former professionals drawn from within the system and who, therefore, understand the minds of the professionals working with them.

The authorities and officers of open universities

Open universities, having been established largely during the last three decades of the past millennium (the oldest of them, the UK Open University was established in 1969), are, by and large, fortunate in not being weighed down by traditions, precedent, or archaic bodies like the court or senate. Hence, compared to the traditional universities, they have a simpler structure for governance. Most of them have three principal authorities or decision-making bodies. These are:

- The *planning board* which is mainly responsible for policy formulation and planning of developmental activities.
- The *board of management* or the *executive council* which is the decision-making and implementing body and which wields considerable power as much administrative and financial authority is vested in it. It also has some say in academic matters, being the body that grants final approval to academic decisions.
- The *academic council* which is concerned with all academic matters, including starting of programmes, framing of curricula, grant of equivalence to degrees, recognition of institutions and award of degrees and diplomas. Its recommendations are almost invariably accepted by the administrative authorities.

The vice chancellor (or president) is the chief executive officer of the university and functions as both its administrative and academic head. He or she is assisted by pro-vice chancellors (or vice presidents or rectors). Other important functionaries are the registrar, finance officer and controller of examinations who look after administrative aspects, and deans and/or directors who supervise academic and para-academic activities.

A number of committees, statutory and non-statutory, function in an advisory capacity under these three authorities. For example, the finance committee, staff affairs committee and campus development committee advise the board of management, and the academic council receives inputs from faculties, boards of study and departmental/school committees. Thus, in the case of the majority of institutions the administration is committee oriented, with the officers being responsible for the implementation of decisions. This often leads to piquant situations, for while the authorities and committees may take difficult-to-implement, and even impracticable, decisions, the responsibility of implementing them rests with the officers.

Managing the subsystems

Because of their varied functions, the constituent units of an open university may be assigned to the following four categories:

- *administrative divisions*, including those dealing with general administration, finance, campus maintenance and development, student registration, and evaluation;
- *academic units*, including faculties, schools and departments, and centres responsible for development of academic programmes, curricula and teaching-learning materials; and also for assessing the work of students or conducting research and/or training;
- *production and distribution units* for the production of teaching materials (print, audio, video and electronic), their storage and distribution;
- *student support services*, including a central library, regional centres and counselling centres.

Each of these categories presents distinct subsystems of the distance education system and it is the responsibility of the senior management to ensure that there is effective coordination between them.

Management of distance education systems is also difficult because of the fact that it comprises various subsystems with different functions and responsibilities. It is necessary that each subsystem work in harmony not only with other subsystems but also with external (sub) systems that provide inputs into the functioning of the system. Powar, Panda and Bhalla (2000) have, for example, recognized subsystems relating to administration and management, development of learning materials, production and distribution of learning materials, student support services, and registration and evaluation, and have described performance indicators for each of them.

The best strategy for the management of distance education institutions would conceivably be to:

- *delegate* authority and *assign* responsibility to heads of different divisions and units to evolve, under the supervision of the central authorities, procedures of functioning that would ensure productivity and quality of outputs;
- *monitor* the progress of each division and unit through a system of constant reporting and feedback;
- *assess* performance, periodically, through the use of recognized performance indicators;

- *coordinate* the activities of different divisions and units through frequent meetings, interactions and dialogue.

It follows that the middle-level management (divisional and unit heads) must be conversant with the basic administrative and/or managerial functions. These (Sengupta, 1996) include:

- *Planning*, which is determining objectives and policies, and formulating systematized programmes according to them. Office planning involves determining the various necessities of the office, selecting the best possible method(s) for performing various operations, and deciding when, where and how they are to be performed.
- *Organizing*, which is identifying and grouping of work, defining and delegating authority and responsibility, and establishing relationships.
- *Staffing*, which is finding the right person for the right job. It could be through the selection of a person having the requisite qualifications and training, but more often than not it is identifying a person who could be trained and assigned the work.
- *Directing*, which is the interpersonal aspect of management through which subordinates are led to contributing efficiently and effectively to the attainment of objectives. This is best achieved through effective communication and providing motivation.
- *Coordinating*, which is keeping the team together and in good spirit, thus ensuring that work is carried out harmoniously. This is best achieved by a suitable and equable allocation of work (according to capabilities) and even-handed treatment.

Management information system

Planning, monitoring, evaluation and promotional activities all require a steady inflow of data and other information from various units within an institution, and also from external sources. In the case of the distance education institutions, the data that are absolutely essential relate to admission and registration of students, evaluation, despatch and delivery of learning materials, stocks of learning materials, paper etc, income and expenditure against various heads, activities at regional centres and counselling centres, etc. All the information needs to be integrated, analysed and interpreted. Hence, it is essential that distance education institutions have an efficient, computer-based, management information system (MIS). Its basic purpose is to provide information to support operational, managerial and decision-making functions. Consequently the MIS has a pyramid structure (Nigavekar, 1994) with the:

- basal layer consisting of information for transaction processing (information relating to acts, statutes, regulations, rules and also precedents);

- second layer consisting of information required for conducting day-to-day operations and control (basic information and data relating to students, faculty, finances, products);
- third layer with information required for tactical planning and decision making (functions and responsibilities of various authorities, different activities);
- top layer, or apical part, containing information critical for strategic planning and policy formulation by the highest authorities (viewpoint, and possible impact on stakeholders).

There has to be a complete flow of data from one level to another. If properly developed, the MIS can be an invaluable aid in institutional management.

A word of caution is necessary. MIS is difficult to use because:

- The major stakeholders of the distance education system, ie students, faculty and administrative staff, operate within a dynamic framework and may, therefore, be disturbed by decisions taken on insufficient or old information. It is possible that they may express their dissatisfaction in different ways.
- Decision making is through the democratic process (by authorities, committees) and, therefore, can be subjective. On the other hand, the implementation is by an executive process (through officers) and is circumscribed by legal requirements (rules, regulations) (Nigavekar, 1994). Implementation may also be difficult because of 'ground realities'.
- Information is partly obtained from spatially separated units that are not under the direct supervision of central authorities. The possibility of data being incomplete, and even non-authentic, cannot be discounted.

MIS facilitates decision making and management if the information is complete and provided to the decision makers in time.

Interpersonal relationships

In a multifaceted system like that of distance education, where there is a need for effective coordination between, and within, different subsystems, there has to be a harmonious relationship between all employees, and interpersonal relationships assume importance. The initiative in this matter has to be taken by the chief executive and his/her senior management.

Following Verma (1994), interpersonal relationships in distance education institutions can be examined in terms of the following dimensions:

- *intra-institutional relationships* involving the central administration, the production units, the academic divisions and the support services;
- *human relationships* involving the members of the decision-making bodies, the academic fraternity, the administrative and production staff and the members of the community;

- *academic relationships* involving the basic academic activities, namely teaching, research, material development and production, and student support.

In each of the above relationships the personal, or human, approach is likely to yield the best results. The head of the institution and senior management must meet the different stakeholders (students, faculty, administrative and technical staff, members of the community) at regular intervals. The policies and programmes of the institution must emerge as a result of interaction and after considering the inputs provided by the stakeholders.

Verma (1994) emphasizes the fact that interactional and bi-directional activities can strengthen interpersonal relationships. The activities include:

- *Involvement*: It is productive to have the stakeholders involved in the decision-making process. The views of the students on the mechanisms of evaluation and the usefulness of a course, and that of the faculty on course development, of technical staff on matters related to production and of the community on the general quality of the programmes offered, are invaluable for decision making.
- *Dialogue*: Unilateral decisions often create unpleasant situations and lead to tensions and even confrontations. It is best to have a dialogue with representatives of students, teachers or employees before taking decisions that are likely to affect many or most of them. Even if there is no agreement after discussions, the two sides know each other's thought process and position. This helps to remove bottlenecks and misunderstandings.
- *Equality*: There has to be a feeling of equality even in a hierarchical system and employees must feel that they are being given their due, whatever the nature of work done. The basic norms and rules must be the same for all categories of employees.
- *Freedom of expression*: Every stakeholder must have the freedom to express his/her view, of course in a disciplined manner; as also the right to be heard. Simply allowing a person to express his/her feelings can relieve a lot of tension.
- *Cooperation*: The cooperation of every member of a unit must be sought. A friendly word, a little encouragement, and permission to innovate generate a feeling of involvement.
- *Motivation*: In order to get the best out of employees, it is necessary to motivate them. This can be done in a variety of ways, including giving them a job of their liking, keeping them informed, soliciting their views, appreciating good ideas, giving adequate incentives and rewards, providing job security and showing concern about their welfare. It is, however, sometimes necessary to stress discipline and instil a modicum of fear.

Financial aspects

Most plans related to the management of an institution, and for its development, are based on the assumption that enough funds are available for their implementation. If resources are readily available institutions can be managed successfully and plans for expansion of infrastructure, activities and programmes implemented. Unfortunately, this is rarely the case, and in reality institutions have to function under financial constraints. Hence, careful budgeting and monitoring of expenditure is an essential part of management.

A characteristic of distance education institutions is that both income and expenditure can be high. The income is from governmental grants (usually for payment of earmarked expenditure like that for salaries, and for developmental purposes) and fees. In the case of many institutions that have huge enrolments, the latter can be considerable. Expenditure on production and delivery of learning material may also be considerable, and in many cases difficult to control because schedules have to be met. However, if the programmes offered are of a general nature, like the Bachelor's programme in the liberal arts, and the learning material mass-produced according to the 'Fordist' production strategy (Raggat, 1993), then considerable savings can accrue. This is the position in the case of certain distance education institutions, especially the dual-mode universities. In such a situation, the additional revenue generated may be diverted to other expenditures within distance education.

As Rumble (1986) points out, when funds are in plenty, institutions expand with a proliferation of programmes and activities, the growth, however, being relatively unplanned. When funds are constrained, institutions have to make effective and efficient use of resources. This succeeds only to a certain extent, and if the situation of reduced resources continues there is an ultimate curtailment of activities. As, in most cases, the resources are limited, the efficient management of finance is crucial to the functioning of an institution. This can be achieved through efficient functioning and careful budgeting. Tightening up of performance is possible only to a certain extent. Financial managers often take recourse to an all-round financial cut of equal proportion (say 10 per cent of budgeted amount). This is an unhealthy practice for it favours the proliferate spender, while penalizing the efficient. It's also a case of the financial personnel taking decisions which others (administrative and academic heads) have to implement. Financially constrained institutions usually resort to revenue budgeting (when there are tight but predictable resources) or to zero-based budgeting when resources are scarce and the future uncertain. It is a good practice in such cases to have a 'core budget' that can take care of all essential requirements and an 'additional' or 'peripheral budget' to meet the optimum needs of a programmme. Constant monitoring of expenditure should be able to control the overall situation, and with the availability of many financial software packages this should not prove to be difficult.

Conclusion

The distance education system is polycentric, having a number of subsystems with disparate functions and requirements; therefore, the management of distance education institutions is relatively complex. It is controlled by the organizational structure of the institution and its working culture. The chief executive and other senior management personnel have a key role to perform. Within this dynamic system, there needs to be a continuous exchange of information among the various units/subsystems, and management can be made easier with support from a fully functional and efficient management information system. Interpersonal relationship is a key factor and has to be fostered. As most institutions work under resource constraints, there has to be carefully planned budgeting and monitoring, along with an efficient functioning of all subsystems.

References

Checkland, P and Scholes, J (1990) *Soft System Methodology in Action*, John Wiley and Sons, Chichester

Cohen, M D and March, J G (1974) *Leadership and Ambiguity*, McGraw-Hill, New York

Davies, John L (1996) Higher education management, training and development quality indicators, *New Papers in Higher Education Studies and Research*, UNESCO, Paris

Mugridge, I (n.d.) Managing the institution, *Course Material, M.A./Diploma Course 4, Block D, Unit 13*, UK Open University, Milton Keynes

Nigavekar, A S (1994) 'Management information system for university administration: concept, structure and development', in *University Administration and Management*, eds K B Powar and S K Panda, pp 49–63, AIU, New Delhi

Paul, Ross H (1990) *Open Learning and Open Management*, Kogan Page, London

Powar, K B, Panda, S K and Bhalla, V (2000) *Performance Indicators in Distance Higher Education*, Aravali Books International, New Delhi

Raggat, P (1993) Post-Fordism and distance education – A flexible strategy for change, *Open Learning*, **8** (1), pp 21–31

Rumble, G (1986) *The Planning and Management of Distance Education*, Croom Helm, London

Sengupta, S (1996) 'Office administration and management', in *Staff Development in Indian Universities*, eds K B Powar and S K Panda, pp 9–20, AIU, New Delhi

Verma, S K (1994) 'Management in university administration: interpersonal management', in *University Administration and Management*, eds K B Powar and S K Panda, pp 35–40, AIU, New Delhi

Chapter 6

Institutional leadership and the management of change

Ross H Paul

Introduction

In this age of high technology, there are many prophets with breathtaking visions of a very different future for postsecondary education. They foresee empowered learners with ready and inexpensive access to a huge array of learning materials in all sorts of media pursuing learning opportunities throughout their lives. In their future, both formal and informal education take place in all sorts of institutions, public and private, and the relatively autonomous student is in charge of his or her learning.

At the same time, there are many sceptics who fail to appreciate the value of the new visions or who are dubious about our ability to achieve even their most desirable aspects. They cite such barriers as strongly entrenched faculty resistance to change, the glibness and superficiality of much writing about technology and its application to learning or the high front-end costs of a significant investment in new technologies. They also wonder about the readiness and ability of students to assume the responsibility for their own learning inherent in most of these models.

In contemplating the implementation of a radical new vision for education, it is relatively easy to imagine the establishment of new institutions that incorporate its central premises, a few of which have already been established. They might be (as has been described in Chapter 1) updated versions of the British Open

University and its many imitators around the world, 'niche' institutions directed at professional education, or bold new corporate ventures like the University of Phoenix.

This vision notwithstanding, it is highly likely that most postsecondary education will continue to be provided not through brand new institutions but by updated versions of what we have now. Instead of building institutions from scratch, the major challenge will be to work to change our established institutions to adapt and adapt to the new information technologies, as has also been echoed by Haughey in Chapter 4.

The pressures are for transformation, not incremental change, and, if a recent major speech by the UK's Education and Employment Secretary David Blunkett is anything to go by, the stakes may be very high indeed for an incumbent university president:

> Universities are autonomous institutions, and rightly so. But as the Prime Minister put it in his Romanes lecture last year, in the knowledge economy, entrepreneurial universities will be as important as entrepreneurial businesses, the one fostering the other. The 'do nothing' universities will not survive – and it will not be the job of the government to bail them out. (Blunkett, 2000: 2)

It is the central premise of this chapter that bridging the gap between the vision and the reality is the primary challenge for those leading today's (distance teaching) universities and colleges, one that will require a wide range of management and leadership skills. The immediate challenge is to find ways to preserve the strengths of the current system while taking advantage of new technologies to produce learners who have the independence, skills and motivation to take responsibility for their own learning.

In this chapter, some of the common components of a future vision for postsecondary education are reviewed; the primary barriers to its realization are suggested and discussed; and a strategic approach is outlined that best ensures the realization of the vision within existing educational institutions.

The vision

There are many writers with quite dramatic visions of change in postsecondary education over the next decade or two, fuelled by the tremendous advancements in information technology and the growing recognition of knowledge as the currency of power in the information age (see, for example, Dolence and Norris, 1995; Downes, 2000; and Langenberg and Norris, 1998).

Common themes among these writers include empowered and more autonomous students, freed from time and geographic constraints through access to a glittering array of information technologies; a much greater variety of educational institution, both public and private; a true commitment to lifelong learning; a separation of course development from course delivery; and a competency-based approach to learning.

Langenberg and Norris (1998: 5), for example, cite four key adjectives for what they call 'transformed' learning in the Knowledge Age. It will be 'perpetual' in that it is fused with work and other activities; 'distributed' as students are exposed to pervasive virtual, online resources; 'interactive' as opposed to the more unidirectional traditional model of education; and 'collaborative' as students work increasingly in teams or in communities.

In a stimulating paper prepared for Contact North, Ontario's distance education consortium in Canada, Downes (2000) presents a wide-ranging vision of how a sophisticated technological environment can place the student much more centrally responsible for his or her own learning. He likens it to the model of video games, whereby the learner adapts to a demanding environment where the requisite knowledge and skills must be actively sought and learnt for success.

Institutional support would be provided through 'the triad model' (Downes, 2000: 14) whereby the student interacts with both the instructor, who is responsible for content and evaluation, and the facilitator who is there to motivate and to provide personal support.

In projecting this model into the mainstream, Downes (2000: 15) envisions increasing differentiation between 'host' and 'provider' institutions. The latter are apt to be large-scale and global in outlook, producing learning modules and 'courses' for international distribution. The host institutions are local in orientation, providing the social environment and access to technology and the personal support required to understand and make best use of the learning materials. Host institutions would be smaller and more personal, often with areas of fairly narrow specialization.

A strength of Downes's paper is that, while presenting a rosy future for online learning, it recognizes that today's version is a long way from the dream and that its development is very demanding on initiators and practitioners.

In contemplating a decision to adopt a vision like Downes's, it is quickly obvious that it would be much cheaper to adapt existing institutions than to create a whole new network of host and provider institutions. At the same time, such adaptations must confront significant barriers that rapid change always faces – resistance from the prevailing organizational culture, very practical issues of costs and systems, and a huge challenge to communicate with, persuade and recruit faculty, staff and even the students themselves to participate actively in the new directions. It may be cheaper, but will it be easier? Will it be more effective?

It is this management challenge, to provide the leadership necessary to change our existing institutions, that is of central interest in this chapter.

Difficulties inherent in adapting an established institution to the new vision

In an established mainstream university, there are many reasons why implementation of a Downes-like vision is difficult:

- Faculty were hired primarily for their disciplinary skills and commitment to research.
- Faculty have not been trained as educators and are likely to teach the way they were taught in university. Hence, any significant change in teaching and learning methods in a university requires a huge investment in faculty training and education.
- Faculty workloads have escalated with a decade of cutbacks in resources coupled with expanding enrolments and the exponential increase in the pace of institutional life associated with new communications and information technologies.
- The front-end costs of preparing online courses, both financial and in terms of faculty time, are huge and require enormous investments of both at considerable risk and uncertainty that the new product will be 'better' and more popular than the current offerings.
- Institutional reward systems do not usually encourage significant experimentation with models of learning and are skewed in the direction of disciplinary research activity and publication.
- Support systems are geared to traditional modes of operation. Everything from the physical plant (classrooms and laboratories) to the limitations of a fixed course timetable and academic regulations that require regular and specified hours of formal academic contact contributes to the difficulty of change.
- Distance education and the intrusiveness of new technologies means that traditional ways of dealing with copyright and ownership of knowledge are no longer appropriate and their resolution is complex and controversial.

Institutional management and leadership – responding to the challenges

One of the central strengths of a university is its climate of academic freedom and the relative autonomy of its faculty. With the search for truth as its principal value, such an institution is designed to encourage the diversity of opinion and autonomy of practice that are its prerequisites. These present a significant management challenge, however. In fact, those responsible for 'university management' frequently joke either that it is an oxymoron or that it would be easier to go out and herd a bunch of cats!

Ironically, however, as more and more private corporations hire highly specialized professionals in a society where knowledge is increasingly the currency of power, they are organizing themselves more like universities and recognizing that previous hierarchical forms of management are no longer effective (Handy, 1996: 113). This trend places a higher premium on examples of successful change in a university setting as they are increasingly of interest to corporate theorists as well.

Drucker (1999: 73) argues that the great resistance to technological change of the 1980s has been largely dissipated, now that everyone understands the need for continuous change. Even if he is right, this news has not yet reached many universities where faculty are extremely critical of threats to the way their institutions have long functioned.

It is a serious mistake to castigate opponents of major change in our universities as dinosaurs or Luddites. Instead, the effective leader must encourage real debate on issues of change and capitalize on the positive energy that can be generated by an open and thorough consideration of alternatives. University faculty members are highly articulate and forceful in the presentation of their opinions and, while that doesn't make change any easier, at its best, it can ensure that every major step has been well thought through and really does have significant support in the institution.

The point is that there are legitimate concerns about both the direction and pace of change in our institutions in the current age. These include such diverse issues as the compartmentalization of knowledge, the 'dumbing down' of the curriculum, shorter interest spans among students, the glibness and superficiality of some of the claims for new technology, its glorification at the expense of thoughtfulness and perspective, and the overall assumption that, because something is brand new, it must be good. While universities must be in the forefront of change in the knowledge society, their faculty members have also long played the equally important role of social critic, wondering aloud if newer and faster necessarily means better.

In arguing for a balance between change and continuity, Drucker (1999: 90) recognizes the importance of involving staff and clients/customers in the change process. Real and permanent change is usually much more likely where those most affected by it are a fundamental part of its processes, even if this does somewhat slow the immediate pace of change.

A four-year analysis of major change agendas in 26 diverse colleges and universities conducted by the American Council on Education (1999) found the most effective strategies to be those that fully involved all key stakeholders in an ongoing collaborative venture. It was also important for leaders to view change not as an event with a beginning, middle and comfortable end point, but as a much more complex 'ongoing, organic process in which one change triggers another, often in unexpected places, and through which an interrelationship of the component parts leads to an unending cycle of reassessment and renewal' (ACE, 1999: 1).

While recognition that the times are changing is a prerequisite, it is an insufficient condition for successful leadership. Especially in a university environment, the institutional leader must be well prepared before launching an overt attempt to induce change. The approach must be strategic, systematic, open, informed and long term to be effective. Such 'strategic planning' involves several stages and components as given below (these may be related to strategic versus overall/contexual planning discussed by Haughey in Chapter 4).

Environmental scan

A well-informed environmental scan that stands up to rigorous scrutiny is a good starting point, outlining the strengths and weaknesses of the institution and of its competitors, demographic and political trends, and alternative courses of action. By articulating and analysing the strengths and weaknesses of and opportunities for an institution, a good strategic plan clearly establishes the case for change and the major factors that must be considered in the process.

Vision development and articulation

From this strong information base, the leader must develop and communicate a clear vision for the future of the institution, one that builds on current or potential strengths and which can be carried out by a core group of in-house leaders. Nothing is more central to institutional change.

While there are many strong advocates for strategic planning, it is also useful to read the sceptics, such as Henry Mintzberg (1994) and Gary Hamel (cited in Langenberg and Norris, 1998). Mintzberg cautions against top-down strategic planning while Hamel notes that it is all too frequently not strategic at all, but simply incrementalism, projecting into the future what is already going on. True strategic thinking must be subversive, putting the strategy back into planning, encouraging the revolutionaries that every organization has, and recognizing that the end product may be very different from that originally envisioned (Langenberg and Norris, 1998: 12–13).

One of the most important components of developing a vision is the overall identity of the institution and which 'niche' it will serve. For example, in looking to the future, Langenberg and Norris (1998: 7) identify three kinds of learning which will flourish in various combinations in an institution:

- traditional courses and degrees, delivered on-campus, a mature market which will continue to thrive in regions where the proportion of 17–24-year-olds is still growing;
- virtual and distributed learning, off-campus, which will enjoy substantial growth in a great variety of settings;
- transformed learning, incorporating all their previously noted components of future learning (perpetual, distributed, interactive and collaborative) and leading to specific certificates of mastery, which they portray as a massive growth area that is application-driven and geared to the workplace.

A useful perspective on the choices that must be made from an institutional viewpoint is offered by William Massey's three categories of institutions of higher education (cited in Donnelly et al, 1998: 95). These are:

- 'platinum cards' – highly prestigious universities, the visibility and reputation of which are usually based on faculty research and traditional educational values;
- 'wannabes' – prestige-seeking universities that lack the market power to achieve that status;
- 'entrepreneurs' – those that build a market niche by catering to student needs and whose market potential depends on delivering quality as defined by the 'customer' rather than by more traditional academic values.

Notwithstanding the IT revolution, it is highly likely that the 'platinum cards' will continue to thrive as their ongoing attraction of the best students will reinforce the reputation of their graduates. They will, of course, adapt to new technologies and approaches to learning, but not at the expense of their critical social and political roles of producing a nation's elite.

The real challenge is for the 'wannabes', whose deeply entrenched cultures make it very difficult for them to aspire to anything else. Under bold new leadership, a few may transform themselves into the kind of institution described as entrepreneurial, but the danger is that they may gradually lose out to both other categories, unable to match the prestige of the 'platinum cards' or the 'student as customer' orientation and flexibility of new 'entrepreneurs'.

Another option is for a given institution to compete differentially for different programme areas. Hence, a given university might strive for 'elite' status in one or two areas of real strength, while emphasizing a much more student-oriented flexibility and outreach in others. This is the strategy currently in place for my own institution, the University of Windsor, building on its natural advantages in the automotive and environmental sectors while endeavouring to improve the quality of service to students across all others.

Communications

Once a vision has been adopted, the leader must be tireless in its articulation and communication in language that is clear and optimistic for the future of the organization. Internal leaders must be identified, cultivated and encouraged to work with others who are sympathetic to or excited by the prospects for change. It is vital in these communications that the case for change is made positively and focuses on improvements without assigning blame. Especially where faculty and staff have invested a great deal of time and energy in an institution, they are apt to react defensively if the proposed new directions can be seen as criticizing what has gone on before (ACE, 1999: 3). Sensitivity to such feelings and concerns is an important characteristic of an effective leader.

Investment of resources

It may be trite to state that new ventures must be solidly funded and supported, but inadequate funding is one of the most common reasons for failure. This is strongly underlined by Drucker (1999: 88) who advocates the creation of two ongoing budgets for a given area – a regular operating budget and a special allocation of as much as 10–12 per cent as a budget 'for the future'. A willingness to invest heavily in a new venture demonstrates the leader's confidence in its importance and potential for success, it recognizes that those responsible for it need strong support and recognition and it removes any subsequent blaming of inadequate resources as the reason for failure.

Pilot project

While it is hard to disagree with the need to invest suitable resources in a project, an institution can pay a high price for a major failure. It is, thus, usually advisable to start with a pilot project that has every opportunity for success. It is much easier to ensure proper staffing and financial support for a pilot project, working with those who are already positively disposed towards the experiment, than it is to try to reform an entire institution all at once. As well, success breeds success and it is extremely important that a first venture be given every opportunity to succeed.

However, there is a danger that even a successful pilot project will not integrate well into the organization. Leaders must anticipate this challenge in advance and build in as many links as possible across the institution.

Reward systems

Every effort must be made to adapt the reward systems so that they are consistent with the new directions and vision. This is particularly challenging where they are entrenched in collective agreements or senate bylaws. Given that issues may be complex, as in ownership of intellectual property or how one recognizes good teaching, the importance of open and serious discussion is reinforced. This area requires a particular combination of persistence and patience from institutional leaders. The challenge is to help those opposed to changes to come to appreciate the overall benefits to the institution and, hence, to themselves, in the long term.

Training needs

These must be identified early in the process and faculty and staff must be given every encouragement and incentive to participate in them. This requires consider-able sensitivity to workloads and recognition that release time and other support may often be necessary if the change is to be given every opportunity to succeed. It should also be recognized that this is not 'training' in a traditional hierarchical sense. It must be delivered in ways that take full account of established faculty values and practices, so that it facilitates rather than inhibits the enhancement of the quality of teaching and learning on campus.

Information base

Leading change in an established organization forces one to confront the institution's culture and its mythologies. It is not enough to rely on the initial environmental scan if an institution is to adapt continuously to today's rapid pace of changing conditions. Good institutional research, especially as validated by objective, external sources, can be extremely useful in this difficult challenge. Hamel (in Lagenberg and Norris, 1998: 13) emphasizes the importance of perspective in developing a deeper understanding of an institution's strengths and weaknesses as a prerequisite to good strategic planning.

Accountability

Openness is central to effective management, especially in times of major change. Everything, from the central vision to the means adopted to achieve it, must be open to ongoing evaluation and, where necessary, reformulation.

There is a too prevalent tendency to use 'input' rather than 'output' measures in assessing the effectiveness of educational institutions. Hence, a university may be valued more for the high marks of its entering students than the subsequent performance of its students in graduate school or in the job market or, using an even more difficult measure, the responsibility subsequently taken by graduates for their own learning.

As critical as these public and external commitments to accountability are today, even more important is the internal accountability of the institutional leadership. Especially in a university, where faculty autonomy and collegial governance are so entrenched, the authority of the president and other institutional leaders is more moral than statutory. It follows that an open leader who performs in a manner fully consistent with the vision and the values originally espoused will have a much better chance of perpetuating that moral authority than someone with a more closed style.

Strategic alliances

There are many important advantages to developing strategic alliances in adopting a strong change mandate for an established institution. Appropriate partnerships can do much to help institutions deal with the huge initial investment costs of new technologies and of training staff to use them effectively. They can provide access to those with complementary competencies rather than having to develop all of these within one's own institution and the synergy between compatible partners can encourage both to be more innovative and ambitious.

At the same time, and especially in an increasingly competitive environment, collaborative ventures are effective only when the roles, responsibilities and benefits are clearly specified for and well understood by each partner. Without strong mutual benefit and understanding of each other's cultures, partnership agreements will be increasingly seen as time-consuming, frustrating and counterproductive.

Conclusions

Donnelly provides a very useful comparison between the future development of higher education and what has already happened in the healthcare sector, at least in North America. After tracing the development of the latter from 50 years ago, when it was essentially a collection of local cottage industries, to today's huge, market-driven corporate complex, he concludes that the lesson for higher education is very clear:

> Technology holds great promise to improve the efficiency of higher education management, teaching, and learning, but change will come only slowly and at a higher price than expected. That cost will not be measured only in dollars, but also in profound changes in prevailing values and the sacrifice of some sacred cows of the academic environment. At the same time, some 'end-runs' are likely, in which new providers of direct training and then education . . . will capture a measurable share of the current college and university market, by exploiting the power and cost-effectiveness of new information and communications technologies without the transition costs and dislocations that existing traditional institutions face. (Donnelly *et al*, 1998: 87)

It is those transition costs and those dislocations that are of most interest to an incumbent university president. They are occurring in a highly competitive, increasingly complex environment and traditional student bases can no longer be taken for granted as the choices and opportunities widen at a phenomenal rate. At the same time, they offer an opportunity for institutional leaders to reverse the recent trend of what Mitchell (1999: 20) has identified as a 'topsy-turvy process of ad hoc development' by narrowing their missions and bringing their institutions back together in a more common purpose.

It is probably still the case, then, that those in well-established, credible institutions of higher learning have the best chance to continue to dominate the market, but only if they adapt much more quickly and much more openly to it than they have in the past. The need for strong, open and sensitive leadership has never been higher.

References

American Council on Education (1999) *On Change: Reports from the road – insights on institutional change*, ACE, Washington
Blunkett, D (2000) Speech by the Secretary of Education and Employment, University of Greenwich, England, 15 February (www.dfee.gov.uk/newsnews.cfm?prnumber=064&pryear=00)

Dolence, M G and Norris, D M (1995) *Transforming Higher Education: A vision for learning in the 21st century*, Society for College and University Planning, Ann Arbor, MI

Donnelly, T R *et al* (1998) 'The revolution in health care and a prognosis for higher education', in *Reinventing the University: Managing and financing institutions of higher education*, eds Clark L Bernard *et al*, pp 69–98, John Wiley and Sons, New York

Downes, S (2000) *The Future of Online Learning*, Contact North/Contact Nord, Sudbury, Ontario

Drucker, P F (1999) *Management Challenges for the 21st Century*, Harper Collins, New York

Handy, C (1996) *Beyond Certainty: The changing worlds of organizations*, Harvard Business School Press, Boston

Langenberg, D N and Norris, D M (1998) 'Expeditionary strategy and products for the knowledge age', in *Reinventing the University: Managing and financing institutions of higher education*, eds Clark L Bernard *et al*, pp 3–40, John Wiley and Sons, New York

Mintzberg, H (1994) *The Rise and Fall of Strategic Planning*, Free Press, New York

Mitchell, T N (1999) From Plato to the Internet, *Change* (March/April), pp 17–22

Chapter 7

Management of academic development

Graham Webb

Introduction

The outcome of academic development for flexible learning is to produce an academic workforce with the understandings and skills necessary to produce good educational experiences for students in the wide variety of settings that flexible learning makes possible. However, the nature of the involvement of staff in producing those experiences is the subject of some debate. This introduction will therefore consider what is meant by:

- academic work (relating to flexible learning);
- academic development;
- flexible learning;
- good teaching and good educational experiences.

Academic work

Much has been written lately on the changing nature of academic work (Coaldrake and Stedman, 1999; Marginson, 2000; Martin, 1999; Taylor, 1999). One of the central concerns is the degree to which academic work will become more or less professionalized and skilled. One major trend is de-professionalization and de-skilling, with economies of division of labour being sought in the separation of programme planning and the production of instructional materials from teaching, and both from assessment/evaluation, and quality assurance. This means that three separate workforces may plan and prepare courses, teach courses, and mark, evaluate and set standards for courses.

At the same time there is also a trend towards increasing professionalization as university teachers are encouraged or required to obtain a credential in teaching (usually a Graduate Certificate), join a professional teaching association and demonstrate continuing professional development in order to retain professional standing. Credentialing in teaching mirrors the longstanding (and far more intensive) credentialing in research as evidenced by the PhD, and membership of a professional teaching association equates with the normal practice of most other professional groups. The point to make here is that Graduate Certificate courses together with the notion of teaching as a professional practice, generally, favour a view of teaching based on a reflective practice cycle of planning, teaching, assessing, observing, evaluating and improving. While others (such as materials production and instructional design people) may well be involved in the process, there is a strong sense of academic involvement and participation in the complete cycle of course planning, delivery and evaluation. This stands in contrast to a reflective practice cycle seen as limited simply to 'delivery', for example.

It is obvious that the nature of staff development will depend on an organization's view of academic work and that the reflective practice model suggests that academic development integrates understanding and skills across the whole cycle. This chapter views academic development from the latter view.

Academic development

The term 'academic development' is used in this chapter to indicate that we are dealing with academic programmes that are for the most part developed, taught, assessed and evaluated by academic staff, and therefore that academic staff are a central concern. 'Educational development' is often used as an alternative. 'Academic staff development' can have a wider meaning (including development for research and/or leadership and management) and both 'professional' and 'staff' development are often applied to non-academic staff.

While it is undoubtedly true that academic staff will work increasingly with non-academic staff (instructional designers, Web programmers, multimedia producers, project managers etc) in team situations, it is academic staff who usually have overall responsibility for initiating curriculum development, defining the major dimensions, determining content material, selecting and refining teaching approaches, determining assessment regimes, designing and conducting evaluations, and making subsequent improvements. This is all grist to the mill of academic development.

Flexible learning

In Chapter 1, Peters referred to the focus on increased accessibility and individual learners. The term flexible learning is used here to convey the desire to provide students with increased access to learning and greater choice within the educational environment:

> Flexible learning can thus be seen, not as an alternative mode of education, but as an overarching driving force, a move to allow students greater choice in how, when and where learning takes place. This has prompted teachers and administrators to reflect on the teaching and learning environments they have created, and determine new ways to engage with their students. (Murphy, Jamieson and Webster, 1998: 2)

Flexibility may or may not be found in the large variety of 'on-campus' learning contexts, distance education, open learning and so on. It may be developed in terms of course structure, course content, teaching and learning methods, interaction and assessment. The central assumption is, however, that academic development to help achieve good flexible learning experiences for students depends on the development of academics as good teachers.

Good teaching and good educational experiences

Just as there is rarely a clear, causal and linear relationship between teaching and learning, so too is it rare to see a clear linear relationship between academic development, teacher behaviour and student learning. In each case the 'teaching' experience has to be embodied in the participant, imbued with their own background and understanding, and played out through their various intentions and motivations. However, from the discourse of academic development that has emerged over the past 40 years or so it is possible to suggest a number of key points for teaching that will tend to lead to good educational experiences for students. Here are 10 key points that are repeatedly suggested in that discourse:

- building relationships between staff and students;
- modelling scholarly values;
- encouraging cooperation;
- encouraging active learning (eg being actively engaged in talking and writing about learning experiences, relating these to past experiences, daily lives and prospective careers);
- providing appropriate teaching through different teaching approaches to meet different learning objectives;
- providing appropriate assessment;
- providing prompt and helpful feedback;
- encouraging productive use of time;

- communicating high expectations;
- respecting diversity in the background and experience of students.

These 10 key points provide an outline for the content and direction of academic development in helping staff to provide 'good educational experiences' for students.

Institutional context

Before considering academic development strategies for flexible learning, it is worthwhile to consider the context within which these work and the measures necessary to align institutional goals, policies and academic development.

Staffing policies

Trying to effect academic development for flexible learning in a hostile environment is a waste of time. Most notably, if institutional practice is to promote people disproportionately on research publication as opposed to teaching, then academic development will have a poor chance of effecting change. Other measures to support teaching, such as awards for teachers, teaching development grants and the use of leave for pursuing teaching development projects, can augment but cannot replace a carefully thought through and thoroughly implemented staffing policy (see Ramsden *et al*, 1995). In other words, staffing policy and implementation must stress the production of evidence, through performance management (or appraisal) by academic staff and heads of schools/departments, concerning the scholarship of teaching, quality of teaching, including evaluation of teaching, development of flexible learning approaches (where this is an institutional priority) and continuing professional commitment to, and achievements in, educational development and the scholarship of teaching.

At the level of recruitment it is necessary for advertisements, job descriptions, short-listing and interview processes to address this area, and so too must probation and promotion processes. Evidences for teaching development need to be made explicit in promotion policy and development activity needs to be undertaken to ensure that promotions committees adequately understand the policy and the interpretation of relevant evidence.

Planning, educational policy and review

It is necessary to ensure alignment between the policy and plans of the university, academic development and the development of flexible learning. This includes such documents as the university strategic plan, education policy, assessment policy, teaching and learning plan, information technology plan, service/support area plans and faculty or departmental plans. Again, for academic development to be successful the direction of development needs to be clearly outlined in the plans and educational policies of the institution. Further, the review mechanisms of the institution should also pick up the most important elements of policy and assess the degree to which these are being implemented.

Key strategies for academic development

In this section a number of key central university strategies for academic development will be outlined. This is not to suggest that worthwhile development does not occur at the level of faculty, school, department or the individual academic. However, if a university wishes academic development to be strategically focused, consistent, efficient and effective across the whole organization, then central planning and provision are required.

Thick and thin strategies

In order to use academic development resources efficiently and effectively, some decisions need to be made with regard to the level of service or provision that any academic can expect, as opposed to resources being concentrated in areas of high strategic priority. *Thin* strategies are those that any and every academic can expect by way of support. These might include such things as 'Guides to Flexible Learning' and 'Case Studies in Flexible Learning' (see, for example, http://www.adm. monash.edu.au/ched/) together with introductory workshops to teaching generally and flexible learning in particular. *Thick* strategies, on the other hand, aim to concentrate academic development resources in high priority areas. It may be, for example, that a university has a fund for strategically important course or teaching and learning development. If there is no central means for identifying strategic initiatives, then faculty plans or consultation with heads or those charged with faculty course or teaching and learning initiatives can establish priorities.

Professionalization strategy

As outlined earlier in this chapter, academic work may be at a crossroads between increasing professionalization and increasing de-skilling, fragmentation and casualization. In choosing the direction of professionalization, an institution must be prepared to reward those attaining a professional teaching credential and continued professional standing, mainly through the appointment, probation and promotion system.

The most important aspect of the professionalization strategy is that it recognizes the need for a grounding in the discourse of university teaching and learning for *all* teachers, and that teachers who have developed skills and understanding through such a process will tend to adapt better to the ever-changing context of flexible learning and new technology environments. On the other hand, development that is more technically focused (eg technical training for Web-based teaching) does not allow the teacher to see the role of teaching within the larger framework of educational values and understanding. The teacher with a thorough appreciation of the theory, values and perennial paradoxes of teaching and learning will tend to make better use of changing technologies in developing good educational experiences for students.

When a Graduate Certificate in Higher Education course is itself offered flexibly (eg with choice in pacing, place of learning, negotiated projects, face-to-face introductory sessions, online activities, online discussion, print materials etc), participants in the course gain an intensely authentic appreciation of flexible learning from the student's perspective. Again, this is a far deeper and more authentic learning experience than simply attending a half-day workshop on flexible learning, for example.

Quality-related strategies

With the adoption of quality assurance and improvement processes in many countries, new possibilities for academic development have already emerged and continue to do so. Although a defining line is sometimes drawn between quality assurance and academic development (policing/enforcing as opposed to supporting/ developing), this has always been questionable. As the point of quality assurance is increasingly seen as being necessary to effect improvement, and improvement and development are inexorably tied, it is likely that the traditional area of academic development will be drawn ever closer towards quality processes.

There will be a need to work with course teams (and others) in identifying performance indicators and benchmarks for the success of their course, collect evidence from a variety of sources, monitor performance, identify areas for improvement and introduce development activities to these areas. This will be necessary across the whole university and will include support areas for flexible learning, for example, together with the academic programmes themselves. Routine planning, monitoring and development will feed into rolling reviews that again will unearth opportunities for academic development. It may well be, therefore, that internal university arrangements for quality assurance and improve-ment include academic development functions that historically have stood apart, and often been marginal to such institutional concerns.

Leadership strategy

As academic leaders such as heads of department are crucial in changing the way in which teaching is valued and implemented within an institution, it is necessary that they be evaluated according to their performance in the development of academic programmes and staff. At the same time, staff development is important in introducing academic leaders themselves to the discourse of teaching and learning improvement and to the scholarship of teaching.

Management issues for academic development

This section considers some issues pertaining to the positioning and management of academic development within the institution, followed by some issues relating to the 'internal' management of an academic development centre.

Institution-level management

The way that academic development is structured and organized varies enormously by country and by institution. Some themes have included:

- individuals having responsibility for institutional and teaching research in a 'Higher Education Office' (1960s and 70s);
- audiovisual units developing educational technology materials and providing advice and training (1960s and 70s);
- student evaluation of teaching operations (1970s to present);
- ubiquitous adoption of workshop series, especially for new staff (1980s to present);
- merger of academic and general staff development and later separation (1990s);
- academic development placed with instructional design and media production (1990s to present);
- new relationships between quality assurance, improvement and academic development.

There is obviously no right way to structure academic development within a university. That having been said, the themes above suggest some convergence on how academic development has been structured at various times.

Within universities there has been a general trend to identify a senior management position (eg deputy or pro-vice chancellor) with the responsibility for academic or educational matters. Under this management umbrella, the modern structural trend is to develop a 'one-stop shop' providing all support for teaching and learning, including academic development. Especially in universities with developed distance education or educational production services, the 'one-stop shop' concept has led to academic development finding itself in joint centres dominated by materials production and instructional design (and in some universities library and information technology support). This raises significant challenges, including: academic leadership; work practices and culture; the 'product' and 'system' focus of instructional design versus the 'people' and 'adaptive' emphasis (starting with where the person is) focus of staff development; maintaining the credentials and credibility of academic developers; credibility of Graduate Certificate programmes offered; and support for academic research.

The other recent trend relates to quality assurance and improvement. Universities are presently creating centres to oversee quality assurance, especially given the development of national external audits. However, given the destructive effect of quality assurance dissociated from quality improvement, and the need to link quality improvement to developmental mechanisms and structures, it is possible that some redefinition and restructuring of academic development around the quality assurance–improvement–development continuum could occur.

Centre-level management

Many of the general issues concerning the leadership and management of an academic area addressed by Ramsden (1998) apply equally to an academic development centre. To put some of these into context as well as adding additional operational issues, this final section will briefly consider a few key issues in centre-level management.

Staffing: qualifications and performance

An academic development centre is only as good as its staff, and staffing for academic development is a crucial if difficult area. In order to have credibility in working with academic staff, academic developers must have PhDs themselves, an appropriate teaching qualification, and experience of teaching in flexible learning settings. In terms of performance, staff must also be seen as exemplary in terms of producing good quality research and publications, and in terms of teaching as evaluated through normal processes. Similarly, where staff take on management responsibilities, it is necessary to induct and mentor where necessary.

The most difficult area of staffing is where the staffing profile does not meet the requirements of the work to be undertaken or where performance is poor, and staff development is not appropriate or has been unsuccessful. Just as departments throughout universities have had to make hard decisions with regard to ending contracts, offering early retirement and redundancy packages or simply termination, so too academic development centres face similar decisions.

Staffing: flexible learning and technology

We have seen how the career path for academic developers tends to mean that they are mid-career and move into the area having already had experience in universities. As such, they can reflect some of the 'older' values and attitudes of the university as a whole; and, on the other hand, may also resist change, especially in the uptake of modern information and communication technology. It may lead to new technology areas (flexible learning or multimedia centres) being set up outside of academic development. There must therefore be management commitment to ensure that all who are responsible for academic development themselves not only understand, but are skilled in the use of new information and communications media. Minimum competencies to be developed could include: word processing and tracked editing; e-mail, address books and lists; initiating and running an electronic discussion group; chat; teleconferencing; videoconferencing and desktop videoconferencing; Web navigation, searching and bookmarking; electronic filing and databases; PowerPoint; multimedia audio and video players.

Staffing: budget and flexibility

The budget of an academic development centre can be tied up to a large degree (eg 80 per cent or more) with long-term staffing. Again, this mirrors the situation in many departments of the university and it does not ease the leadership and management task. Wherever possible, reducing fixed staffing costs down to a core, long-term minimum, and then hiring in short term for specific projects, allows a centre to take strategic priority initiatives that otherwise would not be possible. Similarly, having a flexible 'outer' workforce, particularly of people who only wish to work part-time, or who are at the same time contracted with others, allows for growth and reduction of staffing as budgets, contracts or external earnings fluctuate. By such means the centre's own initiatives to provide flexible learning academic development opportunities for staff can be supported.

Just as many universities are looking to diversify their funding sources, so too can academic development centres seek to diversify income. In many places the pattern of block central funding for university-wide workshops and academic development activities remains, with cost recovery operating for 'tailored' or contract work. Research contracts and outside consultancies have long been a feature in the work of some centres, but for the most part these have been seen as offering development opportunities and exposure for centre staff, rather than as a serious vehicle for income diversification.

Modelling flexible learning

As more flexible approaches to learning gain ground it is inevitable that academic development centres will use similar processes. This means making staff development materials and opportunities more accessible to all staff by utilizing modern communications and multimedia approaches. Effecting academic development more flexibly, including the development of a flexible Graduate Certificate type of course, presents opportunities for academic developers themselves to model many of the characteristics they endeavour to promote in others. For example, the centre may: adopt a team approach to developing and teaching both a Graduate Certificate course and other development events; seriously commit to student-centred learning; define and base courses on articulated educational values; link local teaching issues to the broader international discourse; use educational media appropriately and for particular purposes; develop exemplary Web-based, print and other multimedia materials; and use modern outsourcing methods for materials planning and production. Seeing these things done well sets a good example to staff committed to the development of both flexible learning and professionalization.

Supporting distributed academic development

As a central unit strives to deliver academic development for flexible learning throughout the university, the issue of the interface with faculties or schools comes up. It is likely that faculties or schools will develop some educational materials production capacity (eg Web) of their own, along with instructional design. These may be located within the faculty or externally contracted. The question then is: how does the central unit work with the manager of the faculty and with these local developments?

One solution has been the development of 'Associates' schemes in a number of universities to link the central effort with faculty-based activity. Not all have been successful, with a major stumbling point being ownership by the dean of the faculty (or similar). The other matter, which can cause problems, is that 'Associates' may not be granted any relief in order to pursue academic development activities. For such schemes to succeed, therefore, it is necessary to have the faculty dean, relevant sub-deans and the director of a central staff development unit all agree on the appointment (of the person) and the extent of relief from other duties. It is also necessary to negotiate a clear position description that reflects faculty strategic directions, and if a particular project is a part of this, to specify clearly the parameters of the project. This presents an ideal opportunity for determining priority areas for faculties in terms of the development of flexible learning and for ensuring central academic involvement, through the associate scheme, in such projects.

Routine management

These last words on the management of an academic development centre concern routine matters, as it is in the routine of management that the strategies and directions outlined above can be effected, or fail. For example, while a yearly retreat to consider general directions and performance may be common, more targeted and shorter retreats to consider particular areas may be less so. Further down the hierarchy, whole day, half-day or even one-hour (anticipated and planned) sessions devoted to 'brainstorming' an issue or requirement may be useful.

Similarly, 'management' meetings to consider work requests coming in, progress with strategic priorities and the allocation of workload need to be held on a very regular basis, whereas whole staff meetings in larger centres may be held less regularly. The planning, preparation and sharing of duties for meetings and events of all kinds is an important management responsibility.

Finally, and especially with regard to work practice-related issues, there needs to be a central reference point (probably Web based) for decisions taken with regard to such things as workload, conference attendance, working from home, technology support and so on. This also applies to other policy decisions such as the kind of support that can be offered to teachers within the university presenting for promotion. It is surprising how often the same issues come forward, and how quickly decisions that have been thoroughly talked through and agreed are forgotten.

Conclusion

With the present urge for technology-based solutions to teaching and learning, especially the rush to 'get on the Web', it is not surprising that academic development is finding itself located alongside instructional design and production functions. In recapitulating the past, it may be anticipated that academic development will emerge from this trend to express once again the wider understandings of teaching and learning (see Webb, 1996) that it has helped to develop. Part of that emergence could well be associated with the need to tie development to institutional quality improvement and assurance. Indeed, working in this way would take account of many of the considerations that Boud (1995) outlines as being important for the staff development of the future. It is to this area that we may perhaps look for future management options.

References

Coaldrake, P and Stedman, L (1999) *Academic Work in the Twenty-First Century: Changing roles and policies*, Department of Education, Training and Youth Affairs, Canberra, Australia

Boud, D (1995) 'Meeting the challenges', in *Directions in Staff Development*, ed A Brew, Society for Research into Higher Education and Open University Press, Buckingham

Marginson, S (2000) Rethinking academic work in the global era, *Journal of Higher Education Policy and Management*, **22** (1), pp 23–35

Martin, E (1999) *Changing Academic Work: Developing the learning university*, Society for Research into Higher Education and Open University Press, Buckingham

Murphy, D, Jamieson, P and Webster, L (1998) *What is Flexible Learning? Flexible learning guide number 1*, Centre for Higher Education Development, Monash University, Clayton, Victoria

Ramsden, P, Margetson, D, Martin, E and Clarke, S (1995) *Recognizing and Rewarding Good Teaching in Australian Higher Education*, Australian Government Publishing Service, Canberra

Ramsden, P (1998) *Learning to Lead in Higher Education*, Routledge, London and New York

Taylor, P (1999) *Making Sense of Academic Life: Academics, universities and change*, Society for Research into Higher Education and Open University Press, Buckingham

Webb, G (1996) *Understanding Staff Development*, Society for Research into Higher Education and Open University Press, Buckingham

Chapter 8

Management of research and development through the support of action learning projects

David Kember

Introduction

Research and development (R&D) is crucial to any open or distance education institution; and such operations may occur and be managed at various operational levels of the institution. There may be exclusive units or centres dealing with this; and the institution or the centre may base its activities on any framework it decides to be most appropriate and feasible. This chapter looks at the management of research and development initiatives through an action learning or action research framework. To do this it draws upon the Action Learning Project (comprising 40–50 projects) in Hong Kong. This initiative funded and managed 90 action research projects across the eight higher education institutions in Hong Kong. As the Action Learning Project was itself conducted as an action research project into how to manage this type of development and research activity, there are valuable lessons to share. This is also an example of academic development, and of managing a wide variety of research and development activities (including those concerned with open and flexible learning) undertaken collaboratively across institutions.

Action research framework

Terminology within the chapter will slip somewhat loosely between *action learning* and *action research*. The literature on action research is much better developed so it is easier to describe a framework based upon action research. The initiative drawn upon, though, used the word *learning* in its title to make it clear that it was not purely a research project, but was concerned with the development of learning initiatives and the improvement of learning quality. It is, therefore, necessary to explain the relationship between action learning and action research.

Both action learning and action research assume that learning results from active experience. Learning and improvements to existing situations come about through iterative or cyclical processes. Initial ideas can be examined in concrete applications. Observation then leads to reflection and the formulation of ideas for improvement the next time the activity is performed.

Action research is a more systematic and rigorous form of action learning, and its outcomes are normally made public. Action research gathers systematic data during its observation phases, whereas action learning usually relies only upon critical discourse (McGill and Beaty, 1995). Action research projects are, then, action learning projects, but the converse does not hold true. In general, research is always a learning process, but a methodical and rigorous form of learning in which results are published (Kember, 2000).

Action research

The characteristics of action research listed below have been distilled from a number of accounts representing the major typologies (Carr and Kemmis, 1986; Elliott, 1991; McKernan, 1991; McNiff, 1992; Stenhouse, 1975). In the following text in this section each of these aspects of action research will be briefly discussed.

Action research is applicable in situations in which participants wish to improve their own practice. The mode has been called participative action research, indicating that it is normally a group activity involving those affected by the topic being investigated. There may well be an attempt to widen the circle of involvement to include others involved in the practice. There is a degree of divergence of opinion as to whether it is essential that action research be conducted by a group or if it can be conducted by an individual as a problem-solving activity or through reflection on practice.

The roles of the practitioner and expert researcher also influence the subject matter of action research. It has been claimed (Carr and Kemmis, 1986; Stenhouse, 1975) that educational researchers following other paradigms commonly concentrate upon theoretical issues which are of little interest or relevance to teachers. In action research, though, it is the participants or teachers who decide the subject or topic for research. It can be something they feel is interesting or important or it can be a problem they want to solve.

Perhaps the clearest distinction between action research and other types of research lies in the attitude to changes to what is being researched. Other paradigms tend to avoid perturbing the subject of their research. Action researchers set out with the avowed intention of improving their practice. Lewin (1946) and Rapoport (1970) both maintain that research should go beyond the production of books and papers to achieving social change.

Action research is portrayed as a cyclical or spiral process involving steps of planning, acting, observing and reflecting. It is normal for a project to go through two or more cycles in an iterative process. Improvement is brought about by a series of cycles, each incorporating lessons from previous cycles.

It should not be thought that action research is a soft or imprecise mode as rigorous systematic inquiry is as integral as for other paradigms. The action research cycle incorporates systematic observation and evaluation. Outcomes of systematic inquiry are made public and subjected to normal criteria for scrutiny and acceptance. Action research does, then, contribute to both social practice and the development of theory. Its advocates claim that it brings theory closer to practice.

Characteristics of projects

To translate these general characteristics into something rather more concrete, following is a list of characteristics which would apply to all the projects supported by the Action Learning Project:

- Project teams are composed of small groups who share a similar interest or concern.
- The topic for the project is chosen by the participants, to fit within the broad aim of investigating and improving some aspect of their own teaching.
- Project groups meet regularly to report observations and critique their own practices.
- Projects proceed through cycles of planning, action, observation and reflection. At least two cycles are normally necessary to implement and refine any innovatory practices.
- The observation phase makes use of a variety of evaluation methods so that triangulation can occur.
- Lessons learnt from the projects can be disseminated to a wider audience through publications and other methods of dissemination.

Introduction to the action learning project

The most important evidence that action research is an appropriate framework for managing research and development projects is the fact that it has been effectively put into practice through a large-scale project, namely the Action Learning Project (Kember, 2000). Theory that cannot be applied in practice is not useful theory.

Virtually all of the participants in the supported projects felt the action research framework was appropriate, even though the majority had no prior experience of the mode of research.

The Action Learning Project is an inter-institutional project encompassing the eight institutions in Hong Kong funded by the University Grants Committee. Academics in each of the institutions were invited to submit proposals for funding from an Action Learning Project Fund. The initial round of the Action Learning Project funded 50 projects and, in the second round, it supported 40 projects, which are now drawing to a close. Each project was an action research project by a group of academic staff, with its own focus consistent with the overall goal of enhancing the quality of student learning by improving the quality of teaching.

Not all of the projects could be described as concerned with open or flexible learning in the artificially constrained way in which the terms are commonly used. About a third of them were concerned with the development of multimedia packages or Web sites. The remainder were research and development projects concerned, either with a wide variety of innovative forms of teaching and learning, or with tackling a range of identified issues. Regardless of the nature of the innovations or the type of education, the important lesson for the purpose of this book is that the framework was applicable to managing a large number and a wide variety of research and development initiatives.

The management structure

There are three main aspects to the management of the initiative. The first is the organizational structure through which the Action Learning Project, as a whole, was run. The second is the nature of the support offered to the individual project teams. The third is the associated dissemination activities.

The Action Learning Project was, as noted earlier, an inter-institutional initiative operating across the eight institutions funded by the University Grants Committee of Hong Kong (UGC). It was governed by a management committee with a member from each of these institutions. On a day-to-day basis the project was run by a small team consisting of a coordinator with between one and six associate coordinators at various stages.

In awarding grants the Action Learning Project was structured as a conventional research programme. It seemed sensible to follow well-known and established procedures. Structuring the initiative in this way was also part of a bid to enhance the status of teaching and learning as a valued academic activity.

All academics in Hong Kong were invited to submit grant proposals for action learning projects related to some aspect of courses they taught. The most significant criterion for awarding grants was whether the proposals contained a convincing rationale for how the potential project would have an impact on improving the quality of student learning. It would seem to be good practice in allocating resources for flexible learning initiatives always to make the requesters justify what they intend to do in terms of why they think it will improve learning outcomes.

Supporting projects

The Action Learning Project had a small coordinating team who provided support to the project teams. A large majority of the participants in the projects felt that this support was necessary, as did an independent evaluation panel. Evidence was also gathered which showed that the provision of the supporting infrastructure helped to ensure that the projects led to worthwhile outcomes (Kember, 2000).

In view of the nature of action research it is not appropriate to think of support by an external facilitator or adviser as 'management' in the way the term is normally used. The orientation of the coordinating team to the participants was important. Carr and Kemmis (1986: 161) felt that the relationship between the action researcher and teachers was important. The researcher should become a 'critical friend' helping the insider to make wise judgements in the process of educational transformation. Stenhouse (1975: 142) believed that proposals should be presented as provisional specifications to be tested rather than unqualified recommendations. This orientation or approach seems highly appropriate for staff in educational institutions who are often sceptical of didactic pronouncements.

The 'critical friend' orientation provided a suitable level of support while still permitting ownership of projects by participants. This led to greater involvement and allowed participants to develop valuable skills and appropriate perspectives. The coordinators worked together to fulfil this critical friend role. The associate coordinators acted as the first point of contact with the project teams. Each had responsibility for liasing with 10 to 12 projects. To strengthen the contact, for the first round of the project, each took responsibility for a different university.

The involvement of the coordinating team varied from project to project and defining the role was an evolving process. There was an initial meeting with each project team at which the level and type of involvement was negotiated. The development of the supporting role evolved throughout the project. The Action Learning Project was itself an action research project into how to organize and support a teaching quality enhancement initiative along action learning lines.

The critical friend role in supporting educational action research projects has evolved towards a multifaceted role. Important facets of the role are discussed below and metaphors given:

- The ideas for the projects came from the participants themselves but some did need help in planning so this led to the role of *project design consultant*. It should be noted that action research plans are not the detailed and rigid plans of positivistic research. Action research is an iterative process so plans are changed and refined as the cycles progress. Hardly any of the projects in the Action Learning Project stuck closely to their original plans and many participants seemed surprised that they were allowed and encouraged to deviate from them.
- Establishing a viable relationship with a team brings in the facet of *rapport builder*. Once a relationship is established, this needs to be developed into an ongoing relationship of mutual respect and trust which has been christened the *coffee maker* facet of the role.

- Reflection upon practice is an essential component of action research for it is through this that lessons are learnt from initial cycles which can guide practice in future ones. It is also through critical reflection that attitude change can occur. The critical friend can play the role of *mirror* by asking questions, prompting and challenging the teams while engaged in their critical discourse.
- The most significant facet of the role has been that of *evaluation and research adviser*. It is important that appropriate evaluation is conducted during each cycle so that appropriate lessons can be drawn for future practice. The orientation here has been that of helping the participants to develop the necessary expertise rather than doing the evaluation for them. In this way the teachers can become equipped for ongoing monitoring and improvement of their own teaching.
- The research element enters as most teams have wanted some means of proving that they had achieved what they set out to.
- As the initiatives are treated as akin to research projects, university academics can benefit from the traditional reward structures of universities by publishing the outcomes. Some participants have sought advice from the *writing consultant*, as they were unfamiliar with writing papers in an appropriate format for educational research.
- An important aspect of the Action Learning Project has been encouraging teams to share lessons learnt with other teams and with academics not involved in projects. This started in an informal way with the *match maker* putting participants in touch with those working in similar areas.

There are several more facets to the role but these are less relevant to the discussion at hand. Further discussion of the critical friend role is given in Kember *et al* (1997a).

Dissemination activities

Dissemination of ideas and information from the supported projects has been an important facet of the overall project. The dissemination activities served several purposes. Firstly, they were a way of passing on what was learnt to other teachers who were not involved in the initiatives. The hope was that others could incorporate into their teaching what had been learnt from the projects. The requirement to report on their projects at meetings and a conference served as a check on progress and a quality assurance mechanism. The Action Learning Project dispensed with the form-filling type of reports normally associated with research grants as the reporting through meetings gave a better picture of progress and, at the same time, communicated what had been learnt to a wider audience. The final function of the dissemination activities was that of developing a belief in research into teaching as a legitimate scholarly activity.

To establish the mode of reporting through the dissemination activities, the project teams awarded grants in the Action Learning Project were asked to sign an initial agreement which included the requirement of participating in meetings and the conference and producing a final report. It seemed sensible to incorporate these obligations in a written agreement, though it must be said that the participants saw the dissemination activities as events they wished to participate in rather than things they were forced to do. Similarly, the production of reports was accepted as a necessary final outcome, though some teams did seem to find difficulty meeting the deadlines.

Interest groups were formed to encourage the sharing of expertise between projects. The interest groups focused upon a particular discipline, such as language teaching, or upon the nature of the project, for example problem-based learning or developing multimedia packages.

For the second phase of the Action Learning Project, the following interest groups were formed:

- developing critical thinking and clinical reasoning;
- English language teaching;
- learning through doing;
- multimedia;
- Web site development;
- teacher education.

The participants valued the informal networking experiences and the more formal ones through the 'interest group meetings'. These brought together participants in projects of a similar nature or in the same general discipline area. They aimed to stimulate learning across projects and to pass on lessons to others not involved in projects, for example to a wider audience of Hong Kong academics. This process surely had some impact in promoting teaching as a scholarly activity.

Each of the interest group meetings was held in conjunction with an appropriate department from one of the universities in Hong Kong. The event for the multimedia and Web site development group was in the form of a display of educational packages developed for the computer. The display attracted a wide range of presentations from projects supported by the Action Learning Project, plus others from universities and the Vocational Training Council (VTC). The teacher education meeting formed part of an international conference promoted by the Hong Kong Institute of Education. The remaining meetings were in the form of seminars or mini-conferences held in conjunction with an appropriate department or university.

A conference was held at the end of each of the two rounds to give all project teams the opportunity to report and discuss their projects. The sessions were arranged in parallel streams which approximated to the groupings used for the interest group meetings. The conferences were open to all academic staff so as to widely disseminate findings from the projects. The first conference had 343 registered participants, and the second nearly 600 registered participants. These included staff from each of the eight UGC institutions together with participants from the school sector, the Open University of Hong Kong and the VTC.

The papers for the conference were posted on the Action Learning Project's Web site so that interested participants could read them prior to the conference. The aim was to maximize discussion, rather than presentation, but few participants appeared to have taken advantage of this facility.

After the conference the project teams were given two weeks to modify their papers in the light of any discussion. They were then expected to submit the modified version as a final case study report on their project. These were then compiled into a bank of case studies of action research projects for a range of discipline areas and diverse types of teaching initiatives. The first of these has been produced (Kember *et al*, 1997b) and the second is well on the way.

Maintenance of quality standards was important in respect of the dissemination activities. In these the projects are portrayed as paradigms of good practice. If they are not, then the worth of the dissemination aspect is seriously undermined. Maintaining rigour and quality is seen as important otherwise research on teaching and learning will be seen as an inferior form of research activity. Final reports were only included in the respective collective volumes if approved by two independent reviewers. Many of those that were included were asked to revise their initial drafts.

Participants in the projects also report on their activities in seminars, papers, articles and conferences other than those commissioned by the Action Learning Project. Through these reporting activities the participants make a major contribution to dissemination within their own universities and to academics in other universities.

The Action Learning Project developed a Web site. The site includes information about conducting action research and educational evaluation techniques. It has information about projects supported in both the first and second rounds of the Action Learning Project. The Web site (http://alp.polyu.edu.hk) has had a substantial number of visits from Hong Kong and overseas.

Overall conclusions

This chapter has described and discussed a management structure for research and development projects which has been operationalized on a large scale through the Action Learning Project in Hong Kong. The overall initiative was formulated with an explicit action research framework, which had marked implications at each level of operation.

At the individual project level it meant that each of the 90 projects was both a research and development project. Although the phrase 'research and development' is a common one, in academia the two are not often combined, just as teaching and research are normally separate or competing entities.

Another implication of the action research philosophy at the individual project level was that the teams were fully responsible for, and had ownership of, their own initiatives. The approach, therefore, is quite different to the management structure for course development commonly employed in distance teaching organizations.

In these it is common for development to occur through a very organized structure with a central development facility and with significant input from instructional designers and other experts. The difference between these two course development paradigms is discussed more fully in Kember (1997, 1998).

The relationship of the coordinating team to those participating in the projects developed over the course of the initiative and we came to describe it as that of a 'critical friend'. We prefer to talk of providing support to the project teams rather than utilizing the term management.

The final part of the structure put in place was the important one of the dissemination activities. This fulfilled the important role of passing on lessons learnt from the projects to a wider audience. It led to the development of mutual support networks between project teams. It also provided a mechanism for ensuring progress and quality appropriate to the action research philosophy.

References

Carr, W and Kemmis, S (1986) *Becoming Critical: Education, knowledge and action research*, Falmer Press, Brighton, Sussex

Elliott, J (1991) *Action Research for Educational Change*, Open University Press, Milton Keynes

Kember, D (1997) Action research: Towards an alternative framework for educational development, *Distance Education*, **18** (2), pp 43–63

Kember, D (1998) 'Staff development from an action research perspective', in *Staff Development in Open and Flexible Learning*, eds C Latchem and F Lockwood, Routledge, London

Kember, D (2000) *Action Learning and Action Research: Improving the quality of teaching and learning*, Kogan Page, London

Kember, D *et al* (1997a) The diverse role of the critical friend in supporting educational action research projects, *Educational Action Research*, **5** (3), pp 463–81

Kember, D *et al* (1997b) *Case Studies of Improving Teaching and Learning from the Action Learning Project*, Action Learning Project, Hong Kong

Lewin, K (1946) Action research and minority problems, *Journal of Social Issues*, **2**, pp 34–46

McGill, I and Beaty, L (1995) *Action Learning: A guide for professional, management and educational development* (2nd edn), Kogan Page, London

McKernan, J (1991) *Curriculum Action Research*, Kogan Page, London

McNiff, J (1992) *Action Research: Principles and practice*, Routledge, London

Rapoport, R N (1970) Three dilemmas in action research, *Human Relations*, **23** (6), pp 499–513

Stenhouse, L (1975) *An Introduction to Curriculum Research and Development*, Heinemann Education, London

Chapter 9

Management of resources

Greville Rumble

Introduction

Educational enterprises consume resources. Conventionally, accountants identify four categories of resources: human resources; premises and accommodation; equipment and furniture; and stocks (inventory), supplies, consumables and expenses. Typically, budgets reflect these costs in a series of budgetary lines that are more or less detailed, depending on managerial requirements.

The budget is seen as one of the most important communication devices in an organization, helping to make sense of the organization by reflecting its objectives, and helping to measure and define the inputs required to achieve a given output. At the same time, it also helps organizations evaluate their plans since it enables them to establish input–output relationships between the level of resource put into a plan and the level of output achieved. These relationships can then be built into predictive models to help decision makers determine what may or may not be possible in the future.

Different kinds of organizations adopt different budgetary structures. Figure 9.1 is a diagrammatic representation of the budget structure in a distance teaching organization.

Like other enterprises, distance education institutions need to start with their revenue budget for the year. In commercial systems income derives from student

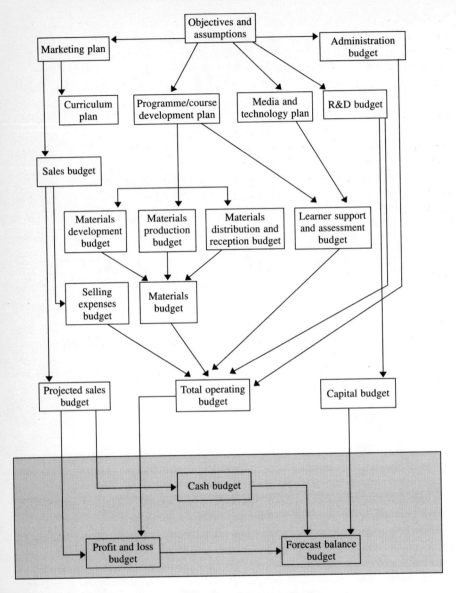

Figure 9.1 *Budget structure in a distance teaching organization*

enrolment fees and/or materials sales. In publicly funded systems the resources come from government or from a mix of government, student fees and materials sales. In some cases government money is generated largely from student numbers, with the government in effect providing a per capita grant for each student enrolled. Because the cost structure of distance education is very different from that of traditional education, not least because of the very considerable investment that needs to take place to develop the materials before a single student can be enrolled, this is a crude approach to funding distance education. Some funding regimes therefore separate the funding of course development, course presentation, student support and overheads. Such an approach has the advantage that it explicitly recognizes the fact that distance education involves high fixed costs (the costs of developing materials and administering a system of a certain size), and low variable costs (the costs of reproducing the materials, and of supporting and assessing students), while enabling the funding agency to control not just the size of the student body, but also the size of the curriculum and the rate at which it is replaced. In this approach the course load was in effect a function of three variables: the total number of courses presented in any one year, the average life of each course, and the total number of courses to be developed each year. A funding formula could thus be derived:

$$E = f + iD + pC + vS \quad \text{[Eq. 1]}$$

where:

E = the total expenditure
f = fixed costs of the institution (ie administration)
i = the direct course-related cost per course of developing a course
D = number of courses (of a standard type) developed in any one year (eg costs of staff to develop the course, costs of copyright clearances for third-party materials used in the course)
p = the direct course-related cost per course of presenting a course in any one year (eg cost of broadcast transmissions, fixed costs of printing materials for that year)
C = the number of courses of a standard time presented each year
v = the variable cost per student (eg costs of tuition, assessment, postage of materials to the student etc)
S = the number of students (attracting a standard support and assessment package)

and where the number of courses in development (D) is equal to the total number of courses presented (C) divided by the average life of the course (ie number of years a course would be presented before it is withdrawn or remade) (L), such that:

$$D = C/L \quad \text{[Eq. 2]}$$

This second approach to funding emphasizes the crucial importance of two institutional plans: the marketing plan – which should cover the recruitment of new students, the retention of existing students and the re-enrolment of old students – assumes prime importance in forecasting student-number-driven income; while the curriculum plan not only becomes a major element of the marketing plan (in as much as it determines the 'products' that the institution is trying to sell), but also assumes a key role in the control of expenditure on course development and production, and in some cases in the funding of the institution.

As with other organizations there will be a sales budget. Institutions operating in jurisdictions where there is an existing shortage of educational provision may find that they have little need to advertise. There are indications that successful commercial correspondence colleges invest no more than 15–20 per cent of their income from fees in the advertising for new students. Certainly, any figure beyond that suggests that the market is saturated, the institution is offering courses that the market does not want, the institution is perceived to be too expensive or of poor quality, or a mix of any of these.

Success in student recruitment will depend on the appropriateness of the curriculum plan and the extent to which this meets demand. For any given number of students, the more options there are, the lower the average number of students there will be on each course. Because of the cost structure of distance education, low course numbers are a problem. The more students that take the course, the lower the average per capita cost of this development effort. It is this fact, coupled with the generally low direct costs of student support, that makes distance education an attractive economic proposition compared to traditional forms of face-to-face teaching (Rumble, 1997).

To an extent, course designers can adjust the mix of media (that is, of print, audio, video, face-to-face, and computing), and the actual technologies used to deliver the media, in order to ensure that the cost per student is kept within reasonable bounds, but, in the end, low-population courses tend to be expensive. Each medium, and each technology, has its own pedagogic advantages and disadvantages, level of accessibility to students, and cost structure (Bates, 1995; Rumble, 1997). Some technologies have high fixed costs (eg television, computer-based learning, multimedia approaches), others low fixed costs (eg print, radio, audiotapes). Some have high per capita student costs (eg tuition – whether it is delivered face-to-face, by audio- or videoconferencing, or electronically, computer-based learning, multimedia approaches), others have low or even no per capita costs (eg radio, once the transmission network is in place). Sensible distance teaching institutions will consider not only the cost of the technology to the institution, but also its cost to their students, since high technology costs (both of buying into the technology and running it) can impact on the students and on demand (elasticity of demand), and hence on the institution's ability to achieve its sales budget and any access mission that it may have. Finally, the costs of technologies are in general coming down, so that what is an 'exotic' and expensive technology now becomes commonplace and affordable within a few years. A key element in any distance teaching institution's plans must be its media and technology plan, and the extent to which it invests in research and development to explore, and in capital equipment to support, particular technologies (cf. Daniel, 1996; Bates, 2000).

Media and technology are used to deliver learning materials and experiences to the students. Working within the overall media and technology strategy, the main 'users' of media are the courses within the academic programmes. Adequate control of resources will require each course to work to a budget. The best way of doing this is to build up an accurate description of what the course will look like when it is being delivered to the learners, and then to cost this description. Thus, a course description will cover not just the aims and objectives of the course, and its likely contents, but also indicate the number of texts that it will have (usually based on some standard of length and quality), the number of audio and video programmes (of x minutes of a certain standard quality) and their mode of distribution or delivery (cassette delivered by post, broadcast), the amount of face-to-face tuition that will be available in local centres (in hours) and the average size of the learning group, the number of assignments that students will do for marking, the examination arrangements, the IT components of the course etc. Standard costs (developed over time and regularly monitored) will enable course budgets to be built up.

Once this has been done, the overall course development, course production, course distribution, course reception, learner support and learner assessment budgets can be worked out. With the exception of the first, these will require some estimate of the student numbers likely to take the course (though guesstimate may be the better word at this stage). Also, one needs some idea of the number of years over which the course will be presented before it is withdrawn or remade. The latter depends in part on the speed with which knowledge or content is changing, and in part on changes in the market.

If cost-efficiency is an objective, then balance has to be drawn between the likely student population each year, the choice of media, the number of years the course will be presented, and the maintenance of academic credibility in the light of the rate of obsolescence of content. However, one of the major constraints on the life of courses is the ability of the institution to redevelop materials. The UK Open University originally aimed to replace its courses after four years but it quickly became apparent that the academic productivity rate (the volume of materials one academic could produce in any one year) was insufficient to enable this to happen (Rumble, 1997: 78–81). With the Department of Education and Science refusing to provide funds to increase the University's teaching staff, the University had to take the other option and increase the length of life of its courses to eight years – making some of them look decidedly dated by the time they came to be replaced. However, even those institutions that rely on contracted authors to develop materials can face difficulties when it comes to redesigning courses. Productivity rates are a useful way of modelling and controlling the size of the establishment (Rumble, 1997: 78–83).

The next stage is to ensure that the total production and delivery load can be accommodated within the budget and within the capacity of the production facilities. There may be particular constraints on the development, production and delivery of some technological options (for example, a maximum to the number of video programmes that can be made in a given year, or the total hours of broadcast television airtime available). Here too there are balances to be achieved – in this case between the number of programmes allocated to each of the courses and the number of years they will last before being replaced, the production capacity, transmission resource, the availability of alternative distribution technologies such as video cassettes, and the relative cost of distribution by broadcast versus cassette.

The overall materials budget is made up of the materials development, materials production, and the materials distribution/reception budget. These budgets will each be made up of different elements – direct labour, materials purchases, and overheads, as appropriate. The learner support and assessment budget similarly embraces labour, materials and overhead elements. This budget, together with the consolidated materials budget, the selling expenses budget, the administration budget and elements of the R&D budget, make up the *operating costs* of the institution.

Capital costs deserve a particular mention. In theory, at least, capital expenditure is expenditure that is non-recurring, in the sense that once a building is erected, it will last for many years. However, the erection of a building will lead to increased maintenance and running costs which will need to be reflected in the administrative operating budget. Equally, not all capital goods last as long as a building. Vehicles, computers and furniture will all need to be replaced at some time. Money therefore needs to be set aside to fund this replacement. One way of doing this is to think of the expenditure not as a capital expense at all, but as an operating expense. Thus, Thames Valley University in the UK took the total value of the equipment in its student computing service and divided it by three – the number of years that it felt the equipment would last before it had to be replaced. This sum was then written into the operating budget of the unit. This ensured that provision was built in for replacement.

Keeping costs down

There are a range of factors that affect the total costs in distance education systems, including, for example:

- the total number of learners in the system and on individual courses, and the extent to which small-population courses are a necessary part of the curriculum;
- the level of student support built into the system, and particularly tuition and individualized guidance and counselling;
- the number of awards (degrees, diplomas etc) and courses on offer, including the balance between mandatory and optional courses within any one award;
- the number of years over which awards/courses are presented before they are withdrawn;
- the frequency with which materials have to be updated;
- the choice of technologies (and the relationship between this choice, the cost structure of the technology, and student numbers at both institutional and course level);
- the way in which technology is used (ie product quality issues such as print quality and use of colour, paper quality, video quality etc);
- local prices (costs of labour, broadcast transmission time, access to facilities etc);

- the extent to which costs are passed on to the students, or carried by the institution;
- organizational structures;
- working practices;
- the nature of the internal labour market.

The importance of many of these factors will be clear from what has already been said. However, the last three may need some further explanation. *Organizational structures* are important because they may affect the costs of distance education. It is often said that single-mode distance education systems have a capacity to achieve economies of scale that can never be achieved in dual-mode systems. It is certainly the case that the largest distance teaching systems – the mega-universities – are, with the exception of Anadolu University, single-mode systems, but there is some evidence that dual-mode systems, by capitalizing on economies of process, can bring the costs of developing materials down below the levels achieved by single-mode distance teaching institutions, while at the same time using the materials to bring down the costs of their on-campus teaching. They can certainly offer a wider curriculum. Thus, the advantages do not necessarily lie with single-mode institutions, as is commonly thought (Rumble, 1997: 152–59; Renwick, 1996: 59–60).

Working practices are important because they can affect costs drastically. Multi-author course team models are known to be expensive, compared with having one or two authors create materials; developing all the materials from scratch is expensive, compared with the possibilities of developing wraparound materials to accompany an existing textbook; electronic tutoring looks as if it takes more tutor time, and will therefore be more expensive than face-to-face tutoring. The nature of the *internal labour market*, and particularly the practice of hiring consultants to write materials and tutors to teach by the hour and mark by the script, rather than employing a full-time staff to do any of these jobs, can reduce costs significantly (though consultant-written materials may need more editing).

Enormous energy tends to be spent on keeping the costs of an organization in check. Of course, accounting information is necessary to track financial results and plan activities – but the emphasis on costs can cause employees to put accounting results above customer satisfaction. There are some real difficulties here. To begin with, there is a major problem with cost and management accounting systems. The practice, adopted around 1900, of abstracting financial data from the operation of the firm to provide information for the profit and loss account and balance sheet, and in particular the asset value of inventories (including finished goods and work in progress), ensured that asset values reported originated in the costs reported in the cost and management accounts, rather than outside them, as had been the previous practice. (Figure 9.1 shows this in the relationship between the internal budgeting and accounting structure and the master budgets used to provide shareholder information.) However, the allocation of overhead costs to products and hence to inventory value seriously distorts management information on product (and by extension service) costs. Unable to do anything about the overhead costs being allocated to their products, managers focus instead on the factors that drive the allocation of overheads – typically direct labour costs or machine hours, rather than on the factors that actually drive the costs of the products. As a direct result, managers lose sight of the activities that are actually driving costs (Johnson and Kaplan, 1987). Activity-based costing is one way in which some firms have tried to improve the quality of the information available to them. This has had two main effects: it has drawn attention to the factors (activities) that drive costs, including overhead costs, with a view to providing managers with a better focus on the control of cost-inducing activities, thus getting round the problem that costs reported in accounting-based budget reports are generally too aggregated to enable real control to be exercised; and it has shown how product costs can be distorted by not recognizing the drivers that affect costs. The latter is of particular importance. For example, in distance education, course costs may be driven by the number of student places on the course, or by the fact that the course is being presented. Using drivers triggered by units of output (student courses) to allocate overheads triggered by course presentations will lead to the systematic under-costing of low-volume courses, and the over-costing of high-volume courses. Although these distortions tend to cancel each other out at the macro level, fee decisions based on these distorted figures can be seriously wrong, leading to a net loss on each low-volume course sold. Modern cost management approaches are designed to get round some of these difficulties (see Brinker, 2000).

However, the real problem is not just the quality of the available accounting information but the fact that it is being wrongly used to control business operations (Johnson, 1992: 31). Johnson argues that 'companies . . . must remove accounting information from their operational control systems and relieve their accounting departments of responsibility for providing information to control business operations' (1992: xi). Illustrating this, Johnson points to the case of training: 'Decisions on employee training will be very different if they are based on cost information rather than information about customer satisfaction' (1992: 14). If performance evaluation systems place the emphasis on costs, then efficiency-minded managers will try to cut costs by cutting back on training; but, on the other hand, if the emphasis is on customer satisfaction, then the decision may well be to increase employee training.

Johnson's overall message is that in today's marketplace, providers have to be responsive and flexible, and they can only do this if they empower the workforce 'to learn and make changes that continuously improves processes capable of satisfying customers' (1992: ix).

We can illustrate the problems by looking at some of the behaviours the traditional approach to cost control engenders in distance education systems. It is a truism that distance education involves high fixed costs and lower variable costs. What distance educators seem to do in many ways parallels the wasteful practices of the post-World War II American automobile industry (see Johnson, 1992: 44–46) by assuming that the high overhead costs 'inherent' in distance education can be 'controlled' by expanding student numbers. Thus, the emphasis is placed on driving expansion fast enough to cover overhead costs that are, to a considerable extent, caused by scale and complexity, and that are deemed to be 'fixed' and hence beyond control. But most of the economies of scale are reaped early on in expansion. The nature of the average cost curve is such that the more students there are in the system, the harder it becomes to achieve significant economies of scale (see Table 9.1, which reports on data drawn from a cost study of the Indira Gandhi National Open University, India) (Pillai and Naidu, 1991).

Table 9.1 *Economies of scale at the Indira Gandhi National Open University (based on Pillai and Naidu, 1991: 53)*

Number of students	Total costs (Rs/millions)	Average cost (Rs)	%age rate of decline of average cost
5,000	59.522	11904.47	–
10,000	62.508	6250.77	−113.07
20,000	68.478	3423.92	−28.27
30,000	74.449	2481.64	−9.42
40,000	80.420	2010.50	−4.71
50,000	87.520	1750.40	−1.89
60,000	96.218	1603.64	−1.45
70,000	104.916	1498.81	−1.05
80,000	113.615	1420.18	−0.79
90,000	122.313	1359.03	−0.61
100,000	131.011	1310.11	−0.49
200,000	217.993	1089.97	−0.22
300,000	304.975	1016.58	−0.07

In mass education systems, small cuts in services will produce large savings. A saving of £2 per student course in a system that has 300,000 student courses will deliver savings of £0.6 million. As a result, much effort is put into reducing the variable costs of the product (the value that the student most perceives), in order to increase the contribution margin (the difference between the fee charged for a course place and the direct cost of the providing that place), and thus bring the breakeven rate of output at which production covers overheads down. So, for example, great efforts may be made to shave money off the tuition budget by cutting back on the number of hours of tuition offered to students (thus reducing the level of service received by customers), by increasing the tutor:student ratio (leading to fewer tutorial groups and hence to a poorer geographical spread of provision, as well as overloaded tutors), by cutting back on the number of assignments (and reducing the amount of formative assessment), and by reducing the number of clerks processing corrected assignments (and so increasing assignment turnaround time and hence student dissatisfaction). None of these touches the costs of overheads, nor does it consider what students want.

Institutions that focus on a provider-determined product may well experience initial sales, but these will fall off as the latent market for that product disappears. Organizations that centralize their customer contacts around remote and impersonal selling, invoicing, despatch and help-desk facilities – often to save money – are likely to lose contact with their customers, while those who build their capabilities around local dealerships and sales staff are likely to have a better chance of understanding and responding to their customers' wants. Such organizations, having identified what those wants are, must then deliver – irrespective of the cost – because this creates loyal customers who want to repeat business. That means collecting appropriate information that promotes long-term relationships with customers.

The problem with accounting systems is that 'they provide almost no information about customers, other than revenue data' (Johnson, 1992: 106), and are, therefore, of no use in building up customer loyalty based upon an ability to satisfy customer wants. On the other hand, what is being argued here is the need to keep an eye on measures of performance that reflect customer satisfaction, rather than on measures of cost *per se*. If distance teaching institutions listen to what their customers want and respond quickly to their desires by empowering their workforce to learn and make changes that continuously improve processes capable of satisfying customers, while eliminating those that are dysfunctional in this respect, then student numbers will be kept up and costs will be driven down.

References

Bates, A W (1995) *Technology, Open Learning and Distance Education*, Routledge, London and New York

Bates, A W (2000) *Managing Technology Change: Strategies for college and university leaders*, Jossey-Bass Publishers, San Francisco

Brinker, B (2000) *Guide to Cost Management*, John Wiley & Sons, Chichester

Daniel, J S (1996) *Mega-Universities and Knowledge Media: Technology strategies for higher education*, Kogan Page, London

Johnson, H T (1992) *Relevance Regained: From top-down control to bottom-up empowerment*, The Free Press, New York

Johnson, H T and Kaplan, R S (1987) *Relevance Lost: The rise and fall of management accounting*, Harvard Business School Press, Boston

Pillai, C R and Naidu, C G (1991) *Cost Analysis of Distance Education: IGNOU*, Indira Gandhi National Open University, Planning Division, New Delhi

Renwick, W (1996) The future of face-to-face and distance teaching in post-secondary education, in *Information Technology and the Future of Post-Secondary Education*, OECD, Paris

Rumble, G (1997) *The Costs and Economics of Open and Distance Learning*, Kogan Page, London and Stirling

Part 4

Management of processes

Chapter 10

Management of instructional design and development

Olugbemiro Jegede

Introduction

As has been often mentioned in this book, open and flexible learning has become the fashion and is now a mainstream activity after several decades of struggle. One of the reasons that open and flexible learning (OFL) has become more robust and tremendously successful in meeting the needs of the greater majority of people is the fact that the planning and management of all the complex activities and operation within OFL are well structured to lead to visible outcomes which all can see and appreciate. Central to this is the role that instructional design and development plays in the provision of education through this alternative route. The design of instruction using a set of tested theories and strategies has distinguished OFL from the face-to-face teaching mode and has singularly conferred on OFL the characteristic of quality and an effectual mode of teaching and learning. Instructional design and development needs to be integrated into the management processes of OFL to make this mode of teaching and learning responsive to the popular need to study at one's own pace, anywhere, anytime and through any medium.

This chapter will therefore focus on the management of instructional design and development with a view to itemizing the various milestones which have to be reached to make distance and open learning what it should be. The chapter will first discuss what instructional design means, its history and its elements. In the second part, it will focus on how it is undertaken and how it is managed within an overall system of an institutional framework to deliver instruction by distance mode.

In an apt write-up illustrating the need for constant change, Oliver (2001) describes the lessons humanity has learnt from the story of the dinosaurs. More instructive is the fact that the dinosaurs disappeared because they were not able to adapt to whatever sudden climatic, biological or other changes they might have faced several millennia ago. This again underscores the dictum that the only constant aspect of human existence is change. What we now have as open and flexible delivery of instruction has undergone several changes, from correspondence studies through home study to distance education. Coupled with these changes have been the emergence and influence and constant changes of instructional design. It is the management of these changes that has accorded OFL the success it now enjoys. How did instructional design emerge and what are the evolutionary changes it has undergone within OFL?

History of instructional system design

The history of instructional systems design (ISD) has been traced to a modest beginning triggered by John Dewey's presidential address to the American Psychological Association in 1899 when he called for the development of a 'linking science' between learning theory and educational practice. Jerome Bruner at the 1963 Conference of the Association for Supervision and Curriculum Development (ASCD) also called for a theory of instruction. Almost all instructional design theoreticians, practitioners and professionals subscribe to the use of the systems approach to developing instruction. A system is an aggregate of components; each interacts with and influences others. They work together towards achieving a common goal (see Naidu, 1993). This systems approach to meeting the needs of human performance has several components serving distinct and specialized functions.

That linking science which John Dewey called for and which Ralph Tyler described as playing the 'middleman' role is what is now popularly called, and which has led to a distinct field of practice called, instructional design. As represented in Figure 10.1, ISD links the learning theories of famous psychologists such as Dewey, Thorndike, Bobbitt, Tyler, Montessori, Bruner, Skinner, Gagne, Ausubel, Glaser, Anderson, Piaget and Resnick to educational practice. Instructional design has now become a 'linking science' which prescribes instructional actions in order to optimize desired instructional outcomes.

Many would argue that the Instructional Systems Development (ISD) Model was first used by the United States of America's military during the world wars and

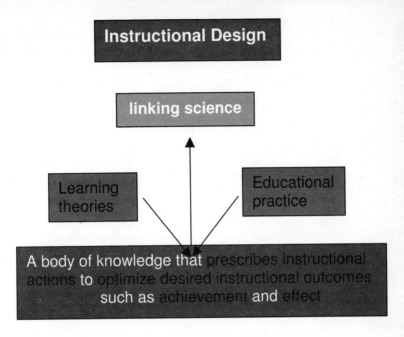

Figure 10.1 *ISD emergence and position as a 'linking science'*

was based on the General Systems Theory Approach (Bertalanffy, 1968; Romiszowski, 1981). ISD was actually devised by experimental psychologists employed by the military to improve the job performance of military personnel during the war. The Second World War created an immediate need to increase the effectiveness and efficiency of military training. It was from this moment that ISD became accepted worldwide and was infused into educational practice.

Components of instructional design

ISD is concerned with understanding, improving and applying methods of instruction. As shown in Figure 10.2, it should be seen as two distinct elements: as a professional activity and as a discipline.

As a professional activity, it is a process of deciding what methods are best for bringing about desired changes in learners' knowledge, skills and attitudes. To draw upon an analogy, as an activity, instructional design is to instruction as the architect's blueprint is to the design and building of a house.

As a discipline, it is a process of producing knowledge about optimal 'blueprints'. It provides knowledge about diverse methods of instruction, effective and efficient combinations of methods and situations in which each of those instructional models is applied.

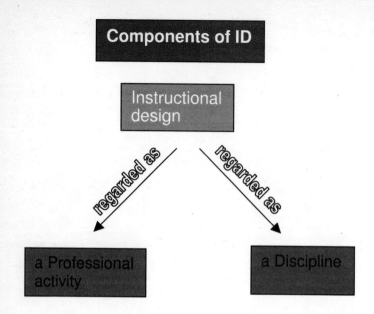

Figure 10.2 *Components of instructional design*

Since the use of the ISD during the world wars, and its refinement over the years, educational psychologists have had a breakthrough in instruction. ISD is now widely used for management, personnel selection, personnel development, job design and automation. But it is most widely used in distance education because it has been found to be useful in designing instruction for learners who are remotely located and do not have constant interaction with their instructors but need to embark on individualized learning. I need to mention here that in education ISD is called ID. It is ID that gives OFL the distinctive edge over the traditional face-to-face mode in which lecturers do not have to plan their teaching or at least do not have to either publish it or have it go through a systems approach to designing instruction using a unit or course team design environment.

Approaches to ID

There are several approaches to instructional design (Figure 10.3) based on several psychological and instructional theories. The first was the behavioural approach to ID traceable to the influence of ISD during the Second World War. At that time the theories of behaviourists like Skinner, Thorndike, Bloom etc became dominant, and formed the basis for designing instruction. This is the structuralist approach that was modelled from Gestalt and Piagetian psychology. There is the not so popular apprenticeship approach – the oldest form of learning in the history of human beings – which seems to have made a comeback in recent years through

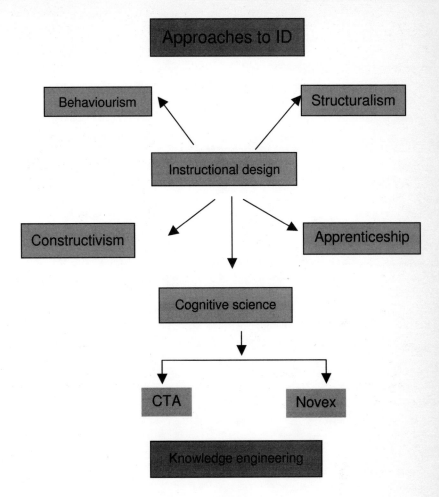

Figure 10.3 *Approaches to instructional design*

situated learning and has brought new ideas to conventional teaching strategies.

The cognitive science approach follows the work of early psychologists, including Bruner, Ausubel, Glaser, Anderson and Resnick. As opposed to the behaviourists, cognitive scientists say that cognitive operations are unobservable. They therefore focus on performance analysis, memory, transfer requirement and mental models. Two variants of the cognitive model of instructional design have surfaced within the past two decades, although they are yet to be popular. These are Cognitive Task Analysis (CTA) and Novex Analysis (NA), both of which lead to knowledge engineering. CTA is a model of instructional design which organizes instructional materials around the results of a cognitive task analysis that identifies the optimal knowledge structures, mental models, strategies and skills underlying expertise in the subject matter (Redding, 1995). Novex Analysis uses cognitive structures and processes, metacognitive strategies and affective dimensions of the human information processing model to design instruction in order to promote meaningful learning and effect the novice-to-expert transition (Taylor, 1994). Knowledge engineering is therefore the design of instruction which uses a combination of expert systems and metacognitive strategies to structure knowledge, information and data for the purpose of meaningful learning.

There is a relatively new philosophy of pedagogy called constructivism, which has emerged in education and has received considerable attention, especially in science and mathematics education, but tragically little in OFL because of the rigidity of practice (Jegede, 1995, 2000). Constructivism talks about the learner's construction of his or her own knowledge, and indeed the focus is now on social constructivism.

The constructivist approach views knowledge as an entity which is mentally constructed via the actions and experiences that the learner undergoes, in a sense, dialogically with the immediate learning and broader social environments. Knowledge is actively constructed by the interaction between the learner and external objects through adaptation of and to the experiential world. Consequently, through the establishment of malleable mental constructs (Driver, 1988; Glaserfeld, 1987; Wheatley, 1993), learning occurs. The meaning of the external world, according to constructivism, is socially negotiated. Thus, external reality is likely to be perceived differently by different learners, and it is through social negotiation that common meaning is constructed (Candy, 1991). Constructivism is more relevant for the OFL environment, which promotes individual self-study and flexible delivery of instruction to take account of the particular learning styles of students. It has benefit not only for instruction at a distance but for the design of the materials and also for the management of the process and development.

Need for ID

There are five major justifications for ID:

Ineffective general methods of instruction

The general methods of instruction do not allow for the chunking of the 'message', nor do they permit the extensive use of all available learning theories and teaching strategies. Indeed, because instructors in the face-to-face mode hardly undertake any design of their instruction, and because the absence of teams to develop courses provides a fertile ground for idiosyncratic instructional delivery practices, to that extent ID is often seen as interference. But the knowledge explosion, the need to cater to heterogeneous groups and a long list of variables for course planning necessitate ID.

Catering for educational as well as intellectual needs

While some believe that instruction should provide mainly for the educational (general) needs of a learner and others believe it should cater for their intellectual/academic needs, what would be preferred and would make for a comprehensive education is for instruction to meet both these needs. The design of instruction adequately takes both of these into consideration.

Learners have poor conception of their own learning ability

More often than not, apart from learners not familiar with the content, both in scope and in depth, of what they are to learn, many are often not sure of their learning requirements and have a poor perception of their learning ability. This is particularly so for adult learners who are going back to study after a long pause for whatever reasons. Designing instruction using all the theories and strategies which take into consideration learners of this category provides tremendous motivation and guidance for the new or the not-so-confident learner.

Reduces the time needed for training

User-friendly courses or teaching materials, which are well sequenced and synthesized using instructional design principles, will considerably reduce the time needed for training, especially in industry or in specialized instructional situations.

Reduces attrition in adult, distance and open learning

The enormous enthusiasm and motivation which learners often bring into adult, distance and open learning situations fizzles away as soon as they experience the reality of studying in a remote location on their own, with very limited personal interaction with the provider of the instructional packages. Furthermore, distractions from family, work or social obligations often make matters worse. These are some of the reasons that account for the usually high rate of attrition in distance education as opposed to the face-to-face mode of education. Using a systems approach to structure the instruction for adult learners, taking into consideration all the useful theories and strategies, would reduce attrition.

Limitations of ID

There are contexts in which ID may not be extensively useful or cost-efficient. ISD is not used in the educational system because of several limitations. ID in an educational setting requires that instruction is relevant, effective and efficient. ID, therefore, needs to be looked at from several perspectives.

Some of the reasons given for its limitations are as follows:

- ISD as an industrial model may not be appropriately suitable for instructional management.
- It does not prescribe actual procedures for development and analysis.
- ISD as practised today is still almost totally behavioural, and does not reflect contemporary developments in the psychological, cognitive and philosophical areas.
- Adequate use of ID is time consuming, restrictive and rigid.
- ISD is often not relevant, effective and efficient for educational situations.

Management issues in ISD

A systematic approach to packaging instruction in a bid to address issues such as what the learner's needs are, what solutions are available, how the solutions to the problems should be planned and designed, how the design should be implemented, and how to evaluate the outcome of the design, would require comprehensive management. In ISD it is often thought that management begins and ends with the design and packaging of instruction. In reality, it goes beyond this to include the management of several other processes and aspects, including instructional, personnel and the management cadre. It also involves the interaction of the design team with the various quality assurance committees and checks, the faculty, school and/or subject-matter experts (SMAs), and the governing body of the university or organization such as the Academic Senate or the Governing Council. The second segment of the chapter will deal with all of these. However, as a beginning, we must consider the various elements which make up the ISD model, and how each is involved with management or can or should be managed for effective instructional outcome.

Generic ISD model

As mentioned earlier, various psychological, philosophical and pedagogical orientations have evolved different ISD models. There are instructional design models such as the Dick and Carey model, Kemp model, Gerlach and Ely model, Gagne and Briggs model, Merrill's model, Jonassen model, those supported by Reigeluth's elaboration theory, Romiszowski's systems approach, Landamatic theory, and the Information Mapping model of Robert Horn. While they all vary in one form or another, they also have many aspects in common. As a result, instead of discussing the individual models of ISD, it will be more expedient to discuss the generic model whose features are common to all of the models available. As shown in Figure 10.4, ISD, which derived from the General Systems Theory, has five generic phases: analysis, design, development, implementation, and control/

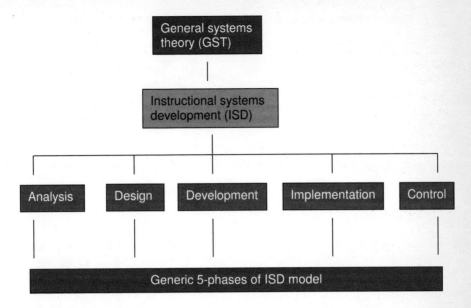

Figure 10.4 *The generic ISD model*

evaluation. Let us mention the highlights of each phase, showing why their management is essential in the overall process of instructional design.

Focus

Let us put in perspective the whole process of instructional design, reminding ourselves for whom we are designing. Our focus is OFL, and Chapter 1 describes the unique characteristics of open, flexible and distance education which make it a very elaborate system. As a result, DE/OFL systems are engaged in teaching–learning situations where the learner and teacher are physically separated and instruction must be designed to fit this, and its management taken into account. Instruction at a distance demands that all educational principles are applied, with carefully planned and designed instructional materials. ISD is always undertaken by a multidisciplinary team, with the need to use flexible delivery and probably to combine face-to-face with the distance mode in some circumstances, especially where students require tutorial support. If properly done, good instructional design ensures a successful and effective DE tailored to the needs and situations of each learner.

This is why the various phases of the ISD model are important and have to be properly managed. The important aspects of each phase are briefly highlighted as follows.

The analysis phase

This is the initial stage in which the problems and all the issues involved are identified, analysed and prioritized in terms of seeking solutions. Data about the learners, their environment, what is available by way of student support from the institution or the local environment, etc are collected. Decisions are also taken about each of the four levels of design: course systems, lesson, instructional event, and learning steps attached to specific learning tasks.

The design phase

This phase is about how to sequence and synthesize the content or skills that will be taught to the learner. Many practitioners see this phase as the 'heart' of the matter as this stage develops the blueprint of instruction. The development is based on the theoretical models of designing instruction. For instance, in sequencing instruction, the ISD team must consider strategies such as scrambled versus logical sequences, micro-level sequencing and macro-level sequencing. At the macro level, an approach or a combination of approaches must be chosen from a long list, including Bruner's spiral approach, Ausubel's general-to-detailed approach, Gagne's hierarchical approach, Merrill's shortest path approach or Reigeluth's elaboration approach.

To sequence instruction, several strategies such as Reigeluth's elaboration theory synthesizers, Anderson's mapping, Dansereau's networking, Ausubel's advance organizers, Novak's concept mapping or Jonassen's approach are considered for their efficacy and appropriateness.

The development phase

This phase is where the professional expertise of the instructional designer in the material development team comes in and where major management issues surface. During this phase, instructional goals are set on the basis of needs assessment. This leads to the writing of the performance objectives based models such as the Mager model, the Gagne–Briggs model, the Audience–Behaviour–Condition–Degree (ABCD) model. Learning strategies must be embedded in the development or the materials structured in such a way that the learner generates his or her strategies for learning. Issues such as deep or surface learning, meaningful learning and collateral learning (Jegede, 1995) are evaluated for the specific audience.

The implementation phase

This phase is when the reality of what has been developed comes to the fore with the formative evaluation of the materials. A representative sample of would-be customers is used in a variety of patterns and formats to assess all the aspects of the development. The results collected are used to revise the materials before they are sent to the students. Some development models use other evaluation routes such as the 'external course assessor', 'peer group assessor' etc to check the quality of the content.

The control/evaluation phase

This stage is an elaborate form of the assessment carried out in the previous phase. After the first full-scale implementation of the instructional materials, several things are examined, the most important being whether the instructional goals identified for the course have been met. A summative evaluation is used to do this. There are at least five styles of evaluation, which must be used for the ID activities: decision-oriented evaluation, value-oriented evaluation, naturalistic evaluation, systems-oriented evaluation, and utilization-focused evaluation. In many design systems, it is often recommended that both formative and summative evaluation are used throughout the life of the course, so that by the time a review of the course materials comes up, enough information has been collected to take certain critical decisions about the course and its performance.

Media and the delivery of instruction

One issue, which affects all design phases, is how the media should be incorporated or integrated in the course being developed. Media development and its management is discussed in the next chapter. A popular and classical reading is *Understanding Media: The extensions of man* by Marshall McLuhan (1964). Clark's (1983) publication is also a good guide. Although there are many other guides and publications on the use of technologies, especially the new and emerging technologies, Heinich, Molenda and Russell (1989) came up with a model which has proved very useful for instructional design. The model, called ASSURE, outlines how to do this using the following process:

- **A**nalyse learner's characteristics.
- **S**tate objectives.
- **S**elect media and materials to bridge the gap between where the learner is and what he or she should have learnt by the end of the course.
- **U**tilize materials.
- **R**equire learner performance.
- **E**valuate and revise.

As you may have experienced, the development of instructional materials for OFL involves a team effort, which needs input from various experts to carry out the five phases mentioned above. The success or otherwise of the team depends on the institution and the quality of management of the efforts of the team members. What many systems do is to have some procedural guidelines and benchmarks to ascertain efficient and effective management of the design process, including all members of the team, and how to track the document or materials through the design process.

Other areas for management

As mentioned earlier, there are other areas which require the serious consideration of management. They are itemized in Figure 10.5. This demonstrates two things: there are other aspects involved or implicated in the design process which require management, and ID is a pervasive element in many DE institutions or organizations. The three broad categories shown in Figure 10.5 overlap in some areas and any OFL system or organization that is functional must exhibit all these characteristics. These include educational factors, which relate to the design and development of a specific unit, course and programme, and organizational matters such as personnel and management relating broadly to the administration of a distance education programme.

Features that ID must meet in DE

Instructional	Personnel	Management
Highly planned, organized and delivered	Design and development	Academic leadership
Interactivity	Subject-matter experts	Humanizing and personalizing
Flexibility	Site facilitators (RLO)	Contingency plans
Instructional feedback	Production	
		Free flow of communication
Advanced organizers/overviews	Student support	Scheduling instruction
Evaluation of instruction		Evaluation of Systems

Figure 10.5 *Features of ID systems which require management*

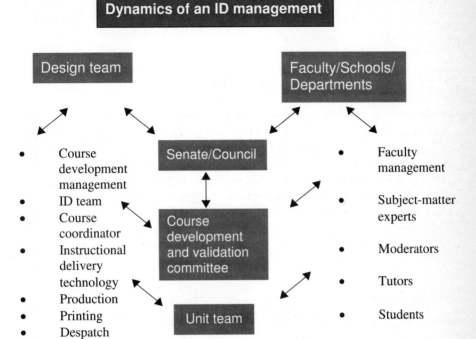

Figure 10.6 *The dynamics of an ID management system at the macro level*

There are other macro areas which impact on the management of instructional design. They are listed in Figure 10.6, which details the dynamics of an ID management at the macro level. It includes the several areas of the design teams in which the various committees, such as the academic unit of the organization and the overarching management and quality control systems such as the Senate or Academic Board and the Council, are involved.

Future of ID and management

I would like to conclude this chapter by looking at the future of ID and management issues. The world is changing, ISD is changing and the use of several types of technologies is also changing. Therefore, the management of ISD must keep abreast of such changes, tracking them for the benefit of quality instruction in OFL.

Any forward-looking DE system that wishes to survive the competition and phenomenal development in the educational scene must be mindful of these changes and their catalysing factors. The management of an OFL institution must be familiar with these factors and develop plans accordingly. They must realize that a lot of changes are afoot, including:

- new and different design paradigms;
- changes in future learning environments;
- performance technology;
- influence of micro-worlds, hypermedia, multimedia;
- changes in general systems, learning, communication and instructional theories.

At the individual level, the people who manage each of the units involved with ISD must display qualities including leadership and administrative ability, a strong commitment to collegiality, and the willingness and ability to be an energetic advocate of the DE system; they must lean towards people management, create a happy working environment, have commensurate scholarship, commit to professional development and have a proactive perspective of global changes in OFL and ISD, and their management in particular.

References

Bertalanffy, L von (1968) *General Systems Theory*, Braziller, New York

Candy, P C (1991) *Self Direction for Life Long Learning*, Jossey-Bass, San Francisco

Clark, R E (1983) Reconsidering research on learning from media, *Review of Educational Research*, **53** (4), pp 445–59

Dick, W and Carey, L (1990) *The Systematic Design of Instruction*, Scott, Foresman & Company, Glenview, IL

Driver, R (1988) 'Theory into practice II: A constructivist approach to curriculum development', in *Development and Dilemmas in Science Education*, ed P J Fensham, pp 165–88, The Falmer Press, London

Glaserfeld, E von (1987) 'Learning as constructive activity', in *The Construction of Knowledge: Contributions to conceptual semantics*, ed E von Glaserfeld, pp 212–14, Intersystems Publication, California

Heinich, R, Molenda, M and Russell, J D (1989) *Instructional Media and the New Technologies of Instruction*, Macmillan, New York

Jegede, O J (1992) 'Constructivist epistemology and its implications for contemporary research in distance education', in *Research in Distance Education Vol. 2*, eds T Evans and P Juler, pp 21–29, Deakin University Press, Geelong

Jegede, O J (1995) Collateral learning and the eco-cultural paradigm in science and mathematics education in Africa, *Studies in Science Education*, **25**, pp 97–137

Jegede, O J (2000) 'Constructivist pedagogy in distance education: myths and realities from OUHK tutorial practices', a paper presented at the *5th Research in Distance Education Conference*, Deakin University, Geelong, Australia, 5–7 December

Jonassen, D H (1991) Objectivism versus constructivism: Do we need a new philosophical paradigm? *Educational Technology Research and Development*, **39**, pp 5–14

Keegan, D (1990) *Foundations of Distance Education*, Routledge, New York

Kaufman, R and English, F W (1979) *Needs Assessment: Concepts and applications*, Educational Technology Publications, Inc, Englewood Cliffs, NJ

Lunenberg, F C (1998) Constructivism and technology: Instructional designs for successful education reform, *Journal of Instructional Psychology*, **25**, pp 75–82

McLuhan, M (1964) *Understanding Media: The extensions of man*, Signet Books, New York

Naidu, S (1993) *Instructional Design for Distance Education*, Unit 88031, Study Book for M.Ed Course, University of Southern Queensland, DEC, Toowoomba

Oliver, C (2001) Global demand for local logistics expertise, *Career Post, South China Morning Post*, Thursday 8 March, pp 1–36

Redding, R (1995) Cognitive task analysis for instructional design: Application in distance education, *Distance Education*, **61** (1), pp 88–106

Reigeluth, C M (1992) Elaborating the elaboration theory, *Educational Technology Research and Development*, **40** (3), pp 80–86

Romiszowski, A (1981) *Designing Instructional Systems: Decision making in course planning and curriculum design*, Kogan Page, London

Spigner-Littles, D A and Chalon, E (1999) Constructivism: A paradigm for older learners, *Educational Gerontology*, **25**, pp 203–10

Taylor, J C (1994) Novex analysis: A cognitive approach to instructional design, *Educational Technology*, **34** (5), pp 5–13

Tenenbaum, G, Naidu, S, Jegede, O and Austin, J (2001) Constructivist pedagogy in conventional on-campus and distance learning practice: An exploratory investigation, *Learning and Instruction*, **11** (2), pp 87–111

Tennyson, R D (1992) An educational learning theory for instructional design, *Educational Technology*, **32**, pp 36–41

Wheatley, G H (1993) The role of negotiation in mathematics learning, in *The Practice of Constructivism in Science Education*, ed K Tobin, pp 121–33, AAAS Press, Washington DC

Chapter 11

Management of media development and production

Santosh Panda and Sohanvir Chaudhary

Introduction

Distance teaching institutions and programmes, training institutions in industries, and government and non-government sectors employ a wide range of media for distance education and training. Broadly, there are five categories of media: human interface, text, audio, television and computing (Bates, 1995). These media can be classified into print and non-print categories. This chapter considers the non-print media like audio, video, radio, television, interactive television, interactive radio, and audio- and videoconferencing, and excludes Internet-based and networked learning which are discussed in Chapter 14. The delivery of these media through telelearning centres is the focus of Chapter 15.

Each of the above media is delivered through certain technologies individually or in combination with each other. They have specific distance education applications: 1) audio applications in forms of cassettes and broadcasts, telephone tutoring, interactive radio counselling and audioconferencing, and 2) video applications in educational programmes, broadcast lectures and videoconferencing. There are other considerations, including whether the medium offers one-way or two-way interaction: 1) one-way applications include cassette and broadcast programmes, and 2) two-way applications lead to audio- and videoconferencing, telephone tutoring, interactive radio counselling and interactive television. Besides audio and video cassettes, broadcast programmes and conferencing, other related technologies available to a distance educator include view data, teletext/videotext, video disc, CCTV – and all these can be effectively integrated into any form of computer-mediated communication. In distance education and training situations, cassettes, broadcasts and conferences are common and popular non-print and non-computing media applications; and, therefore, a judicious choice has to be made in selecting these media either as individual applications or in combination with not only each other but also with human interface, print and computer-based technologies.

Media selection

In distance education and training, crucial decision making, debate and sometimes conflict centre round media selection and deployment. Bates aptly remarks:

> Because of a lack of generally agreed criteria for media and technology selection in education and training, crucial technology decisions have tended to be made primarily for commercial, administrative or political reasons: the availability of spare broadcasting capacity; an offer from suppliers of free or cheap equipment or services; the comfort level of academics with technologies that replicate the lecture format; or the enthusiasm of a key decision-maker for a particular technology. (1995: 33)

In the absence of clear criteria and institutional policy, either no decision is taken, or it is left to individual academics to select media as per their choice, or the institution arbitrarily decides to deploy a certain number of audio and video and conferencing programmes to a course, or the institution may even decide to go for a single (master) medium and invest heavily in that. With the advent of newer media options, media selection has become more difficult, and on–demand individualized learning has made it more demanding. The humanistic and flexible approaches to learning advocate selection of media as per the needs of the stakeholders. The ideal requirements of a medium, pointed out by Rowntree (1994), should be generally helpful; and Koumi (1994) noted three important criteria (as a three-stage scheme) for media selection:

1. List comparative merits and distinctive teaching points for each medium.
2. Devise a procedure for media deployment based on your list.
3. Fully exploit the potential of each medium.

A very simple but extremely useful suggestion has been made by Bates: '. . . in distance education, media need to be simple, widely available in students' homes, low-cost to produce, easy to design well, interactive, and integrated with other media' (1990: 104). An organization needs to decide for itself as a whole or for individual courses on a case-by-case basis whether to use any of the media as the master medium and the rest as either supplementary or complementary to it, or to go for integrated use of media – for each of these situations, the design of media at the stage of course design will be different for the course team to consider.

Some of the media researchers have pointed out that variance in media inputs does not affect the learning outcome. For instance, Clark (1983) pointed out no significant difference in the learning effects from different media. While these kinds of studies need further investigation, this finding is simply not applicable because even if experiments have been conducted in full controlled conditions, the distinctive potential of each medium in relation to particular content with different instructional designs needs to be exploited for greater learning effectiveness, rather than just comparing them while keeping the remaining variables constant. The latter practice has been noted by Bates as 'equivalent to cutting two legs off a horse to see if it can run as fast as a man' (quoted in Koumi, 1994: 43).

From the pedagogic point of view, the institutional managers and course team chairs need to see that extra objectives are not formulated just to justify audio or video, a fixed number of audio or video is not allocated for all the courses, and that the matching of media and course objectives takes into consideration the affordability and easy access of those media to the learners at home, workplace and learning centres. Sometimes, exclusion of non-print media in learner assessment restricts its production quality and use: if the producers and students know that these media are being used only as supplementary without any weightage for learner assessment, the producers may not deliver a good production, and the students may not use them.

Bates (1995) has provided an extremely useful ACTIONS framework for decision making at each institution:

- **A**ccess: includes access to individual learners, and flexibility of media for specific target groups.
- **C**osts: includes the unit cost per learner, as also the institution's ability to afford that cost.
- **T**eaching and learning: includes the pedagogical strength of each medium to meet specific learning objectives.
- **I**nteractivity and user-friendliness: includes the ease of handling and the kind of interaction provided by the media.
- **O**rganizational issues: includes organizational preparedness and restructuring for deploying any of the media.
- **N**ovelty: includes the newness of the medium so as to attract the learners.
- **S**peed: includes the quickness with which courses can be created as well as revised with the help of such media.

Further, interactivity and learner control are important considerations for media selection. In the case of real-time presentations like radio and television broadcasts, student interaction is strictly controlled and limited, whereas teleconferencing interactions can be properly designed to get the dual benefits of interactive media and a face-to-face lecture. However, it does not mean that all course contents need the same degree of interactivity; also, not all courses may need synchronous interaction. One-way technologies, with careful planning, can contribute to a high level of interaction. Further, while learner control of interaction is ensured through telephone tutoring, audio and video cassettes also provide for learner control of learning.

Instructional design for media

In choosing media, it is not worth comparing various media; rather it would be desirable to consider which media can perform which teaching functions and for which topic. This holds good even if media are used as supplementary to the printed course materials. Therefore, comparative evidence of the effects of multiple media for teaching the same topic would have less research value; what is valuable is to consider and judiciously develop the criteria for use of media to achieve the learning outcomes most effectively. Nevertheless, one must be aware of the strengths and limitations of individual media being used.

Mechanical selection of media will not serve any purpose unless the learning concepts are intelligently designed and delivered through these media. The design variables that both the academic and the producer need jointly to consider involve decisions on the achievement of cognitive, experiential, affective and psychomotor objectives. The categorical specifications of these objectives for each medium and for each topic/teaching point will facilitate further considerations of the specific format(s) and word–picture combinations to best achieve those objectives.

The teams involved in media production differ in their perception of instructional design for various non-print media. While teachers and trainers follow a rigorous procedure of curriculum design and instructional design for course material development for print, laxity is observed in the case of non-print media development and production. Each medium addresses different teaching functions and learning tasks. Instead of comparing various media, it is desirable to develop criteria for media deployment to best achieve the learning objectives. There exist differences among media producers on the need for a pre-production instructional design, and between academics and producers on media selection and different teaching functions of various media. The problem is found among those producers who are trained in the production of general programmes which demand a more artistic approach rather than pedagogic considerations. Further, institutional considerations for media deployment are based on robust estimates and logistical factors, rather than the pedagogic attributes of the media. These flaws have been attributed by Koumi (1994) partly to the absence of design theories for educational media, and he further points out that decisions based on media comparison research are biased because 'media comparison research in the past has been severely flawed' (Koumi, 1994: 48). The inventory of distinctive audio/visual techniques and their teaching functions given by him will be extremely useful to both academics and producers in making the best use of non-print media (Koumi, 1994; also see Bates, 1988; Koumi, 1991).

Production and distribution

Audio/video production, like print, also has to be undertaken keeping in mind the distribution or delivery mechanism. Audio/video components of the learning package involve the stages of finalizing the content, format, production, reproduction (multiplication) and distribution. Once the academic content of the course to be developed in audio and/or video form has been decided, the question of its production has to be tackled. The production of audio/video requires specialist professionals. Apart from academics, the other professionals required are producers, researchers, sound recordists, camera persons, editors and a host of other technical staff.

The activities of design, production and editing may be undertaken in-house, outsourced or a combination of the two can be used. The policy decision makers should keep in mind the following: 1) The overall production workload must be determined. In the case of audio/video production, the capital investment is high, and highly sophisticated equipment and specialized staff to use and maintain it are required. Is it possible to justify the creation of facilities in-house in terms of audio/video production costs and enough regular work to make the best use of the personnel and infrastructure throughout the year? This is pertinent since there have been wide variations in the annual production load of video producers across open universities: 6.5 hours programming for the UK Open University, 12 hours each for Indira Gandhi National Open University and Sukhothai Thamathirat Open University, 80 hours for Central Radio and Television University, and 200 hours for Taiwan Open University (Koumi, 1994). 2) In the case of in-house production, should it be centralized or decentralized to various schools of studies and/or discipline areas?

A major area of management decision is the recruitment of producers and their training, and resolving the academic–producer conflict. While it has always been to the institution's advantage to recruit reputed academics as producers or production assistants, and promote them with major responsibilities and significant workload after substantial grounding in the process of production, it has been difficult to expect quality production from those with significant general production skills but without much grounding in the academic discipline concerned. Irrespective of the source of academic–producer disagreement and conflict (which, if not channelled towards quality programming, eventually ruins the programme), a major management decision involves sufficient orientation and training for both to better appreciate each other's language. Soliman and Holden (1988), in a study on co-production and the relationship between an academic and a media specialist, concluded, among other suggestions, that 'The ideal would be attained if AV

Table 11.1 *Delivery of audio/video material*

Method of delivery	Final product	Method of distribution	Learner requirement	Remarks
Direct broadcast or telecast to learners	Master tape	Radio/TV station	Equipment to receive it (radio/TV)	The timings are fixed, therefore the suitability for learners must be kept in mind
Use at study centre	Copies made after duplication on suitable tapes/CDs (audio or video)	Through post/ courier with suitable packing to protect	Equipment available at study centres with access to learners (cassette player, CD player, TV, VCR/VCD)	The points to consider are: At what time can it be played at the study centre? Is it suitable for learners? Proper maintenance of equipment
Despatch to individual learners	Copies made after duplication on suitable tapes/CDs (audio or video)	Through post/ courier with suitable packing to protect	Suitable equipment available with individual learners	Instructions to be provided to learners about how to use them along with print media

centres were staffed with media personnel trained in both the theory and practice of education and the technical aspects of production …' (1988: 311). Furthermore, with increasing miniaturization, convergence of skills is being called for.

Media production needs teamwork and very close cooperation between the academics, producers and editors who need to jointly consider the method of delivery and decide the form of the final product and its distribution (Table 11.1).

In all cases, the learners need to be briefed about the interrelationship of audio, video and print material, and their proper usage so as to derive optimum benefits.

Depending on the delivery and distribution mechanisms, a decision needs to be taken about getting duplication done in-house or through outsourcing. This is one activity where outsourcing may be economical both in terms of procuring blank tapes/CDs/VCDs and duplicating them. The equipment to perform these activities and the personnel required to run it may not be needed for long enough to justify their location in-house all year round.

In deciding on delivery and distribution, a combination of the strategies listed in Table 11.1 can be worked out. Along with centralized broadcast/telecast, these can be provided either through learning centres, or made available at low cost to individual learners who can afford to buy and own the equipment to use them.

(The Indira Gandhi National Open University has adopted this combination with a fair amount of success.) Further, the method of delivery may also vary across academic programmes, and this is guided by the learner groups, their learning needs, the availability of resources, and the way the audio/visual media have been conceived as part of the learning package. Questions such as whether these are complementary, supplementary or integrated, and whether they will be used under the supervision of instructors, must be addressed.

Institutions have to be very careful in choosing not only the most suitable medium but also the finer details of form because media require sophisticated and expensive equipment. The viability of the medium and its delivery assume significance for its use in a given time frame. A few notes of caution are required here: 1) Audio cassettes are being replaced by audio CDs. Though the production of CDs is cheaper, the equipment to play these is relatively expensive. The same is true of video tapes and video CDs. 2) The quality of audio and video CD can be much superior in the case of digital technology, but the equipment to play them is more sophisticated and costly.

The fast-changing technology requires careful forward planning, keeping all the finer details in view while framing the institutional policy on non-print media. Another aspect to decide within the institutional policy is co-production of audio and video programmes, in parallel with joint development of courses. Koumi (1992) points to both the positive aspects and the limitations of such an exercise. In a study involving 10 countries, he compared co-production on the basis of seven aspects: producer, director, academic, script, technical aspects, use, and funding; and concluded that the following (selective) factors contribute to either the success or the failure of co-produced programmes: 1) Factors facilitating success: commitment, meticulous planning, respect for and diplomatic handling of cultural differences, on-the-job training; 2) Factors jeopardizing success: obsession with academic purity, non-respect for partner's status, conflicting ideologies, difficulties of translation/dubbing, rushing through planning and production, unstable collaborators (Koumi, 1992: 10).

Conclusion

While non-print media production and delivery need specialized skills, significant management decisions centre on proper recruitment, training and grounding for those involved in it, as do decisions on infrastructure and issues of access and equity. However, pedagogic requirements and functions are basic to all other decisions. Given the media hype with which distance education and training specialists are grappling, audio/vision as a medium of teaching–learning has achieved more effective learning at a lower cost than most of the other print and non-print media (Koumi, 2002), and may be given a trial. Further, not only does the Internet require significant audio and video inputs, but the pedagogic requirements for audio and video media will continue to haunt educators and trainers for quite some time to come.

References

Bates, A W (1988) Television, learning and distance education, *Journal of Educational Television*, **14** (3), pp 213–25

Bates, A W (1995) *Technology, Open Learning and Distance Education*, London and New York, Routledge

Bates, T (1990) 'Audio cassettes in the British Open University', in *Media and Technology in European Distance Education*, ed A W Bates, pp 101–04, Heerleen, EADTU

Clark, R E (1983) Reconsidering the research on learning from media, *Review of Educational Research*, **53** (4), pp 445–59

Koumi, J (1991) Narrative screen writing for educational television: a framework, *Journal of Educational Television*, **17** (3), pp 131–48

Koumi, J (1992) 'Types of co-production: case studies from 9 countries', paper presented at the international conference on European Issues in Educational Media, 9–11 September, Strasbourg

Koumi, J (1994) Media comparison and deployment: a practitioner's view, *British Journal of Educational Technology*, **25** (1), pp 41–57

Koumi, J (2002) 'Audio vision-audio cassette, guiding learners through visual materials', paper presented at the XV Conference of Asian Association of Open Universities, 24–26 February, New Delhi

Rowntree, D (1994) *Teaching with Audio in Open and Distance Learning*, London, Kogan Page

Soliman, I K and Holden, N F (1988) Video production for distance education: a collaborative enterprise, *Distance Education*, **9** (2), pp 298–311

Chapter 12

Material production and distribution, and operations management

A R Khan and Suresh Garg

Introduction

The structures and practices of open and distance education systems have used conventional resources. It is, therefore, reasonable to assume that there would be convergence in the educational provisions in the two systems. However, the evolution of open and distance learning (ODL) systems has been such that their requirements and functioning vastly differ from those of conventional institutions. The most important difference is in the substitution of the conventional teacher by self-instructional study materials. 'Building the teacher into the text' demands considerable effort in the design of an innovative curriculum and development of quality materials (Sparkes, 1993). This is facilitated by multiple channels of learning through print-based self-learning materials (SLMs) and electronic media (audio and video, teleconferencing, interactive radio, television, CD-ROMs, computer-mediated learning, WWW/Internet). Moreover, for the success and growth of ODL systems, learner satisfaction is crucial. This necessitates the production and distribution of materials to a timetable and the availability of mechanisms for learner support in a manner that facilitates the pacing of individualized learning.

As such, the production and distribution of materials are two distinct processes, and we propose to discuss these separately. But they are so closely connected that their policy decisions are mutually inclusive and one has quite often to refer to the linkages and effects of the policy formulations of one on the other. For this reason, many open universities position these operations within a materials production and distribution division.

Production of self-instructional materials

The use of the term 'production' of materials in ODL focuses upon the printing of study materials (SLMs, assignments, programme guide/study guide, student handbook, prospectus etc), duplication of audio/visual (A/V) media and availability of digital media. However, the development and production of learning materials is a multi-stage process. It begins immediately the course is approved. A decision is then made on the nature (certificate, diploma, degree) and the level (continuing professional development, undergraduate, postgraduate) of the programme in a particular area. Following curriculum design, the strategy to develop the materials is evolved in keeping with the profile of the learners – age, qualification, experience – and practices of the institution. Since the entire process is complex, specific plans have to be put in place. In particular, a decision is required on the type of media, mode of presentation, number of modules, printed block(s) in each course, programme guide, A/V cassettes/CD-ROMs etc to be sent to individual learners and/or to be used at study/regional centres (Bates, 1993). For smooth running of the process, it is advisable to appoint senior academics as experts/resource persons in the design and development of the curriculum (Perry, 1987). Since the distance education system is akin to an industrial operation, the following issues assume significance:

- whether materials production is to be an in-house or outsourced activity, and if in-house, centralized or decentralized;
- availability of infrastructure for quality printing/desktop publishing (depending on the size of enrolments);
- staff managing various operations leading to production.

While learning materials may be presented through a variety of media, most of the ODL systems, particularly in the developing world, place a heavy reliance on print. For this reason, our discussion in this chapter focuses on print materials. Issues related to audio/video media and networked learning are presented in Chapters 11 and 14 respectively.

Production of print materials

Issues in presentation

In general, print materials comprise self-instructional texts, assignments, programme/study guides, and additional readings as supporting components. Distance educators have differing opinions on the presentation of such materials. While some advocate one comprehensive volume for the whole course, others believe that the text should be presented in smaller booklets, each dealing with topics having a thematic unity. In our view, both arguments have advantages and disadvantages. For example, while presentation of the whole course in one volume will aid the maintenance of institutional inventories, packaging and despatch/distribution, it may not be learner-friendly. It may not fit through the letterbox and could initially be intimidating! On the other hand, a mature learner pursuing a higher professional course may find it more convenient to manage one book rather than many booklets. However, smaller booklets increase institutional work (of inventory, storage, packaging and distribution), but these are more convenient for the learners to handle/carry. Moreover, smaller booklets may give learners psychological satisfaction and confidence in themselves, so vital for pursuing the course successfully. The choice affects the production costs as well: materials in one volume are likely to be cheaper to produce. However, academic considerations and learner preferences should prevail over administrative and financial conveniences. It may be worthwhile to point out here that the nature of programmes, the learners' profile, and their particular needs (institutional policies and practices) may suggest adopting strategies other than standard practices.

Preparation of camera-ready copy

Once the decision in respect of presentation of course materials has been made, due attention has to be paid to the following aspects, before printing part or the whole of the course, and after necessary approvals:

- copyright/intellectual property right clearance;
- copy editing to ensure quality and consistency of in-house style/format;
- preparation of cover page and illustrations;
- typesetting and design of the booklet for uniformity in respect of size of the block, figure spacing, margin spaces, style and format, colour and code of a block/course/programme;
- preparation of camera-ready copy or electronic copy.

It is extremely important for any institution to have ownership of its materials so that these can be used in any manner it deems fit. This involves obtaining such rights in writing from course writers involved in the development of the course. (This can be part of a standard contract between the institution and the resource persons.) Where the writers plan to use the existing patented works of others, they should alert the institution so that written permission is obtained from the rights holder to use this material. Failure to do so is not only unethical but could result in legal action and subsequent costs. (Such rights clearance includes parts of others' work in literature, where novels, drama, stories, poems etc written by authors are taught, or when maps, photographs, illustrations, articles and the like are included.) In respect of the activities listed above, it is helpful to provide clear guidelines as to how rights are to be secured and to ensure strict adherence and implementation (Bottomley, n.d.). All these tasks can be performed in-house, particularly in institutions with large enrolments, if appropriate expertise and resources are available, requirements are known on time and priorities have been correctly specified. However, much depends on institutional policies. The availability of sophisticated computer software has considerably eased the preparation of such materials. Undertaking this activity in-house gives complete control over quality and production time. Furthermore, one has liberty to make changes/amendments at any stage. This is also true of such documents as assignments, programme guides, the prospectus and student handbook. Of course, fast-changing technology may require continuous retraining of personnel and use of new machines. These issues lose significance for an institution opting for outsourcing.

Printing

Printing is a specialized job and institutions relying heavily on print materials must specify their policies carefully. While formulating such policies, the following points are worth considering:

- quality of paper and cover card to be used;
- quality of printing with scope for multi-colour;
- quality of binding;
- depending on the nature of a programme, the suitability of desktop publishing, developing in-house capacity for printing or outsourcing the jobs.

We now examine each of these issues separately.

   The selection and acquisition of the quality of paper is determined by 1) the shelf-life of materials; and 2) the capacity to withstand handling by a learner. The paper should be of an optimum quality, weight and finish. Using lightweight paper may compromise print quality and reduce its integrity in use. On the other hand, heavyweight/finished paper may be expensive and its dispatch will cost more, though it will last longer. So, decisions on the quality of paper for different programmes and/or requirements should be made only after cost–benefit analysis. Whatever the decision, an institution can provide a print specification. The decision regarding multi-colour printing should be guided by academic requirements – where colour is a vital and integral part of teaching. However, in our experience, by creative use of icons and various typefaces it is possible to highlight salient features and/or details even with one-colour printing. In this process, the following considerations may facilitate decision making:

● cost of the final product;
● fee to be obtained from learners and the life of the course;
● balance between enhanced cost and effectiveness of learning materials.

If an institution decides to generate in-house capacity for desktop publishing or printing, it must be convinced that there is sufficient volume of work to keep the equipment and personnel busy all year round (Bottomley, n.d.). While in-house capacity has advantages as far as control over production schedules is concerned, it involves high initial costs and recurring maintenance expenditure. It may, however, be desirable to put in place basic arrangements to print smaller or urgent jobs (Dodds, 1983). In general, outsourcing this activity has distinct advantages:

● availability of latest state-of-the-art printing technology and expertise;
● no limit on magnitude of job(s);
● minimal initial investment in printing infrastructure at competitive rates.

Machines which can reproduce, print, collate and staple, on the basis of an assembled computing file delivered remotely, are now available. They involve a substantial investment, yet a computer operator alone can handle all the operations.

For outsourcing to be viable, the educational institution must:

● assemble a list of 'quality' printers who have the necessary infrastructure and technical skill;
● enter into a memorandum of understanding with the printers, offering uniform rates to all for similar job;
● appoint its own production staff, copy editors, designers, artists etc with the necessary technical expertise to supervise the various operations, liaise with outsiders and maintain quality content.

Of course, all such staff should be exposed to the latest technological developments through regular training.

Storage and inventory maintenance

Storing materials and maintaining proper records of incoming and outgoing stock are crucial operations in the ODL system. When designing stores, one has to keep in mind that they have easy access to transportation and good ventilation and lighting. Depending upon the local conditions, one may need to take precautions against rodents, termites and humidity. The storage racks should be arranged so that there is sufficient space between them for the movement of persons and material. Where the build-up of dust may be a problem, a regular cleaning cycle may be needed to avoid long-term health risks to workers. Inventory maintenance needs meticulous planning and execution. In this connection, the following points need consideration:

- keep the number of stock items as low as possible;
- develop systems/software which indicate the stock position at any given time;
- provide for quick storage and retrieval of materials;
- computerize inventory maintenance;
- provide for annual stock verification.

The learning materials should be stored in the order they are to be dispatched and delivered to learners. Thus if materials are dispatched in two cycles, the respective materials of each cycle should be stored together. Moreover, the inventory should be made in terms of the basic learning unit. Assignments, programme guides, admission brochures etc should be stored and entered separately because they are quite likely to be replaced every year. If a course comprises a few booklets, they should all be stored together and may be treated as one item for handling. If courseware is updated/revised, earlier booklets should be declassified and disposed of. They should never be kept with updated materials. Moreover, the stock position should be notified to the corresponding faculty as soon as stock verification has been completed. This will inform decisions regarding revision or reprinting of stocks.

It is important to note here that receipt of materials from printers must be regulated to ensure smooth distribution. Printers may be asked to submit an advance copy of the printed booklet(s); after verification, they may be asked to deliver materials at a specified date.

Materials distribution

The distribution of materials should be planned with due regard to the geographical spread of learners, costs to be incurred and time at hand so that every learner receives the materials before the start of the session. To do so successfully, the following options may be considered: 1) materials are posted to learners; or 2) learners are asked to collect the materials from a nodal point (headquarters/ regional centre/study centre) or a distribution centre (community centre/warehouse) according to a particular schedule, at a time convenient to them and in a manner that does not cost too much.

While the first of these options assumes that the institution is willing to discharge its responsibilities in keeping with the basic philosophy of open learning, the second option shifts the onus on to the learner. The Indira Gandhi National Open University (IGNOU) has tried both options over a period of time but our recommendation, on the basis of our experience, is in favour of the first option. Whatever the mode of distribution, materials should be packaged so that they are not damaged and are easy to handle. This involves:

- packaging the materials;
- generating the address labels and pasting these on to the packets to be distributed;
- scheduling the distribution to avoid inconvenience to learners as well as staff;
- updating the inventory;
- obtaining receipts from learners;
- establishing a system to receive undelivered packets and initiating action to know the reasons for non-receipt.

Some learners enrolled in earlier years may like to receive the current assignments and/or updated supplementary materials. An efficient learner support system should ensure availability of the same materials to all learners.

Operations management

Operations management, in reference to production and distribution of materials, relates to issues of policy formulation and its implementation, and to monitoring various activities in this process. The need to have such a system arises due to the complex nature of the activities/operations and their interdependence (Rumble, 1986). It may be noted that although all open/distance teaching–learning institutions seem to perform similar activities, there could be variations in the quality of academic support due to differences in their structure and organization of learner support services (Lockwood, 1998). For instance, an institution may use one or more of the following models:

- Only print materials, with counselling arranged centrally or at select centres. This is widely practised by polytechnics on the African continent, and by university correspondence course institutes in India.
- Self-instructional print materials as well as audio/video programmes to individuals and/or at regional centres/study centres etc. These may be accompanied by radio/TV tutorials and counselling as in IGNOU, India; USP, Fiji; Open University, UK; and many other universities in Asia, Australia, Europe and North America.
- Learning materials in the form of audio/video (ie telecasts), supported by course guides. The tutorial support is through radio counselling/teleconferencing, as in CRTVU, China.
- Learning materials and counselling online as in virtual universities in the developed world.

Quite often, one institution may adopt a combination of such models for different programmes, depending on the learners' profile and their needs. As mentioned earlier, in spite of differences in detail, some operations (such as materials design, development and production, learner support, learner assessment and certification) are basic to each institution. These activities constitute major operations in an open and distance learning institution, and require administrative support and infrastructure for efficient and effective operations management. To some, these may seem to be separate, but one drives the other and an operations management system should provide an interface between them. Moreover, there are various subsystems of materials production and distribution which have to be managed for the smooth functioning of production/reproduction (Figure 12.1) and storage and delivery (Figure 12.2).

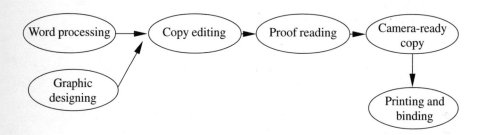

Figure 12.1 *Production/reproduction subsystem*

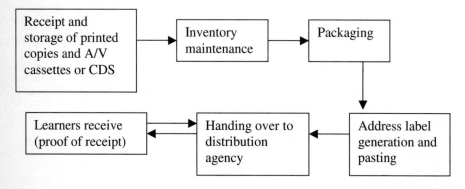

Figure 12.2 *Storage and delivery of material*

Operations management, in respect of materials design and development subsystems, involves planning and development strategies for (Bottomley, n.d.):

- activities to be undertaken in-house;
- activities to be outsourced;

- decision-making authority of an individual in the course team;
- coordination within the course team/group/department and with outside experts/agencies;
- approval of competent decision-making bodies of the institution.

In addition, an institution needs to lay down guidelines for activities such as payments to outside experts/individuals/agencies for undertaking course writing, content editing, language editing, format editing, proof reading, preparation of illustrations, cover design, copy editing, translation, and workload and work norms for the faculty. At the micro level, the production/reproduction subsystem involves:

- assigning responsibility for the production of materials;
- determining the relationship between the printing unit and those developing materials;
- determining whom to assign jobs;
- deciding on the style and the print run, and the availability of printing paper.

The storage and delivery subsystem has its own requirements and strategies which include:

- availability of authentic enrolment data as well as the stock position;
- components of the learning package;
- time to begin delivery;
- ensuring reliable delivery and minimizing damage/loss.

From the point of view of complete systems management, various operations, nodal and sub-nodal agencies are listed in Table 12.1. This is notwithstanding the

Table 12.1 *Operations management*

Operations	Nodal agency	Sub-nodes
Design, development of materials	Academic faculty	Experts from outside
Materials production, storage and inventory management	Production and distribution division	Academic faculty, printing press
Publicity and enrolment of learners	Admission division	Publicity unit
Materials distribution	Distribution unit	Production division
Learner support system	Support services unit	Academic faculty, admission division
Examination and certification	Examination and evaluation division	Academic faculty

fact that every institution will have its own variants – one or more of these – depending on its models of learning and organizational structure. However, some important points worth consideration under any circumstances include:

- not overloading a system/subsystem beyond its known capacity;
- preparation of a master schedule of operations with a well-laid-out calendar of activities, and the role and responsibility of nodal agencies concerned;
- putting in place a monitoring mechanism with the proviso for built-in checks and reviews.

Due to its inherent industrial nature, every aspect of the operation of the ODL system needs clear-cut guidelines, and in spite of the complexities, it should be flexible.

References

Bates, T (1993) 'Theory and practice in the use of technology in distance education', in *Theoretical Principles of Distance Education*, ed D Keegan, Routledge, London and New York

Bottomley, J (n.d.) *Managing Production and Delivery*, M.A. in Distance Education Course 4, Block D, Unit 15, UKOU, Milton Keynes

Dodds, T (1983) *Administration of Distance Education Institutes*, International Extension College, Cambridge

Keegan, D (1996) *Theoretical Principles of Distance Education*, Routledge, New York

Lockwood, F (1998) *The Design and Production of Self-Instructional Materials*, Kogan Page, London

Perry, W (1987) *Open University: Personal account of the first vice chancellor*, Open University Press, Milton Keynes

Rumble, G (1986) *The Planning and Management of Distance Education*, Croom Helm, London

Sparkes, J J (1993) 'Matching teaching methods to educational aims in distance education', in *Theoretical Principles of Distance Education*, ed D Keegan, Routledge, London and New York

Chapter 13

Management of services to students

Alan Tait

Introduction

This chapter engages with the management issues in open and distance learning (ODL) and concentrates on those relating to the delivery of services to students. The chapter attempts, following Paul (1990) and Rumble (1992), to identify those which are specific to the ODL context rather than addressing management issues in general. The chapter also attempts to do this in a practical rather than abstract way. To begin with, there are a number of issues which deserve particular attention. These are:

- Distance education represents substantially an industrialized process of teaching and learning, and support to students is conceived within the framework of a service industry (Sewart, 1993).
- Support to students is often delivered within a decentralized, distributed or franchised model, and accordingly many of the core activities like tutoring and counselling are 'invisible' to those with management responsibilities.
- There are specific issues with regard to the ways in which support services as a sector of activity relate to others within an ODL institution, conventionally divided into course production, operations and administration.

● In ODL as well as elsewhere in education, there is rapid change and at present considerable confusion about the relative status of students, clients and customers, which makes management problematic (Tait, 2000).

The service industry

Education and business have grown up separately over the centuries in most countries, with different purposes and ethics. Over the past 20 years, however, there has been in many countries a deliberate move by governments to diminish the autonomy of education as an activity which exists for its own sake, and to bend it more closely to serving the purposes, generally economic, of the state. Going along with this has been the widespread imposition of a changed attitude to the status of the staff in education, for the most part by bringing in accountability as against professional autonomy. This has been accompanied to a significant extent by related attempts to change the status of students more closely to that of customer. Much of ODL has also developed a separate, but in complex ways related, ethos of student-centredness, which has grown up alongside the inclusive access policies which have empathized with those excluded from more conservative and less student-centred institutions. All this bears on the core managerial question of 'what are we doing in this organization?' The weight of this question revolves around whether the success of our students is a primary or secondary purpose. However, in many sectors of education and training where ODL is used, it is accepted that successful and satisfied students represent primary institutional goals, even within the conflicting value systems in relation to 'customer care' of having to fail students who do not meet required standards. Within an industrialized teaching and learning system, it has now been widely accepted that there needs to be a service industry approach to student support in achieving this primary objective (Sweet, 1993). What does this mean for management of services to students?

Essentially it means a very complex balance between the systems necessarily developed in order to achieve reliability and consistency, along with the capacity to relate to the individual and group in such a way that learners feel recognized in their particularity. There is on one hand a necessary bureaucratic framework which tells students what they can have, and on the other hand a commitment to giving students in various ways what they want. The balance, it hardly needs saying, is difficult to achieve. The success of student services in ODL is built not just on the second of these, although some colleagues seem to think from the best motives that this can be the case. It is also crucially built on the systemic development of services that demand complex routines. In their turn they necessitate management of a kind to which educational institutions have not hitherto, to any great extent, been accustomed, and to which there is an understandable resistance. If those systems, however, are delivered without real understanding of what students need (and this in part grows out of listening to them), without flexibility or transparency, and without a commitment to their success, then student support will remain only a bureaucratic service in the worst sense of the word. This represents the axis on which the rest of this chapter in many ways turns.

The invisibility of service

Where tutoring and student guidance and counselling are delivered on a decentralized basis this creates the significant issue of 'invisibility' of service. The same can apply to small units like study centres, from where administrative services are also delivered. While this might be worrying enough in itself, it is compounded by the fact that a significant proportion of services to students are delivered precisely where management and quality assurance activities find it difficult to operate. While there is no magic wand to wave, there are a number of elements that contribute to the construction and maintenance of good practice which is invisible to the headquarters of the organization. These include focuses on staff and systems.

Management of staff

With regard to staff management, the following elements are identified as important:

- appointment of staff;
- creation and maintenance of job descriptions;
- the induction and initial training process;
- mentoring;
- supervision and appraisal;
- teamwork;
- continuing training;
- value-driven management.

Appointment of staff

Different institutions and organizations will have their own approaches to the appointment of staff. Modern management demands that equal opportunities approaches are taken in order both to contribute to equity in any particular context, and equally to ensure that the best appointment is made to the job. For the appointment, it is necessary to construct a job description which makes clear what is to be done, and a person specification which makes clear the essential and desirable qualifications, experience and skills. The job description should include a passage on the values associated with the job, ie the approach to engaging with students that the institution wants to see in place. The candidates may undertake tasks which are based on the job specification, eg making a presentation to students or tutors, doing some correspondence teaching in advance, or doing an in-tray exercise.

Creation and maintenance of job descriptions

Each person should work to a job description which is current, and which can remind them of their core tasks and responsibilities. While there may seem to be a labour-intensive and bureaucratic element to this, it is surely better in the context of supervision to revise job descriptions annually so that they remain relevant, than to begin to ignore them because they are felt to be useless. Job descriptions should be simply and clearly written, with active verbs, eg manage staff in study centres; advise students on choice of courses; etc.

Induction and initial training process

Induction and training represent key ways in which the practice and values of the institution can be inculcated in those individuals who come to work for it. This is especially important in contexts where other educational systems from which candidates will naturally present themselves have very different values etc from the ODL systems that they are coming to join. Induction and initial training can then follow on from the job description used at recruitment.

There is no doubt that in distributed systems it is more difficult to provide such training than in a campus-based or one-location organization. While some induction is needed immediately in all cases, this can be provided on paper or through computer-mediated communication (CMC), while more interactive forms of induction can be staggered at least to some extent in order to bring new colleagues together if at all possible. The induction and initial training should be as much about values and mission as about immediate tasks in hand.

Mentoring

The allocation of a mentor for the first year or so of appointment for a new member of staff can substantially assist both in supporting that new colleague in his or her work in a non-threatening way through a peer, and also support the institutional agenda of establishing the values which underpin interaction with students or tutors. Mentoring, in other words, supplements the line management relationship (where it is termed so). It can be particularly effective as the values are seen to come from a peer and thus to be accepted by one's immediate colleagues, and do not seem only an imposition from 'management' (see Morgan and Smit, 2001; Panda and Jena, 2001).

Selection and initial training of the mentor are thus essential elements in this approach if it is to be adopted. Key elements in training of mentors should include exercises to:

- develop listening skills;
- allow analysis of boundaries, eg which issues the mentee should be encouraged to discuss with his or her line manager;
- allow discussion of the issues around confidentiality.

Supervision and appraisal

Effective supervision of staff represents perhaps the core condition for the delivery over time of services to students of a quality desired by the institution, however defined. For many staff in education, if not in other contexts such as training and human resource development (HRD), such practices may still be foreign, since the staff inherit elements of a long tradition of being free spirits, accountable only to their subjects and to their peers. This conflicts in many educational contexts with both the scale and complexity of what needs to be done, and also with the widespread interest of the government. Further, ODL using industrialized methods with new divisions of labour in all but the smallest of institutions reinforces the need to develop new approaches to management in general and to the supervision of staff in particular.

A combination of qualitative and quantitative approaches makes up the optimum mix for this demanding situation. Along with the bottom-up approaches which induction and mentoring bring, it can be suggested that those with managerial responsibilities have three key approaches:

- commitment;
- trust;
- conversation.

By the first of these is meant that managers should themselves demonstrate commitment by showing interest all the time in what is happening. If, however, managers are always out of the office engaged with 'more important' activities, this will negatively impact on those they manage. Further, they will firstly not know what is going on, and secondly will demonstrate their contempt for the core tasks to their staff.

The second core component is the notion of trust. Here it is intended that within appropriate accountability and supervision, there should grow out of the managerial style a perceptible understanding by those who provide services to students that they are trusted to do so. In the ODL context this means above all that staff are trusted to work effectively and in accordance with the values of the organization when they are working 'invisibly'. This should grow naturally out of effective appointment, induction and initial training.

By the term 'conversation' is meant that managers should spend time listening to as well as talking to their staff over the delivery of services to students. Much can be learnt of a qualitative nature both about the kinds of services which students are using, about shortfalls in services, and about what is additionally needed. Regular attention through conversational management to the delivery of service can make a substantial contribution to both the building of and, importantly, the maintenance of quality. To achieve this, managers need to be there.

Cultural specifics will determine in any one organization how these or other managerial approaches need to be applied. The managers and staff can sit down together, say once per year, in order to review achievements against historical objectives, revise objectives for the next year, and identify training needs. The revision of the job description can also be undertaken in this context.

Teamwork

Large-scale organizations in many contexts have over recent years moved away from extended hierarchies and watertight job designs towards teams where tasks are managed more cooperatively and flexibly. As ODL in most contexts is a more industrialized form of teaching and learning, this development is of particular interest, no less so in the delivery of services to students.

The creation of teams across traditional boundaries of teachers or academics and clerical/administrative colleagues can do much both to improve and maintain services to students and to build on the values which the organization wants to drive the work. This supports the objective of establishing quality in work which is 'invisible' much of the time. These teams can, for example, review the management of the admissions process, the quality of study centre accommodation, or the timetabling of face-to-face elements of provision, in which all parties have an interest. Leadership in teams can move across hierarchies within education.

There will also be a need to participate in teams outside those concerned immediately with services for students, and which are based more widely within the institution as a whole. This is particularly true for senior staff. As the section below on value-driven management argues more fully, it is essential that the knowledge and values that drive the work of supporting students are represented elsewhere within the organization. It is also conversely the case that those supporting students need to understand, through working in teams, the values and constraints that govern the work of those writing courses or who are responsible for regulatory compliance of one sort or another.

Continuing training

It would be paradoxical if a book in the field of management of ODL were not to endorse the importance of continuing training and development, and the rationale for HRD as a contribution to organizational success does not need to be further rehearsed here (Robinson, 1998). It is, however, worth identifying some of the priorities for training and development after the induction period. The issues can be addressed in a number of ways. Training and development can be conceived to be:

- for remedial purposes for the immediate job;
- preparation to meet change and future organizational needs;
- for individual development.

The first area, that of training for remedial purposes, is likely to be of the most clearly functional nature, eg providing IT skills where these are lacking, or induction to ODL. It will be particularly important where an institution or organization is first going into ODL, as new skills will need to be introduced, such as management of student databases for ODL, the writing of course materials, or the creation of Web-bases. Important decisions need to be made, depending on the local context, as to whether training should be brought in for these purposes or developed in-house.

Responsibility for training must, of course, have home(s) in the organization. Development of such a training function can represent a compromise between the alternatives of in-house and external provision. In-house training may be arranged for those that need to be met on continual basis, while in smaller-scale cases, the training will have to be brought in. Points to be made to any outside training organization or individual training include:

- Has the outside training adequately studied the needs of your specific organization and of ODL?
- Will the training package be tailored or adapted to your needs rather than be an off-the-shelf programme which will have redundant or inappropriate elements?
- Is there space after the event or course for the outside training provider to discuss results of evaluations and other evidence of outcomes?

The second area, preparation to meet change and future organizational needs, is more developmental. In our specific context of supporting students, developmental training might look at:

- demographic trends over the next 10 years;
- historical evidence about recruitment and student success, which can be analysed in terms of its future trends and what activities might be undertaken as a response;
- management exercises in the context of, say, expansion. What would need to be done of an incremental or a qualitatively new nature?
- analysis of perceived competition, and resultant activities;
- implications of new technologies;
- international conference attendance and study tours in order to assess developments elsewhere.

In many of these activities it is very worthwhile to involve students as an element in the mix of participants.

The third element of training relates to that which is primarily for individual development rather than being based on an assessment of the organization's needs. This can include support in terms of fees and time for further study, or the learning of new languages. The extent to which support for training should be restricted to that which seems related to the support of students will vary from one context to another, and there is legitimate variety of view as to the extent to which such training contributes to staff retention or their departure for new opportunities. However, it is worth saying that there is an increasingly influential view that any learning undertaken by employees benefits their organization in some broad ways.

Value-driven management

Lastly, in this section on staff management, comes the issue of value-driven management (Paul, 1990; also see Chapter 6 of this book). What is identified here is that management is not solely a technocratic activity, and in the context of ODL and of supporting students is unlikely to be related only to profitability. The institutional values as they relate to the importance of education and training for the development of people within a regional, national and increasingly international context should underpin all managerial activity.

The support of students in ODL will therefore need value-driven management which is founded on the importance of, not disinterest in, the success of students. This core belief, if acted upon by senior managers, will have a good chance of illuminating the work of all those supporting students, leading to students being treated seriously, with respect, and with care. Such values will inform many aspects of the work, eg transparency, ie the importance of systems and regulations being framed in ways that students can readily understand; and timeliness, ie the recognition that students are entitled to responses which come within an agreed period.

A supporting core value lies in demonstrating understanding of the ways in which educational goals are integrally connected with administrative competence, and overall represents a core managerial achievement.

A further and related core value lies in the ways in which the knowledge that tutors and students have is accorded status and respect. These categories of participants, from the periphery, if you like, in many ODL systems, are marginalized in many societies from a historical point of view in relation to their status as well as geographic location. But the knowledge they have is important knowledge for the institution or organization, and represents a necessary and integral element alongside those of managers and teachers or academics. Those managing services to students may encounter attitudinal difficulties in espousing and operationalizing such values.

Finally, services to students should embody the values of specificity, by which is meant a commitment to the individual and to the locality. Services to students are predicated on the recognition that particular students have specific needs arising out of their local circumstances and, therefore, student-centred values need to be promoted by those staff who serve students.

All these values have further to be represented in other domains of the institution or organization. The core values that are developed in the management of student services are, in the very nature of things, unlikely to be universally shared across the organization. The strategic planning at organizational level should contribute to the sharing of values throughout. Those managing support to students will have, as an important element in their role, the representation of the values which underpin their activities to other parts of the institution, as well as to the colleagues whose activities they direct.

Management of systems

The management of systems, while it has followed the management of staff in this chapter, is in fact no less important. Indeed it stands as a foundation without which ODL of any scale at all cannot be managed. Attitudes of academic snobbery towards those who design and manage systems which support students is entirely misplaced, not least from a practical point of view. The systems which will admit and register a student, ensure the delivery of teaching materials or provide access and troubleshooting to the Web, which allocate tutors to students, accurately and speedily record changes of address, record future course choice, manage historically the accumulation of credit and notification of awards, chart and communicate dates of examinations, manage assessment scores, and so on: all these contribute as much to student progress and success as anything else that the institution does. The development of such systems relies on teamwork: those with responsibility for teaching and learning must work as colleagues alongside those with responsibility for the development and management of systems.

While this calls for professional management where the 'academy', ie the educationalists, are equals, not masters, those who come from administrative or managerial backgrounds have also to change their perspectives. They have to develop a framework of attitude that takes the 'academy' seriously, and they have to engage with the ideas about education and training that colleagues from that background bring. These shifts in attitude can be all the more difficult to manage in dual-mode institutions, where the institution may be dominated by more conventional delivery of teaching and learning, and thus the different needs of ODL are difficult to establish.

The design and management of systems for ODL is a huge topic which deserves a volume of its own. Within the scope of this chapter, however, the following elements can be identified as particularly important for notice:

- systems tailored to available technologies;
- record-keeping and data management;
- communications maps;
- complaints procedures;
- audit and inspection.

Tailoring systems to technologies

Key decisions in selecting and using technologies to support services to students lie firstly in whether they are for internal organizational use only, or are to be accessed by students. In organizations dealing within anything more than a handful of students, computerized data management is essential. However, the step-change for a centre–periphery organization, as many ODL institutions are, lies in the capacity to network computers across a range of locations and their proper maintenance. What this reveals is that technologies have the potential not just to speed up what we do, but to change what we do and how we do it. As new technologies are introduced and facilitate new developments, the following questions become pertinent, and need to be responded to:

- Can we deliver existing services more effectively? What are our criteria and measures?
- Can we deliver new services?
- Do we need different categories of staff for new services?
- Do we need staff in different places for new services?
- Are there implications for change in management activities and structures?
- How much technical support do we need in using new technologies?
- How do we construct a budget for the new services?
- How do we evaluate new developments, including cost-effectiveness measures?

Record keeping and data management

There are a number of key points which can be briefly made about this complex area. They are made in the knowledge that the ways in which data is collected and manipulated is going to vary from the services for students in one institution to another in radical ways that make comprehensive discussion difficult.

Data capture

Careful thought needs to be given to what data is wanted by the institution. There are a range of interest groups or stakeholders who will need to be consulted. These include:

- the admissions and guidance systems;
- the teaching materials delivery system;
- the tutorial system;
- the assessment system;
- evaluators and institutional researchers;
- the strategic planning system;
- marketing;
- outside bodies, eg government departments.

These functions will exist in some form in all ODL systems, and nothing will be more frustrating or damaging to effectiveness or teamwork than to find that essential data needed by one or other function has not been collected. There will certainly be discussions about how much data can reasonably be collected from students or clients at the point of entry or during study. It will be more facilitating if data are collected, analysed and results communicated by one unit.

Data manipulation

Obvious though it seems, in systems of more than micro size students will need a unique identifier, in other words a number or sequence of letters and numbers. This identifier means that the institution will never (or almost never!) confuse one student with another. A further dimension that is essential for almost all systems is the historical one. However data is collected, there need to be ways of using it historically so that you can ask, for example, which courses the student has taken, how much credit has been gained, or when a student is due for an award.

Communication mapping and management

The complexity of the division of labour in ODL organizations means that effective communication is essential. Mapping and management refer to activities which first of all make clear who should talk to whom about what (the mapping); management refers to the operation of systems that build in actual communication, which actually takes place. It also refers to the culture and attitudes that prevail. Most importantly, it means that while customer and service relationships exist between departments, the status of knowledge is one of equals.

There are a number of areas of particular concern within which such concepts can be more concretely understood. These include the following.

Course production and course presentation communications

In second-generation ODL there have been particular difficulties in many systems over the communications between those responsible for producing courses and those responsible for delivering them in the field. The worst scenario is that which occurs when the design and production stage has been all but completed before thought is given as to how students will study, eg how materials will be delivered, how students will be admitted or selected, who will tutor the students, how practical experience where necessary can be incorporated, how examinations can be held etc. In third-generation ODL, where information communications technologies (ICT) provide the essential media, there may be more integration between production and presentation in the actual running of the course.

Centre–periphery communications

From the perspective of communications management perhaps the most important element in any ODL organization that has a centre–periphery structure concerns the ways in which the two elements communicate. The culture in which this is done is as important as the actual activity. In many systems, the culture has grown up that the centre has high status and the periphery – meaning tutors, and staff in regional offices or in study centres – has low status.

There are elements of this which are very difficult to impact upon. Nonetheless, the well-managed organization will at least recognize that the knowledge which is developed in the periphery is essential to the organization as a whole – it is useful knowledge. In particular, it draws on knowledge which is much harder to identify at the centre, namely that which is drawn from the public at large about perceptions of the institution; from students and from tutors. Within dual-mode institutions, this can be especially hard if ODL is already seen as an inferior activity within the mainstream.

Thus, systems need to be developed which draw upon knowledge developed in the periphery. These conventionally are based on meetings at the centre, to which staff from regional centres and study centres, and sometimes students, are invited. Colleagues from peripheral posts can be used as chair-people. Occasional meetings can be held in regional offices or study centres, and ways should be found of involving students on major committees.

Where possible, meetings by telephone or video-conference can be very helpful in diminishing time for travel. They can be especially important for minor meetings, or as elements within a schedule of meetings which take place half on a face-to-face basis and half through one of these technologies.

An enormous amount of communication within the organization and to the external world now takes place by e-mail and CMC. Through its social dimension, CMC allows discussion across a range of locations in ways that resolve issues of time and place in revolutionary ways. In many cases, it offers a medium which is strong on discussion rather than decision making, where often it seems still to be felt that face-to-face meeting is imperative. There seems to be a kind of hierarchy developing within management where e-mail, CMC, video- and telephone-conferencing and simple telephone calls are conceived as being in ascending order, with face-to-face meeting remaining not only a desirable element, but the most desirable element where particularly difficult, important or sensitive issues have to be resolved.

Where all or some of these approaches are well managed through achieving the optimum fit of a particular set of circumstances, the term 'distributed organization' rather than 'centre–periphery organization' becomes more appropriate, and is certainly preferable. As is clear, it suggests a flexible if complex set of arrangements across more than one location, rather than a structure based on a headquarters and outpost mentality.

Institution–tutor and institution–student communications

Particular difficulties arise in the ways in which the organization relates to tutors where they are part-time and distributed, and to students.

These are based around geography: the tutors and students are simply not in the building. They arise also around status, with the knowledge that tutors and students are all too often seen as subordinate to those who work full-time for the organization. However, it has been argued here that the knowledge deriving from one category or another of participants in the overall ODL enterprise should not be seen as subordinate. While tutors and students represent only one element within understanding across the institution as a whole, their contribution should be seen as integral and necessary. This can be very galling for those who perceive their status within the organization as threatened by having to listen, sometimes to criticism, to those they perceive as 'junior'. However, the knowledge that is represented in tutors and students about the success or otherwise of what is happening within the organization is very important in its development and improvement. All, including the most senior, have something to learn.

Academic–administrative communications

Communications about student services can also be diminished by attitudes which derived from former traditions within education about the subservient role of administrators vis-à-vis academics to teachers. As with tutors and students, it represents a false understanding of who has relevant and useful knowledge. In the context of ODL, where in more than micro-systems elements of industrialization are likely to be present, it also represents a particularly damaging diminishment of a range of functions which can be termed administrative, and which are of core and integral importance in the delivery of services to students.

The most effective way of changing both the practice and its supporting culture in an organization where this sort of separatism is present to a greater or lesser degree, is to move towards teamwork rather than the more traditional committee structure. In the latter, those with administrative responsibilities have been seen as servicing rather than participating in discussions and decisions. Their participation is likely to be more assured where they are members of such meetings rather than servants of it.

Communications through time

As well as spanning the organization in terms of horizontal and vertical structures, in terms of geography as well as categories of staff, communications have to be mapped and managed across time. It is clearly good practice to have a record of major issues discussed and decisions taken at any meeting. It is essential that the record of the last meeting is referred to in order to check on who agreed to do what. Further, there need to be indices of decisions taken on a cross-organizational basis, so that when considering an issue it is possible to check quickly when it was previously discussed and what has been done about it.

Complaints procedures

Complaints from students create both systemic and cultural issues for education in general. For ODL, there is the particular issue of how easy it is for students learning at a distance to make their complaints, and the impact on their progress or conversely dropout, if channels are not created (Fage and Mayes, 1997). Thus the first element in any ODL system is that students know how to complain. The second element is that the institution must have procedures for acknowledgement, timescales within which answers will be given, and authority must be developed in order that redress can as easily as possible be made where necessary. At the same time, there must be channels to senior authority, perhaps an ombudsperson in a big system, for students who do not gain satisfaction and still feel aggrieved. Systems for logging complaints transparently must be set up, and management must ensure that student complaints are not swept under the carpet but addressed in a competent way. A central log for all complaints may be advisable so that an overall institutional perspective on what students are complaining about can be gained. While there are of course unjustified complaints, the culture should be that complaints are treated seriously, as are the students who make them.

Audit and inspection

There is not space in this chapter to address fully the issues of quality assurance for student services in distance education, under which audit and inspection can be broadly located (Tait, 1997). However, the terms denote both the regular internal cycles of audit and review which need to be undertaken to assure that service standards are being met, as well as the increasingly familiar process of external inspection from government agencies in many countries to assure that public resource is being effectively used. Services to students delivered out of sight in distance education may present particular difficulties for quality assurance activity. These can, however, be addressed through well-planned activity, gathering information from students and tutors, as well as ensuring that standards, for example of timeliness in services, process in teaching, facilities in study centres etc are met.

Conclusion

For both the staff and systems dimensions of student services, managerial persistence over time is essential, in order to diminish the tendency which appears to be universal for systems overall to atrophy, and for familiarity to engender a relaxation of standards and a loss of commitment and concentration. At the same time, systems have to be developed which do not hamper the organization by their cumbersomeness, either in terms of paperwork, meetings, or a bullying insensitivity to the needs of staff themselves, all of which where the balance is wrong will negatively affect the very achievements that they are intended to support. They will also diminish the potential for the fulfilment of key quality indicators such as respect for students or timeliness of response. The development and running of managerial processes to support the delivery of services to students in ODL, where there is a high degree of invisibility, is no easy task. Clearly, there will be a range of differences in how these elements are developed and applied in different educational sectors with different histories and cultures. The distinctions between single- and dual-mode institutions are particularly significant, and the revolution which new technologies bring is difficult to foresee with any precision. This is especially the case where the call-centre model of customer care begins to impact on large-scale ODL organizations, and where information and advice are increasingly given to students on the Web. (The utility of telelearning centres is discussed in Chapter 15.) However, the commonalities of delivering student services in distributed ODL systems will tend to drive at least some commonalities of practice around the world, which make discussion of this nature worthwhile.

References

Fage, J and Mayes, R (1997) 'Monitoring learners' progress', in *Supporting the Learner in Open and Distance Learning*, eds R Mills and A Tait, pp 206–21, Pitman, London

Morgan, C and Smit, A (2001) 'Mentoring in open and distance learning', in *Innovation in Open and Distance Learning*, eds F Lockwood and A Gooley, pp 160–71, Kogan Page, London

Panda, S and Jena, T (2001) 'Changing the pattern: Towards flexible learning, learner support and mentoring', in *Innovation in Open and Distance Learning*, eds F Lockwood and A Gooley, pp 172–78, Kogan Page, London

Paul, R (1990) *Open Learning and Open Management: Leadership and integrity in distance education*, Kogan Page, London

Robinson, B (1998) 'A strategic perspective on staff development for open and distance learning', in *Staff Development in Open and Flexible Learning*, eds C Latchem and F Lockwood, pp 33–44, Routledge, London

Rumble, G (1992) *The Management of Distance Learning Systems*, UNESCO/International Institute for Educational Planning, Paris

Sewart, D (1993) Student support systems in distance education, *Open Learning*, **8** (3), pp 3–12

Sweet, R (1993) 'Student support services, towards more responsive systems', in *Perspectives on Distance Education*, Commonwealth of Learning, Vancouver

Tait, A (ed) (1997) *Quality Assurance in Higher Education: Selected case studies*, (Perspectives on Distance Education), Commonwealth of Learning, Vancouver

Tait, A (2000) Planning student support in open and distance learning, *Open Learning*, **15** (3), pp 287–99

Chapter 14

Planning and management of networked learning

Alistair Inglis

What is meant by 'networked learning'?

Anyone who has only lately developed an interest in networked learning could be forgiven for assuming that this mode of learning is a recent development made possible by the creation of the World Wide Web. Recently, a team investigating this mode of learning in the UK defined networked learning as 'learning in which information and communications technology (ICT) is used to promote connections: between one learner and other learners; between learners; and tutors; between a learning community and its resources' (Networked Learning in Higher Education Project, 2000). If we accept this definition, then networked learning has a far longer history, albeit under other names.

Before the advent of the World Wide Web, learning supported by ICT was referred to by such terms as 'computer-mediated communication', 'computer-managed learning', and 'computer-assisted learning' (Romiszowski, 1990). Each of these terms signified a slightly different way of using ICT and therefore the term 'networked learning' can be taken to signify a stage in the evolution of the use of ICT in education, but not necessarily a totally new departure.

If we look around the world at the ways in which institutions and organizations are using the Internet to deliver courses online, we can see two reasonably distinct models of delivery being adopted (Inglis, Ling and Joosten, 1999). In one, which we might term the 'resource-based learning (RBL) model', the learner is seen as learning by self-instruction and the Internet is used as the medium for delivery of the learning materials. In the other, which we might term the 'virtual classroom model', the learner is seen as learning through person-to-person interaction. In this model, the Internet provides the medium by means of which interaction takes place. Most courses delivered online combine the use of both self-instructional resources and person-to-person interaction. However, it is the way in which these different components are combined that distinguishes the two models. In the RBL model, conferencing is used to augment what is learnt through use of the self-instructional materials or to compensate for limitations of the self-instructional materials rather than to serve as the principal mode of teaching. In the virtual classroom model, resource materials serve to support the discussion activities rather than reduce the need for interaction.

The definition of 'networked learning' above places the emphasis on person-to-person interaction. Courses that conform to the former model are often referred to as 'Web-delivered'. However, as teachers are becoming more experienced at delivering courses via the Web, the term 'networked learning' is acquiring a broader meaning which encompasses resource-based as well as classroom-based learning.

Networked learning may involve synchronous or asynchronous interaction or both. Synchronous interaction is interaction that takes place in real time. Asynchronous interaction is interaction that allows participants to interact at times that suit them. Most educators consider asynchronous interaction to be more useful than synchronous interaction for planned learning activities, because the former allows participants more time for reflection and greater opportunity to make considered responses and because it is more flexible. Students can participate even when their work and family responsibilities place tight limits on their availability. Asynchronous interaction suits the situation where participants happen to be spread across several time zones. Synchronous interaction nevertheless has a useful role to play in less formal interaction such as online study groups.

Institutional and course-level management and planning

The responsibilities and functions involved in the planning and management of networked and collaborative learning need to be considered on at least two levels – at the organizational level and at the course level. At the organizational level there is the need for establishing and maintaining the specialized technical infrastructure and the technical support services required for this mode of delivery. These responsibilities generally lie with a central unit that may have them as its primary role or that may be associated with the information technology services department or may even be associated with the library.

At the course level, the responsibility of planning and managing teaching–learning interactions in ways that maximize student learning opportunities while ensuring that courses stay within budget lies with the individual teacher or with course teams.

For effective overall management of networked learning the activities at both these levels do, of course, need to be strongly coordinated. However, the types of decisions that will be taken at each of the levels are quite different. They are therefore best examined separately.

Planning the organization-wide introduction of networked learning

Most education and training organizations have already started to explore the potential of networked learning. However, in many cases these initial attempts are of enthusiastic individuals – the idea leaders. Once an organization has decided to proceed to the next stage of development – the creation of an online program, there is need for adoption of an organizational change strategy. The organizational change strategy needs not only to address the scaling up of course development but also how various delivery functions such as the provision of library, tutoring and counselling services, the processing of assignments and handling of communication with students will be integrated into the delivery system. It also needs to consider security issues.

Broadly speaking, the ways institutions are attempting to achieve larger-scale change fall into three categories:

- *seeding*: individuals and groups bid competitively for project funding;
- *'grand plan'*: top management drives a whole-of-organization review and restructuring;
- *incremental*: new projects build on existing strengths.

The seeding strategy has been popular in universities for many years but a major weakness of this strategy is that innovations introduced as a result of the provision of seed funding are seldom taken up by the remainder of an organization. The 'grand plan' strategy can achieve change quickly but the strategy can be risky. If the plan is misconceived the costs of rectifying the mistakes produced by the plan can be high. The incremental approach allows lessons that are learnt in one part of the organization to 'ripple through' to other parts of the organization.

Irrespective of which type of strategy is used, the strategy will need to address six main areas of activity:

1. establishing the necessary technical infrastructure;
2. setting up appropriate technical support services;
3. identifying suitable lead projects;
4. training staff to work with the new learning technologies;
5. implementing projects;
6. evaluating the outcomes of projects.

The planning and management of the first four of these types of activities are generally best carried at the institutional level. On the other hand, responsibility for planning and management of actual projects is generally best carried at the course level. Meanwhile evaluation of the outcomes of projects will usually call for some sharing of responsibilities between staff operating at the institutional and course levels.

Let us consider each of these areas of activity in turn.

Establishing infrastructure

It is quite feasible to set up a delivery system that is capable of supporting several concurrent conferences involving more than 100 participants and several online discussions on a desktop computer. Such a system may be all that is needed to conduct a pilot project or for a specialized training operation. However, if the eventual aim is to extend use of the system throughout the whole institution, then beginning with a desktop system is unlikely to offer a smooth upgrade path. So in setting up a conferencing system it is necessary to keep in mind both the long-term and the short-term goals.

The essential requirement for supporting networked learning is some type of system for online conferencing. There are a variety of possibilities:

- free software;
- commercially available systems (eg FirstClass, WebBoard);
- systems integrated with Web browsers (eg Microsoft Exchange);
- integrated electronic learning environments (eg Blackboard, WebCT);
- other solutions (eg list server software, Usenet Newsgroups).

David Woolley maintains a comprehensive list of Web-based conferencing systems <http://thinkofit.com/webconf/>. A useful tool for selecting integrated electronic learning environments is *Online Education Delivery Applications: A Web Tool for Comparative Analysis* <http://www.olin.nf.ca/landonline/>. This regularly updated site provides a side-by-side comparison of a large number of systems.

Integrated electronic learning environments will generally not incorporate as comprehensive a set of features as dedicated conferencing systems. However, dedicated conferencing systems do not provide support for other delivery functions. The user is therefore faced with making a trade-off between convenience and versatility.

Some of the factors that need to be considered in selecting a delivery system include:

- *scalability*: the capacity to expand the system to more users and more conferences; this factor will be important if the intention is to expand use of the system across an institution;
- *reliability*: the frequency with which the system fails in normal use;

- *performance*: the speed with which the system responds to requests from users; the performance of the system is related to the performance of the network to which it is attached;
- *cost*: this is generally a function of the number of users.

Establishing technical and administrative support services

The level of technical and administrative support needed to maintain the delivery system will depend on an organization's scale of operations, on the delivery model, and on the inherent reliability of the hardware and software that are being used for delivery. Pilot projects are likely to make only modest demands for technical support that can probably be met by existing staff. Large-scale projects present much greater risk of failure and the consequences of such failure are much more far-reaching. The way in which technical support is to be provided then becomes much more important. The minimum response times that need to be set will depend on the teaching model that is being employed. If the teaching model makes considerable use of synchronous interaction, then failure of a server or of components of the network infrastructure will produce much greater disruption of discussion activities than if the model uses only asynchronous interaction. If students are spread out over several time zones, overnight failure of critical items of equipment is likely to be much more disruptive than if all students are located in the same time zone.

The large-scale introduction of networked learning will also result in the need for additional administrative support to deal with registration and deregistration of users, be they students or staff, and provision of help-desk services.

Choosing lead projects

The processes used to select lead projects need to be open and clearly understood and 'owned' by all the major stakeholders. They also need to be informed by an understanding of the costs and benefits to the organization. The most important requirement of lead projects is that they contribute to the organization meeting its strategic goals. These goals will differ from organization to organization. So what may be considered a suitable lead project in one organization may not be considered as suitable in another.

Assuming that the short- and long-term goals have been identified, the types of questions to be asked of proposed lead projects might include:

- Will the project contribute to the institution achieving its overall strategic goals?
- Does the project build on the strengths and existing resources of the institution?
- Does the project draw on the institution's existing resources?
- Is the project likely to lead to further projects in the future?
- Does the project offer opportunities for staff to develop new skills that will be important in the pursuit of future projects?

- Will the courseware that is produced have potential for reuse in other programmes?
- Is the solution that the project offers going to be cost-effective?

The selection of initial projects should be either accompanied by or followed by a formal process of project planning.

Preparing staff for teaching online

Discussions about the introduction of networked learning into institutions frequently revolve around the importance of staff development. Making a shift to networked learning does present a range of staff development needs. However, what is more important than ensuring that there are adequate funds for staff development is ensuring that the funds available are appropriately deployed.

Setting up Web sites, putting course materials into integrated electronic learning environments, and registering users of conferencing systems does involve some technical know-how. However, in most situations it will be more economical for tasks such as these to be given to technical support staff. The technical skills needed to use online conferencing systems and integrated electronic learning environments are generally quickly acquired. However, where staff do often need substantial additional training is in designing and developing courses that make use of new learning technologies.

Teachers who already have substantial experience in teaching at a distance are likely to be able to make the transition to teaching online relatively easily. However, for teachers whose only teaching experience is in face-to-face situations, making the transition is likely to prove more challenging. Adopting a team approach to course development, similar to that which is commonly used in print-based distance education, can produce a better result than leaving teachers to learn by experience. The fact that teaching staff may be skilled facilitators of classroom discussions does not necessarily mean that they will be effective at managing online discussions. Collins and Berge (1997) contend that when conferences fail, it is more often than not because the person in charge is unable to transpose leadership skills in face-to-face settings into the online setting. These authors suggest that the main reason may be the loss of non-verbal cues.

Implementing projects

Responsibility for planning and management in the areas of activity that have been discussed up to this point is most appropriately carried at the institutional level. However, when it comes to implementing projects involving the design, development and delivery of courses, planning and management are most appropriately passed down to staff operating at the course team level.

The introduction of networked learning will call for changes to the approach course teams take to the planning of courses and management of teaching of courses in at least three areas:

- planning learning activities appropriate to this method of delivery;
- induction of students into the new mode of learning;
- management of group interaction in an online environment.

Planning learning activities

One of the keys to the success of networked learning is adequate planning. Many of the tasks involved in planning for online delivery of courses are similar to tasks involved in planning for delivery of courses by more traditional methods. They will include, for example, selecting suitable learning activities and identifying the types of resources needed to support those activities. Where the planning processes differ is in setting up the classroom environment. Different types of activities will need to be devised that take into account the particular characteristics of the online environment. Learning resources will need to be prepared for electronic access.

In planning for the online delivery of courses it is important to allow adequate time for preparation and to start preparing well ahead of when a course is to be offered. While, in theory, it ought to be possible to set up a course in a matter of a few hours once the materials have been assembled, in practice, leaving this to the last minute is to court disaster. The vagaries of the technologies upon which networked learning relies are such that there is a strong likelihood of unexpected problems being encountered even when this stage of the process has been carefully thought through.

Special attention will need to be paid to methods of fostering interaction as the opportunity that networked learning gives for student–student and student–tutor interaction is seen as one of the attributes that sets mode of delivery apart from other delivery modes. It is important that interaction not be limited to unstructured discussion. Table 14.1 provides examples of different formats that online interaction may take. More detailed guidelines may be found in Berge (1995) and Harasim *et al* (1995).

Being able to bring together students from different geographic regions also has the potential to enhance the quality of interaction. Bringing experts from different parts of the world into the discussion allows one to draw on a larger pool of expertise and can make for a livelier and more interesting discussion as well as giving students the opportunity to gain the benefit of the experts' knowledge.

Inducting students into online discussion

Students as well as staff need to be given the opportunity to learn the basic skills involved in this new mode of interaction. Providing students with the tools to interact online is of little value if the students don't know how to engage in effective discussion in an online environment.

Table 14.1 *Activities for networked learning*

Activity type	Activity stages
Tutorial	The instructor sets problems; students provide their answers; the instructor discusses the answers; topics may also be discussed.
Seminar	The instructor assigns readings; the instructor or a student reviews the topic; discussion is started with a short series of questions.
Question and answer	Students raise questions; the instructor and/or other students respond.
Debate	The instructor sets a topic and divides students into teams; the debate is pursued according to a pre-specified set of rules.
Discussion	The instructor sets a topic and identifies a series of key issues; students discuss the issues, perhaps in small groups; the instructor or one of the students summarizes the main points that have been raised.
Collaborative problem solving	Problems are set; groups are established; groups collaborate in obtaining a solution; the instructor monitors solutions and reviews them at the conclusion.
Role play	Students bid for or are given roles; students play out their roles in a scenario.
'Visiting' expert	The instructor provides a short biographical summary of the expert; the expert presents an overview of an aspect of their area of expertise; students ask questions.
Work group	The instructor provides a clearly defined task, a specification of roles, the basis on which work is to be shared, and a timeline for completion of the task; the group works to complete the task.

An induction activity allows students to familiarize themselves with the basic features of the conferencing system. It also allows them to become comfortable with participating in this form of interaction. Students can readily overcome their reticence to communicating online if they are offered the opportunity to gain experience at this form of communication in a supportive learning environment (see, for example, Inglis and Keens, 2000). An induction activity may involve two stages: an initial session explaining the way in which the conferencing system itself operates and is used, followed by some sort of simple activity which requires students to engage with each other by making use of the features of the conferencing system. If there is an opportunity for the initial session to take place in a face-to-face context, that can be helpful, although it is often not feasible in courses taught at a distance.

Students who have not had previous experience of online interaction may not know how to communicate unambiguously. Attempts at humour, in particular, can easily be misunderstood. When students communicate in ways that are offensive to other students, strong emotions can be aroused and the ensuing exchanges can be quite disruptive. It is the responsibility of each teacher to gain the acceptance by each group of the basic rules of etiquette to be followed. This is best dealt with when the group is first formed. Each group needs to agree on what will be regarded as acceptable behaviour. It is universally unacceptable for students to make defamatory statements. However, whether or not the groups agree to use a particular set of abbreviations in discussion is inconsequential.

Managing online discussions

Online discussion takes place differently from face-to-face discussion and demands different skills of the teacher. Some of the techniques that can be used to ensure that students remain engaged include:

- making participants welcome;
- communicating with students individually;
- summarizing the discussion regularly.

Online discussion can make substantial demands on a teacher's time. Keeping the cost of this form of delivery within acceptable limits therefore depends on developing strategies that result in students accepting greater responsibility for the progress of discussion. Some of the strategies that can help include:

- paying adequate attention to prior planning;
- giving students clear instructions on what is expected of them;
- setting time limits;
- encouraging students to help one another rather than relying on the instructor;
- withdrawing from the discussion once it gets going;
- delegating responsibility for leading discussion to one of the members of the group.

Students studying at a distance typically have many work and family responsibilities that make demands on their time and compete with their studies. They may therefore be less active in participating in discussion than one might wish and their participation may be interrupted or may taper off.

One of the limitations of many Web-based conferencing systems, in regard to pacing, is that they require participants to check whether messages have been posted. Systems that e-mail messages to participants in addition to posting them to the discussion board therefore have an advantage. If the system that is being used does not offer this feature, then it will be important to employ some strategy for ensuring that students do visit the conferencing system regularly. One strategy is to require students to post at least one message to the discussion each day. Even if students do contribute to discussion regularly, their contributions may not take the discussion in the direction intended. In that event, it will be necessary to intervene to keep them on track.

Beaudin (1999) asked 135 instructors who had experience in using asynchronous online discussion what techniques they used to keep students on task and what techniques they would recommend. The same four techniques were ranked uppermost:

- carefully design questions that specifically elicit on-topic discussion;
- provide guidelines to help online learners prepare on-topic responses;
- formally present rules of conduct that eliminate off-topic comments;
- formally state the expectation that online discussions stay on topic.

Computer and communications systems are subject to failure. When problems arise it is important to know the procedures to be followed to have technical problems rectified. It is also important to have a fallback programme so students can continue learning while waiting for communications to be restored.

Using evaluation to support quality improvement

The introduction of networked learning involves the establishment of a range of systems and processes and each of these should be subjected to evaluation to ensure that they are functioning satisfactorily. Responsibility for such evaluations is probably best carried at the institutional level, although course teams are likely to have a keen interest in the results of such evaluations. Some of the aspects of a project that one may wish to evaluate could include:

- the effectiveness of the delivery system;
- the 'downtime' of the delivery system;
- the adequacy of student support;
- the costs of the new mode of delivery relative to the costs of the existing mode.

Just as evaluation should play a central role in guiding the implementation of technologies, systems, policies and procedures at the organization level, so it should play a central role in guiding the development of course materials, teaching methods, and provision of student support at the course level. However, the types of evaluation methods and the frequency of evaluation will differ between the two levels.

Course level evaluation should focus on factors such as:

- the extent to which intended student learning outcomes are attained;

- the types of unexpected outcomes obtained;
- students' satisfaction with the quality of their teaching;
- the usability of learning materials.

Evaluation at the organizational level should also be linked with evaluation at the course level in order to establish how introduction of the new delivery mode has affected students' performance.

Conclusion

For many education and training organizations, the introduction of networked learning represents a completely new approach to the way they conduct their core business. There will be a concern to 'get it right'. Yet this is probably an unrealistic expectation. Mistakes will be made. What is important is that once made, mistakes are recognized for what they are, and should be used as an opportunity for learning. At a time of rapid innovation, the organizations that succeed are not those that avoid mistakes, but those that quickly learn from their mistakes, correct them and move forward.

References

Beaudin, B P (1999) Keeping online asynchronous discussions on topic, *Journal of Asynchronous Learning Networks*, **3**, p 2 [HREF:http://www.aln.org/alnweb/journal/jaln-vol3issue2.htm]

Berge, Z L (1995) Facilitating computer conferencing: Recommendations for the field, *Educational Technology*, **35** (1), pp 22–30

Collins, M P and Berge, Z L (1997) 'Moderating online electronic discussion groups', paper presented at the American Educational Research Association Conference, Chicago, IL, 24–28 March

Harasim, L, Hiltz, S R, Teles, L and Turoff, M (1995) *Learning Networks: A field guide to teaching and learning online*, MIT Press, Cambridge

Inglis, A and Keens, J (2000) 'Inducting on-campus students into online discussions', paper presented at ED-MEDIA, Montreal, 26 June–1 July

Inglis, A, Ling, P and Joosten, V (1999) *Delivering Digitally: Managing the transition to the knowledge media*, Kogan Page, London

Networked Learning in Higher Education Project (2000) Effective networked learning in higher education: notes and guidelines [HREF: http://csalt.lancs.ac.uk/jisc/]

Romiszowski, A (1990) Computer mediated communication and hypertext: The instructional use of two converging technologies, *Interactive Learning International*, **6**, pp 5–29

Chapter 15

Managing telelearning centres and telecentres

Colin Latchem

Bridging the educational and digital divide

The major hurdles to successful participation in basic, formal and non-formal education and training by the uneducated and excluded in remote, rural and otherwise disadvantaged communities are:

- lack of educational or training providers or infrastructure;
- limited schooling handicapping access to post-compulsory education;
- lack of a culture conducive to the pursuit of learning;
- lack of comprehensive and up-to-date information about courses, careers, entry requirements, modes of study etc;
- lack of suitable courses and modes of communication for linguistic and ethnic minorities, the socially excluded, older age groups, women, the disabled and the technologically illiterate;
- learners and trainees being unable or unwilling to leave their home areas;
- lack of tutorial or peer support for isolated learners or trainees;
- lack of access to, or inability to pay for, information and communication technology (ICT);
- other forms of exclusion caused by historical, political, economic or cultural forces.

One strategy for overcoming such hurdles is to establish telelearning centres or multipurpose telecentres within these communities. It is being increasingly felt necessary in many parts of the world to extend open and distance education delivery through telelearning centres. This chapter explores this, along with effective planning and management of such centres.

Single-client telelearning centres

The Chinese have a saying to the effect that 'learning without the company of friends makes one narrow-sighted' and many studies testify to the importance of providing psychosocial support to help learners new to distance education cope with the unfamiliar mix of autonomous study, collaborative learning and uses of technology. Some distance teaching universities provide this by establishing telelearning centres.

The Korea National Open University (KNOU) provides teaching, learning materials and student support for degree and non-degree students through a network of regional and local study centres offering cable TV, radio, audio/video cassette, videoconferencing, Internet and face-to-face delivery (Jung, 1999). Similar networks are operated by, for example, Sukhotai Thammathirat Open University (STOU) in Thailand and Universidad Nacional de Educación a Distancia (UNED) in Spain.

Such comprehensive study centre provision is far more difficult for India's Indira Gandhi National Open University with its 600,000 students, some from rural, tribal and disadvantaged urban areas distributed across a country of some 3,287,590 sq km. Besides the 28 regional centres (which are maintained by the university itself), IGNOU's 12 recognized regional centres and 626 study centres are managed locally by various organizations, institutions, agencies, societies, NGOs (non-government organizations) and community groups. It is not easy to recruit local tutors/counsellors for these centres or to ensure that they can bring the necessary knowledge, skills and sensitivities to the task. IGNOU is now applying its considerable experience with the Internet, videoconferencing and localized educational delivery to a 'virtual campus' network of telelearning centres (TLCs). Equipped with Internet-connected computer labs, satellite TV and teleconferencing, these TLCs are used primarily by undergraduate students on business and information technology courses to study online or through telelectures or teletutorials with the assistance of IGNOU-based online 'consultants' and locally recruited 'counsellors'. These TLCs were run initially by private providers but it has been found that the students and the university's reputation are better served by bringing these centres under IGNOU's control and integrating them with upgraded IGNOU-owned regional centres. IGNOU has also learnt that the level of online support needed, particularly by first-time distance learners, demands greater staffing and resourcing than originally envisaged, both at the providing and receiving sites (Panda and Chaudhary, 2001).

Multiple-client telelearning centres

An alternative approach is for governmental or other agencies to establish tele-learning centres to provide access to programmes and services offered by multiple public and private educators and trainers. The Queensland Open Learning Network (QOLN) (www.qoln.qld.edu.au/QOLN.htm) is a prime example of this. Initially established by the state government to enable regional communities in Australia's second largest state to access programmes offered by the local universities and colleges, QOLN now also operates on behalf of private educational and training providers, industrial organizations, businesses, government departments and NGOs within and beyond Queensland. QOLN comprises 50 ICT-based Open Learning Centres and places satellite centres temporarily in smaller communities in response to short-term needs. These centres are variously located in schools, community halls, ex-service clubs, libraries, courthouses and government offices and are designed for face-to-face, online and mediated learning, quiet study and computing.

QOLN's head office in Brisbane coordinates the network, but the centres themselves are managed by local committees and operated by specially trained local coordinators. The beneficiary communities provide the premises, the state government provides annual, recurrent base-level funding, the institutions and organizations using the Network pay annual membership fees in return for certain entitlements, and QOLN contributes significantly to these operations through revenue-generating projects. Such an arrangement ensures that the member institutions' students have free access to the centre's learning resources, that services that have to be charged out to other users are as inexpensive as possible, and that QOLN is able to continually enhance its services.

QOLN also provides programme design, development and delivery for its members and clients. Recent examples include an accredited career planning programme for women wishing to re-enter the workforce, an online project to help rural and remote communities develop the knowledge and skills to participate in the digital economy, and an online clinical legal education initiative enabling law students to discuss legal matters with country people (Gooley, 2001).

The DaimlerChrysler Distance Learning Support Centre in the remote mountainous African kingdom of Lesotho provides a similar service, albeit on a much smaller scale. It is open to all students of educational and training institutions in the capital, Maseru, and enrolled in distance education courses provided from outside Lesotho. The centre is located within the National University of Lesotho's Institute for Extra-Mural Studies but run by a community management committee and operated by a commercial manager (Howard, 2001).

The Kitimat Community Skills Centre in remote northwest British Columbia is also community owned, operating as a nonprofit society and delivering cost-recovery, workplace-focused programmes through its computer labs and C and Ku band satellite access at Kitimat and 'electronic classrooms' in three smaller communities. The KCSC brokers programmes from the Open Learning Agency of BC, the Southern Alberta Institute of Technology, the US National Technological University and other distance education and online providers in response to requests from local industries, unions, chambers of commerce, colleges, schools, First Nations peoples and government agencies (Hartig, 2001).

On an altogether grander scale, the UK government has established a public–private partnership – the University for Industry (http://www.ufiltd.co.uk) – to deliver flexible training to help boost the competitiveness of business and industry and the performance and employability of individuals. Multiple providers deliver their programmes through learning hubs linked to over 250 learning centres and smaller access centres in educational, public library, industrial and community settings (http://www.learndirect.co.uk).

Multipurpose community telecentres

An alternative to dedicated telelearning centres is to establish multipurpose telecentres (MCTs). MCTs, sometimes known as 'telecottages' or 'community technology centres', originated in Scandinavia in the 1980s and are based upon three premises:

● Education and training need to be provided in the wider context of socioeconomic development or regeneration.
● Local communities need to be empowered and supported in self-development.
● ICT and other infrastructure costs can be justified by identifying a range of partners and applications.

MCTs are found from Amazonian Ecuador, Mexico and Paraguay to Ireland, the UK and Central Europe, and from South Africa, Ghana and Uganda to Sri Lanka, Bhutan and Australia. Many are pilot projects, supported by international and national aid agencies, some are government-aided and some are purely private enterprises, but the majority are community owned and managed and seek political, logistical and economic advantage through public–private partnerships. As they evolve, their range of programmes and services extend in response to provider and user demand. The Western Australian Telecentre Network, for example, was originally set up to increase participation in post-compulsory education in the remote and rural areas of this vast state but progressively found opportunity and need to encompass a full range of government, business and community services. The success of this network has helped to encourage the Federal Government to provide 'Networking the Nation' funding for the establishment of similar systems in Tasmania and New South Wales (Short and Latchem, 2000).

Some MCTs are stand-alone, some are networked, and some feed into satellite centres or telecentre access points (TAPs) in smaller communities. All aim to support development by providing:

- access to ICT and information services;
- training and support in using ICT;
- teleeducation, teletraining and job creation;
- telework, telebanking, telecommerce and business support;
- telehealth, telemedicine, telegovernance and other community services;
- new community networks.

Access to ICT and information services

Technology tends to bypass the underprivileged, particularly in the developing world where 90 per cent of the people have never used a telephone, 40 per cent are without electricity, and there are fewer than 5 per cent of the world's Internet-connected computers. Given the parlous economies of these countries, it is unlikely that ICT will roll out rapidly or beyond the main settlements or politically and economically favoured regions. The July 2000 G8 leaders at the Okinawa Summit pledged to help bridge this 'digital divide' and agreed to set up a 'Digital Opportunity Task Force'. United Nations agencies, the World Bank, the International Telecommunications Union and other international development organizations, national development agencies such as DANIDA and Canada's International Development Research Centre and corporate donors such as Siemens and DaimlerChrysler also make a substantial commitment to building inclusive information communities through the establishment of MCTs.

Much is made of the importance of access to ICT and global information for the advancement of nations, communities and individuals. However, this may also lead to yet more cultural colonialism and dependency, and there is a great need to develop indigenous knowledge, collate national and local information and expertise and channel these into local communities via ICT. The coordinator of the African Information Society Initiative (AISA) (Havkin, 1998) argues that the real test of achievement in promoting electronic networking in developing regions is in the content development at the national, institutional and local levels.

It has been shown that telecentres can play an important role in enabling people to access up-to-date knowledge and information in languages and forms appropriate to their needs. In the Indian state of Tamil Nadu, the M S Swaminathan Research Foundation ICT-based 'village knowledge centres' provide agriculture-related education and training and crucial information on weather, conditions for planting and harvesting, market prices, women's health and rural welfare issues (Venkataraman, 1999). In rural Uganda, the Nakaseke Telecentre not only repackages information from multiple sources, including the Internet, and disseminates this in forms appropriate to the local communities but, as part of its indigenous knowledge programme, collects and disseminates local knowledge on such issues as organic farming, traditional birth attendants and the medicinal values of plants (Mayanja, 2001).

Training and support in the use of ICT

ICT training and train-the-trainers schemes are core activities in the telecentres, enabling community members to become telecentre volunteers, gain employment or use the technology for educational, informational, recreational or family purposes. In some MCTs, as in Ghana, the trainers have become so overworked that they have developed self-tutoring materials (Akakpo and Fontaine, 2000). Many centres also open their doors to local schoolchildren, providing them with their first experience of computers and the Internet and enabling them to design their own Web pages, access the Web for their homework and interact with other students overseas.

Tele-education, teletraining

Telecentres enable all types of learning, from basic literacy and numeracy programmes to formal study and from upgrading skills in farmers, fire fighters and factory workers to professional development for teachers, nurses, and doctors, to be available in even the remotest community via the Internet and/or satellite or terrestrial broadcast.

Telework, telebanking, telecommerce and business support

Many rural and remote communities are dependent upon subsistence farming or declining traditional industries, struggling to survive and experiencing out-migration. Telework enables centres' 'graduates' to become voluntary or paid trainers in the centres, or establish new enterprises – community newspapers or online businesses offering such services as wordprocessing, desktop publishing, abstracting, editing, indexing, book-keeping, information broking or multimedia or Web design (Bertin and Denbigh, 2000).

The European Commission has supported a considerable number of telework projects and telework training schemes, including the UK Teleworking National Vocational Qualifications (NVQ) Scheme (http://www.itnto.org.uk), LocalNet (European) Telework Training Project (http://www.bealtaine.ie) and ADAPT-BIS (Building the Information Society) (http://www.europs.be/publica/wdat-en.doc).

Some telecentres, like those in Western Australia, maintain telebanking and telecommerce services when banks and other agencies put profit and performance before people and withdraw their services from the smaller communities. The Western Australian and Hungarian telecentres also provide training and work opportunities for the unemployed under government job creation schemes.

Telehealth, telemedicine, telelaw, telegovernance and other community services

Telecentres can provide vital telehealth and telemedicine services. The Remote Community Service Telecentres of Newfoundland and Labrador (www.rcst.net) facilitate asynchronous 'store and forward consultation' for medical emergencies, wherein remote medical staff capture patient data as text, audio, image, video, and transmit this to a physician at a major centre who reviews the data and then provides a diagnosis and treatment plan. The RCST network also provides teletraining for nurses who perform some physicians' duties when these are unavailable (Sheppard, 2001). The Nakaseke Telecentre in Uganda provides teleconsultation and telehealth services for two seriously under-resourced local hospitals that previously lacked the ICT to communicate with the districts they serve or the outside world (Mayanja, 2001).

The Western Australian and Queensland telecentres have trialled ICT-delivered rural legal services. In the incipient democracy of Paraguay, the AMIC@s tele-centres which serve the poor neighbourhoods of Asunción were conceived of, not only as community learning centres, but as a means of strengthening democratic processes, improving communication between citizens and government and increasing community participation in civic activities by automating and simplify-ing procedures such as registering to vote and applying for licences (Aranda and Fontaine, 2001). The Gaseleka Telecentre in South Africa's Northern Province acts as a service agency for the Departments of Health and Welfare and Home Affairs, saving the local community from an arduous 160 km return journey to the nearest town and increasing the number and range of people using the centre (Benjamin, 2001).

New community networks

Telecentres can also help forge new face-to-face and virtual community networks. The Western Australian telecentres have launched such online initiatives as KidsClub, TeleYouth and TeleSenior (Short and Latchem, 2000). The AMIC@ at the central bus station in Asunción has formed an alliance with a nearby NGO that shelters the homeless boys and girls who shine shoes and sell sundries at the station and these disadvantaged children now visit the AMIC@ regularly, surfing the Web, learning to design Web sites, and on one memorable occasion, participating in a videoconference with the mayor (Aranda and Fontaine, 2001).

Accommodation

The MCTs' accommodation varies according to needs and circumstances. The premises are usually provided by the local communities and may be found in educational or healthcare institutions, local government offices, village houses, shops, demountables and even disused shipping containers. It is found that they need to be centrally located, high profile, user-friendly and accessible to the community at all reasonable times; some are accessible 24 hours a day, 7 days a week by means of swipe cards. They are usually also well secured, although such is the sense of community ownership that there is a low incidence of theft or damage.

Management

Larger networks such as those in Western Australia, Queensland, Tasmania, and Newfoundland and Labrador are managed through central support units which broker government funding, grants and fee-for-service arrangements, manage the contracts and performance agreements, monitor quality, and train the local centres' management committees and staff. Telecentre pilot projects in developing countries are usually overseen by international organizations such as the International Telecommunications Union (http://www.itu.int) or International Development Research Centre (http://www.idrc.ca/) or national agencies such as Telisa (the Technology Enhanced Learning Initiative of Southern Africa) operating under the auspices of the Technikon Southern Africa's Centre for Lifelong Learning. In Hungary, the Hungarian Telecottage Association (http:www.telehaz.hu) fostered the national telecentre movement, successfully lobbied government for support and now represents the interests of and seeks resources for the telecentres through a nonprofit Telecottage Public Purpose Corporation. The UK telecentres, while independent, receive advice and support through the Telework, Telecottage and Telecentre Association (www.tca.org.uk).

At the local level, telecentres are usually run by community management committees with full- or part-time managers responsible for the day-to-day operations. Experience shows that dedicated managers with sound business, financial management, and marketing skills are essential to self-sustainability and establishing services within and beyond the community. Many centres rely heavily upon community volunteers, but it is preferable to have a core of appropriately trained and recompensed staff.

Evaluation

While telecentres appear to be hold great promise, Reddi and Dighe (2000) observe that it is premature to comment on their impact on adult learning as evaluation reports are still awaited. Many telecentres are relatively new and/or pilot projects and Gomez *et al* (1999) suggest that the messages are somewhat mixed in regard to their long-term financial sustainability, socioeconomic impact and benefits to governmental, educational or other providers. Hudson (2001) argues that it is critically important for all aspects of telecentres to be evaluated. Unfortunately, as Scharffenberger (1999) observes, the need for evaluation is raised in multiple conferences and meetings but rarely translated into action or accorded the necessary resources.

Financial viability is obviously essential for telecentres to survive and be replicated on a larger scale. All too often telecentres have been forced to close upon withdrawal of government or international aid (Ernberg, 1998). But some have prospered. In the USA, the Community Technology Centers Network (www. ctcnet.org/impact98.htm) has helped establish hundreds of telecentres in low-income urban and rural areas, enabling users to gain competence in using computers and improve their work performance or find jobs (Murray, 2001). Goussal (2000) reports on the success of the Brazilian MCTs, observing that the educational component proved to be the key factor in this. And the South African Mamelod and Kgautswane Telecentres and Western Australian Telecentre Network have all received major national awards in recognition of their achievements.

The Western Australian, Queensland, Tasmanian, Newfoundland and Labrador and some other telecentres receive ongoing government support, but most centres are community owned and required to achieve self-sustainability through fee-for-service activities. Operational costs and pricing structures, policies and records are not always carefully managed (Khumalo, 1998) and it is yet to be shown how centres in developing countries will cope with technology replacement, maintenance and repairs and whether the technology is sufficiently robust for such environments.

Planning and managing telelearning centres and telecentres

The lessons learnt from telelearning centres and telecentres to date are that they take time to establish and gain community acceptance and that they will only succeed where:

- there is societal/organizational readiness for reform, to enter the information age, and to change traditional communication and learning patterns;
- there is strong and ongoing commitment by the government departments, institutions, community management committees, NGOs etc that are ultimately responsible for the centres;
- there are local champions;
- data on user and provider needs are gathered directly from the beneficiaries and carefully tested for reality;
- there is a clear understanding of what the centres can and cannot achieve;
- there is a core application such as telelearning, teletraining, telemedicine or telehealth and the community awareness of and demand for further services is then progressively developed;
- there are clear, measurable goals and targets;

- there is a sound business plan and timeline for self-sustainabilty;
- there are clearly articulated and transparent management, communications and accountability systems;
- there are sound strategic partnerships for development and delivery;
- the centres are well located, accessible, open at times desired by the users, secure and user-friendly;
- there is ongoing training and commensurate reward for the managers and staff;
- the staff have some involvement with any educational or technological research and development undertaken by the sponsors and providers;
- there are specific interventions to ensure participation by women and other traditionally marginalized persons;
- programmes and materials are customized to suit particular age, language and cultural groups and traditional methods of communication are incorporated into technology-based applications;
- ICT are fully exploited but not deterministic;
- there is a sound telecommunication infrastructure and power supply;
- there is proactive management and recognition that donor, provider and community support has to be worked for;
- there is ongoing evaluation of the educational, training and information topics, delivery styles, costs, technology, marketing and outreach strategies and user patterns.

Conclusion

The OECD/CERI (2000: 34) report *Learning to Bridge the Digital Divide* notes that 'By itself education cannot solve the secular problems of social inequalities, but without equal access and quality learning for all, existing gaps will surely deepen'. Telelearning centres and telecentres represent one means of bringing ICT to the cause of learning, equality and social development. They can provide community-based learning environments for formal and non-formal learning through a mix of public, private and local community inputs. In those regions around the globe where it will be many years before computers are common in the home or the classroom, such centres can help to build bridges between the suppliers of learning and information and communities that are currently deprived of opportunities for educational and social advancement. Important lessons are being learnt by those who manage these systems. What is called for now is political vision and commitment to a socially just society, a clear strategy for development, mobilization of and collaboration between the various sectors and between central and local organizations, innovation in educational and ICT applications and sustainable organizational and management structures.

Note

The author acknowledges the wealth of information and ideas shared by the contributors in compiling The Commonwealth of Learning *Telecentres* book.

References

Akakpo, J and Fontaine, M (2001) 'Ghana's community learning centres', in *Telecentres*, eds C Latchem and D Walker, The Commonwealth of Learning, Vancouver

Aranda, S and Fontaine, M (2001) 'The Amic@s in the municipality of Asunción, Paraguay', in *Telecentres*, eds C Latchem and D Walker, The Commonwealth of Learning, Vancouver

Benjamin, P (2001) 'Gaseleka telecentre, Northern Province, South Africa', in *Telecentres*, eds C Latchem and D Walker, The Commonwealth of Learning, Vancouver

Bertin, I and Denbigh, A (2000) *The Teleworking Handbook* (3rd edn), Telework, Telecottage and Telecentre Association [purchasable online on a chapter-by-chapter basis from the TCA Web site www.tca.org.uk or in print from the Wren Telecottage (E-mail: s.lewis@ruralnet.org.uk)]

Ernberg, J (1998) Universal access for rural development: From action to strategies, www.itu.int/ITU-D-UniversalAccess/johan/papers/NTCA_johan.htm; www.itu.int/ITU-D-UniversalAccess/seminar/buda/final_papers.htm

Gomez, R, Hunt, P and Lamoreux, E (1999) 'Enchanted by telecentres: A critical look at universal access to information technologies for international development', paper presented at the conference *New IT and Inequality*, University of Maryland, 16–17 February 1999, http://www.idrc.ca/pan/enchanted.html

Gooley, A (2001) 'The Queensland Open Learning Network', in *Telecentres*, eds C Latchem and D Walker, The Commonwealth of Learning, Vancouver

Goussal, D M (2000) 'Access to information and community telecentres in South America', in *Telecentre Models Around the World*, ed W Murray, ITU, Geneva, www.itu.int

Hartig, N (2001) 'The Kitimat Community Skills Centre in British Columbia', in *Telecentres*, eds C Latchem and D Walker, The Commonwealth of Learning, Vancouver

Havkin, N (1998) E-mail message in Development Forum: Rural communications in Africa, http://www2.worldbank.org/hm/afrocomm/0010.html

Howard, L (2001) 'The DaimlerChrysler distance learning support centre, Maseru, Lesotho', in *Telecentres*, eds C Latchem and D Walker, The Commonwealth of Learning, Vancouver

Hudson, H E (2001) 'Telecentre evaluation: issues and strategies', in *Telecentres*, eds C Latchem and D Walker, The Commonwealth of Learning, Vancouver

Jung, I (1999) The development of virtual institutions in Korea, Appendix 9.1 to Robertshaw, M 'Virtual institutions in East and Southeast Asia', in *The Development of Virtual Education: A global perspective*, ed G Farrell, The Commonwealth of Learning, http://www.col.org/virtualed/index.htm

Khumalo, F (1998) E-mail message in Development Forum: Rural communications in Africa, http://www2.worldbank.org/hm/afrocomm/0010.html

Mayanja, M (2001) 'The Nakaseke multipurpose community telecentre in Uganda', in *Telecentres*, eds C Latchem and D Walker, The Commonwealth of Learning, Vancouver

Murray, W (2001) 'Training telecentre managers, staff and end-users', in *Telecentres*, eds C Latchem and D Walker, The Commonwealth of Learning, Vancouver

OECD/CERI (2000) *Schooling for Tomorrow: Learning to bridge the digital divide*, Organization for Economic Cooperation and Development, Paris

Panda, S and Chaudhary, S (2001) 'Telelearning and telelearning centres in India', in *Telecentres*, eds C Latchem and D Walker, The Commonwealth of Learning, Vancouver

Reddi, U and Dighe, A (2000) 'Literacy and adult education through distance and open learning', in *Basic Education at a Distance*, eds C Yates and J Bradley, pp 155–72, Routledge/COL, London

Scharffenberger, G (1999) 'Telecentre evaluation methods and instruments: What works and why?', in *Proceedings of IDRC Workshop on Telecentre Evaluation: A global perspective*, Far Hills, Quebec

Sheppard, K (2001) 'The remote community service telecentres of Newfoundland and Labrador', in *Telecentres*, eds C Latchem and D Walker, The Commonwealth of Learning, Vancouver

Short, G and Latchem, C (2000) 'The Australian telecentre experience', in *Telecentre Models Around the World*, ed W Murray, ITU, Geneva, www.itu.int

Venkataraman, B (1999) *Knowledge System for Sustainable Food Security*, M S Swaminathan Research Foundation, Chennai (mimeo)

Chapter 16

Planning and management of student assessment

Charlotte N Gunawardena and Deborah K LaPointe

Introduction

Planning and conducting student assessment at a distance has always been a challenging task. Numerous issues such as accountability in certifying students at a distance, test security, identity and proctoring have to be addressed. How should we plan and manage the process of student assessment at a distance? This chapter will attempt to address this question from the context of dual-mode higher education institutions that teach both on-campus and distance learners using interactive technologies such as the Internet or interactive television. While the networked learning model using the Internet and the World Wide Web (WWW) (see Chapter 14) is becoming increasingly popular, many institutions still deliver a majority of their programmes through the remote classroom model, extending the on-campus classroom through real-time interactive television (ITV) or videoconferencing. Both these models are based on assumptions of interaction and communication, feelings of belonging to and cooperation with a community of learners as well as exchange of questions, answers and opinions. Assessment methods in Web-based and ITV courses are converging. In both the models, instructors integrate the virtues of text, the visual appeal of video and the information-manipulating powers of the PC (McLellan, 1997).

A study of ITV engineering education in the State of New Mexico (Gunawardena and Lowe, 1997) indicated that instructors teaching through ITV were gradually changing the type of learner assessments, moving away from proctored or supervised exams to project-based assessments. Partly due to concerns related to accountability and certification at a distance, and partly due to constructivist philosophy influencing changes in pedagogical techniques, designers and instructors are moving away from traditional modes of assessment that measure knowledge gained through reproduction strategies to knowledge constructed through negotiation of meaning. Assessment strategies are changing from measuring the learning of facts to measuring critical thinking and problem-solving strategies, similar to assessment conducted by professionals in the workplace. As learners gain a sense of responsibility for producing pieces of learning that are useful for the group, cheating at a distance is eliminated (Palloff and Pratt, 1999).

Assessment serves multiple purposes. It generally provides the instructor with the means to assess individual student performance as students work towards achieving course objectives. Additionally, assessment illuminates essential revisions of the instructional materials and strategies (Smith and Ragan, 1999). Assessment determines the learners' level of competence, identifies gaps in learning, and accordingly determines remediation. In addition, in the distance learning environment, assessment provides the designer, instructor and distance learning system manager with essential information about how well the process of getting assignments to and from students is working (Moore, 1999). In this chapter, we will focus on assessment as a means of providing the instructor with evaluative information on student learning and progress towards meeting course objectives. Assessment considers both process and product, and includes both formal and informal assessment. And, in the process, assessment may involve award of scores or grades on student achievement.

Assessment in distance learning

In the distance learning context, assessment must be carefully planned and designed as several factors beyond the instructor's control influence the implementation process. It often helps to have a series of questions such as the following in mind when planning assessments:

- What learning theories underlie the assessment and instructional strategies?
- How will assessment match the learning objectives and instructional strategies?
- What process, product, or use of resources must the learners demonstrate?
- What will be considered evidence of learning in this course?
- What tools and resources are needed to support the learners as they complete the assignments?
- Will assessment be based upon independent or collaborative learning?
- Will the assessment be self-paced or timed?

- Will all learners complete the same assignments? Can learners choose from teacher-provided selection of assignments? Will learners have the opportunity to design their own assignments?
- What kind of scaffolding, coaching and managing will be required?
- Will remediation and supplementation be provided?
- Will learners require feedback before proceeding to the next assignment?

When answering these questions, it is important to look for any conflicts or inconsistencies among the answers. For example, designing a self-paced course may conflict with collaborative projects or weekly class discussions. Assigning independent projects may cause infrequent and irregular patterns of participation in class discussions. Assigning weekly projects creates the potential for delay and backlog for instructors, which may result in learners proceeding to subsequent assignments before receiving essential instructor feedback and grades.

Additional considerations for planning assessment in distance learning include the role communications technology will play in assessment. For example, multimedia technology provides multiple formats of representations that appeal to a variety of learning styles during instruction (McLellan, 1997). In the distance learning environment, those same multiple formats of representations and multimedia can be incorporated into assessment tools. The graphics, images, maps, audio and video used to convey course content or incorporated into learning activities can be easily posted in online tests.

Informal assessment

Assessment at a distance includes both informal and formal assessments. While formal assessment is similar to summative evaluation of student learning and includes exams and projects, informal assessment, which is similar to formative evaluation, provides quick ways for instructors to monitor learning throughout the semester, to discover the more difficult concepts for students to learn, and to guide teaching decisions (Angelo and Cross, 1993). Additionally, knowing how students are experiencing learning during the course helps instructors build connections between course goals and student concerns and expectations (Brookfield, 1986).

Informal assessment at a distance requires thought and planning. While some modes require more logistics and planning than others, all modes require the instructor to consider:

- the importance of retaining student anonymity;
- the speed of providing feedback;
- the sense of trust the students must first have in the instructor.

Asking students to submit feedback through e-mail messages means the loss of student anonymity. Mailing paper-based one-minute papers means that two to three weeks will pass before the instructor receives student feedback and can implement course revisions, corrections or remediation. Posting feedback to a course Web site requires the design and development of an evaluation form. Before expecting students to submit feedback in any mode, instructors will first have to establish a sense of trust and inform the students what he or she will do with the feedback.

One informal assessment technique that has worked well for us is the plus/delta sheet. This sheet contains two columns. In the left column, titled 'Plus +', students quickly note the points of the lesson, discussion or class management logistics that work well for them. In the right column, titled 'Delta', students note the confusing concepts or class management techniques that need improvements. The plus/delta sheet can be modified to ask students to list in the appropriate columns the tasks they are undertaking that are facilitating their success in the course as well as the steps or tasks they could undertake to improve their performance. These may be available to the instructor through fax or e-mail, or on a Web site for all the students.

Earning extra credit, getting the chance to enter a drawing to win a prize, or receiving a coupon to a favourite restaurant may induce students to complete the informal assessments. Essential considerations for informal assessment strategies include providing:

- a clear statement of purpose;
- clear guidance for completing the assignment;
- ways in which feedback will be provided;
- a sample assignment.

Formal assessment

Formal assessment in distance learning requires the designer and instructor to plan for at least three deliveries of assignments and assessments:

- delivery of assignments to the students;
- delivery of completed assignments to the instructor;
- return of graded assignments with feedback from the instructor to the student.

In interactive technology-based distance education systems, several ways to convey assignments and assessments exist. Assignments and assessments can be posted on course Web sites, or posted as Adobe Acrobat pdf files to be downloaded from course Web sites. Students can submit assignments in the body of e-mail messages or as file attachments to e-mail messages, or fax them. Another means is to incorporate assignments into a course handbook sold through the college book-store. Regardless of the delivery method, the assignments must contain the objectives of the assignment, clear instructions for completing the assignment, how to send the completed assignment to the instructor, and how and when feedback will be provided.

An advantage online environments offer is the ease of posting and sharing student work with others in gallery tours (Khan, 1997). With student permission, the instructor can post completed assignments along with instructor comments from which all students can benefit. Posting work provides the opportunity for sequential creations wherein a multimedia document is posted and other groups are challenged to comment, elaborate and revise (Hackbarth, 1997). Software such as WebCT provides a student presentation area, where students or small groups can upload files and create Web presentations to share their work and research with other class members. Designing assignments so that learners can contribute to creating content eases the instructor's burden and gives learners responsibility to contribute to the learning community (Beer, 2000).

We now discuss the planning and management of several formal assessment techniques.

Quizzes, tests and exams

Instructors often assign quizzes or tests to assess student understanding of facts, concepts or principles. Quizzes can be administered in many forms: timed or self-paced, proctored or open-book, graded or self-assessed. Testing can be conducted online, mailed to the students' homes or proctored by a site-coordinator at a distant site. Identity and security issues are major concerns in planning an exam at a distance. For high levels of identity security, some colleges are exploring options such as retinal scans, ear shape, facial identification through thermographs, voice, palm, or fingerprints, hand geometry, and ongoing handwriting analysis throughout the term. However, these technologies are expensive, and the cost may not be warranted (Tulloch and Thompson, 1999). Web-based testing may offer the security instructors want by allowing exams to be password protected and by generating a different test form for each student who logs in.

Online testing offers certain advantages. The software quiz graders give instructors options regarding how many times a student can take a quiz, the dates the quiz will be available, and the time limit for taking a quiz. The instructor receives the completed exam immediately, and the score is automatically posted into the online gradebook. These online testing tools provide statistics about overall test scores, each specific test question, and the frequency distribution of answers per question.

Unfortunately, the quiz generators and graders within Web authoring programmes such as WebCT and Blackboard cannot grade the short-answer or essay questions. The instructor must log into the Web course and grade these. Anticipating technology failures, instructors who use online testing should also develop a 'Plan B' contingency policy that is clearly communicated to the students.

Supervised or proctored testing at off-campus centres is another method of handling testing at a distance. Proctored testing offers secure testing and provides documentation of student identity.

Online testing and proctored testing do have their place in distance education. However, more and more instructors are using testing in conjunction with other techniques of student assessment, or are moving away from proctored testing to other methods of assessment. Assessment alternatives to consider include online discussions, role plays, debates, panel discussions, seminars, self-assessments, peer review and e-portfolios.

Assessing online discussions and networked learning

Online course design generally incorporates computer conferences which provide opportunities for discussion, negotiation of meaning and validation of knowledge. In fact, significant weight is often placed on the level and quality of participating in online courses for a variety of reasons (Palloff and Pratt, 1999). Online class discussions give the instructor the opportunity to 'see' what learners are thinking and to 'see' where the learning difficulties arise. With that information, the instructor can offer help, and build in remediation.

Despite the many benefits of online discussion, assessment of these discussions is a challenging task. Many online course development tools such as WebCT provide quantitative measures that report each student's first and last access as well as total number of conference comments read and posted. However, the number of comments posted reflects neither the quality of the students' participation in the online class discussion nor whether the students learnt or met the expected outcomes of the course.

How did the individual learner make sense of the computer conference? What did he or she learn? These questions are more difficult to assess if we subscribe to a constructivist view of learning where the individual learner is expected to take away a unique perspective from the learning experience. One method is to analyse the computer transcript as it affords an unobtrusive and fairly accurate means of gauging whether participants learnt during the conference. Another technique is to ask participants directly what they learnt, either through open-ended questions in questionnaires, or individual interviews, or asking them to discuss their learning in a separate conference space specially designed for this purpose.

In order to understand the myriad forms of learning that occurs in a computer conference, we have often asked students to keep e-journals documenting all aspects of learning. These journals have given us a unique perspective of each individual's learning process and their self-reflections. The e-journal can take the format of a double-entry journal. In the first column, they note ideas, assertions, and arguments from the discussions. In the second column, they explain the personal significance of the assigned readings or discussion. Whatever form the e-journals take, students submit journal entries frequently.

For assessment, we have found that qualitative approaches work better than quantitative methods in being able to understand the process of individual and group learning. The model developed by Henri (1992) is very suitable for analysing computer transcripts, though three aspects of the model – its basis in a teacher-centred instructional paradigm, its distinction between the cognitive and the metacognitive dimensions and its treatment of the concept of interaction – are not very suitable for assessing learning in constructivist settings. In order to determine if knowledge is constructed within the group by means of the exchanges among participants, Gunawardena, Lowe and Anderson (1997) developed an interaction analysis model based on social constructivist theory which they applied to the analysis of a global online debate. Interaction analysis methods help instructors to determine the quality of message content in a computer conference.

One of the most challenging tasks in assessing online discussions is determining participation criteria. If points are assigned for participation, students might participate for the sake of participation even though they may not have much to contribute. On the other hand, if online education is designed placing a premium on active participation, students should be recognized for their contributions.

Listed below are suggestions for planning the assessment of online participation:

- Tell students how participation calculates into the final course grade.
- Set a minimum number of substantive comments required per week (as determined by course outcomes, content, and level of course).
- Post the grading or evaluation rubric that will be applied. The rubric will include the number of comments required per week; evidence of thought the instructor is looking for based on Bloom's taxonomy or other cognitive and metacognitive taxonomies.
- Post samples of substantive comments that meet the grading rubric, with instructor comments highlighting the portions of the message that meet the participation guidelines.
- Tell students directly what will not be counted as meeting online participation. For example, comments like 'I agree, Amy' or 'Good job, Ted' are important for community building but do not satisfy the criteria of 'substantive' comments.
- Determine and inform students about any deadlines for posting comments to a class discussion.
- Tell students they do not need to respond to every message.
- Ask students to read and lurk before they contribute to the discussion.

Some online courses are designed as seminars with individual students or small groups of students serving as conference moderators or facilitators. The instructor should inform students about expectations for their performance as moderators and facilitators and provide students with moderating guidelines. Planning and moderating computer conferences are discussed in detail in Gunawardena (1998) and Palloff and Pratt (1999).

One technique we have used to assess networked learning of which computer conferencing is one component is the e-portfolio or a digital portfolio that highlights and demonstrates students' knowledge and skills. E-portfolios can contain still pictures, audio, video, or written documents that follow a student's progress through the course and can be posted on the Web site or created on a disk or CD. Students can be asked to self-assess and reflect on the items they placed in the e-portfolio. For the evaluation of student assignments, students should also be asked to engage in peer review and evaluate and receive feedback from each other throughout the course.

Problem-based learning and case-based reasoning

A significant change that often accompanies an instructor's transition from the on-campus classroom to the Web-based environment is reflected in the types of assignments given. Often the emphasis moves from assessing knowledge of content to assessing the application of content to solve an authentic problem. Problem-based learning and case-based reasoning require learners to seek out information and differing interpretations to solve problems likely to be encountered by a practitioner in the field. Information seeking can take the form of reading and listening; conducting interviews and experiments; searching for information in libraries, databases and Web sites; and experience through service learning.

The Web provides a versatile environment for fostering problem-based learning; however, careful planning must occur for the learning process to be effective. In case of problem-based learning in, for example, medicine, the patient problems or cases are posted on the Web, or simulated patients are interviewed via conferencing technologies. Each group uses the conferencing features of the Web to discuss learning issues. The Web is also an excellent medium to point to additional resources such as databases and experts. Hyperlinks point students to relevant diagnostic and laboratory tests such as x-rays that are needed to solve the problem. The application of information gained from the study of learning issues to diagnose the patient's disease is discussed in a group conferencing format that will facilitate collaborative learning among students and instructors. Although it takes a tremendous amount of prior planning to work with a Web developer to design the Web site, it facilitates the learning process.

Role plays as assessment

Role plays, using either Web technology or ITV, are another method of assessing the application of knowledge in the real world. Instructors state the goal of the role play, define the role play's problem, set the scene, create the roles and assign them. Students research the problem and their roles, and set goals for their role. Instructors, with input from students, determine the grading rubric. Grading criteria may include the following:

- Students provide references or resources consulted to research the problem.
- Students state the goal they set for their role and how they met that goal.
- Students review transcripts of the role play and reflect on what they learnt from the role play.

For example, in an introductory business course, students could assume roles and handle an annual employee evaluation, mediate an employee grievance, handle a customer complaint or develop a marketing plan. Some students can play the roles; others can serve as advisers or as evaluators of how the situations were handled. Outside experts could observe the role play and offer opinions from the 'real world'. The instructor, or a student, or a group of students debriefs and concludes the role plays.

Assessing practical skills or laboratory experiences

Perhaps the most challenging task related to assessment is to determine how to assess practical skills or laboratory experiences at a distance. Considering accountability issues related to certifying at a distance, it is important to determine if a practical skill can be assessed at a distance, or not. If the skill cannot be assessed at a distance, then it is important to acknowledge it and arrange for the assessment to be conducted in a face-to-face setting. In some cases, such as advanced engineering labs, which involve very expensive equipment, practice and assessment of practical skills must be conducted face-to-face. In the case of training airline pilots, for example, while virtual reality environments or simulators can provide safe practice sessions, the demonstration of the skill must occur in flying an actual aeroplane.

The College of Nursing at the University of New Mexico, USA, which offers a bachelor's degree in nursing via interactive satellite television to students in rural New Mexico, Colorado and Arizona, have adopted the preceptor model to assess practical hands-on skills. They have made arrangements with certified nursing practitioners who work in supervisory positions in rural hospitals to assess the practical skills of nursing students who work in those hospitals.

The medium of television, with its capacity to show a process and convey visual information, has been used effectively to assess hands-on practical skills. Rao (2000), in a dissertation study analysing a semiconductor course taught at a distance via ITV, determined that technical laboratory skills can be taught at a distance. Naber and LeBlanc (1994) developed an innovative biology laboratory that was taught via the ITV Education Network of Maine. The lecture component discussed the major anatomical systems and functions in an introductory biology framework, while the laboratory centred on the dissection of the systems as seen in a foetal pig. The majority of course objectives required students to identify and describe the functions of tissues and organs of the foetal pig. First, in a face-to-face setting in two different locations in the State of Maine, they oriented students to experiments in measurement, microscopy and biochemistry that were problematic for students to conduct at home. Then, the remainder of the course was completed primarily at students' homes or at off-campus centres where students were encouraged to work in groups to do the dissection of the foetal pig. A videotape containing extensive instructions for preparing and dissecting the foetal pig was developed along with a student laboratory guide. These were distributed to students along with a laboratory kit including all materials they would need to complete the dissection at home, or at a site or centre. The final laboratory exam – a proctored, individual exam – took place over interactive television. Students took the exam at sites and centres around the state. In the origination classroom, the instructor had a fully dissected foetal pig and students were asked to identify and describe the functions of the selected structures that they had observed in their dissections. Naber and LeBlanc (1994) note that it is possible for students to achieve challenging learning objectives at a distance. The key is the degree to which the materials support student engagement in the processes necessary for meaningful learning to occur. With the development of multimedia technologies, simulated lab experiences such as dissections are increasingly being developed on the Web. However, decisions about which types of laboratory experiences are suitable for home study and which are not, and about which experiences have to be completed 'hands-on' and which can be completed using Web simulations, should be carefully made by instructional designers and subject-matter experts.

Conclusion

This chapter has discussed the planning and management of assessment at a distance, providing examples from both informal and formal assessments. It was noted that instructors who begin to teach at a distance are changing the types of assessments, from measuring knowledge of content to measuring the application of knowledge in real-world settings. While it is possible to conduct numerous types of assessments at a distance, including laboratory experiences, it is important to acknowledge the limitations of distance assessments for certain types of course objectives. Above all, ethical considerations related to certifying students at a distance must take precedence when designing assessments at a distance, as the process of assessment may sometimes harm the students or people to whom they are accountable, such as employers, clients or patients. It is also important not to underestimate the time commitment that instructional designers and distance instructors need to develop effective assessments at a distance.

References

Angelo, T A and Cross, K P (1993) *Classroom Assessment Techniques*, Jossey-Bass Publishers, San Francisco

Beer, V (2000) *The Web Learning Fieldbook: Using the World Wide Web to build workplace learning environments*, Jossey-Bass Publishers, San Francisco

Brookfield, S (1986) *Understanding and Facilitating Adult Learning*, Jossey-Bass Publishers, San Francisco

Gunawardena, C N (1998) Designing collaborative learning environments mediated by computer conferencing: Issues and challenges in the Asian socio-cultural context, *Indian Journal of Open Learning*, **7** (1), pp 105–24

Gunawardena, C N and Lowe, C (1997) *Evaluation of The Waste-Management Education & Research Consortium's (WERC) Instructional Television Program* (Grant funded by WERC and Department of Energy), Organizational Learning and Instructional Technology Program, COE, University of New Mexico, Albuquerque, NM

Gunawardena, C N, Lowe, C A and Anderson, T (1997) Analysis of a global online debate and the development of an interaction analysis model for examining social construction of knowledge in computer conferencing, *Journal of Educational Computing Research*, **17** (4), pp 395–429

Hackbarth, S (1997) 'Web-based learning activities for children', in *Web-Based Instruction*, ed B Khan, Educational Technology Publications, Englewood Cliffs, NJ

Henri, F (1992) 'Computer conferencing and content analysis', in *Collaborative Learning Through Computer Conferencing: The Najaden papers*, ed A Kaye, pp 117–36, Springer-Verlag, Berlin

Khan, B (ed) (1997) *Web-Based Instruction*, Educational Technology Publications, Englewood Cliffs, NJ

McLellan, H (1997) 'Creating virtual learning communities via the web', in *Web-Based Instruction*, ed B Khan, Educational Technology Publications, Englewood Cliffs, NJ

Moore, M J (1999) Editorial: monitoring and evaluation, *The American Journal of Distance Education*, **13** (2), pp 1–5

Naber, D and LeBlanc, G (1994) Providing a human biology laboratory for distant learners, *The American Journal of Distance Education*, **8** (2), pp 58–71

Palloff, R M and Pratt, K (1999) *Building Learning Communities in Cyberspace*, Jossey-Bass Publishers, San Francisco

Rao, L (2000) *Can technical laboratory skills be taught at a distance? An analysis of a semiconductor course taught at a distance via interactive technologies*, Unpublished doctoral dissertation, The University of New Mexico

Smith, P L and Ragan, T J (1999) *Instructional Design*, Prentice Hall, Inc, Upper Saddle River, NJ

Tulloch, J B and Thompson, S (1999) 'Identity security and testing issues in distance learning', in *Online Testing: Assessment and Evaluation of Distance Learners*, Dallas TeleLearning (Producer), TX: LeCroy Center for Educational Telecommunications, Dallas

Part 5

Quality assurance and accreditation

Chapter 17

Institutional and programme evaluation

Dele Braimoh

What is evaluation?

The hallmark of any tertiary institution's activities, among other things, is to strive to maintain quality and excellence. This process will be at the levels of institutional performance review and the maintenance of programme quality assurance. Therefore, in order to achieve tangible success at both the levels, it becomes pertinent for tertiary institutions to embrace the philosophy of the 5Ps: *prior preparation prevents poor performance.*

Castro (1989) opines that most evaluation experts seem to agree that the purpose of evaluation is to gather information in order to assist in decision making and to obtain adequate and relevant information regarding the possible effects of education/training programmes as well as assess the value of the education/training to the final consumers of such an activity, and the degree to which the intended objectives have been achieved (Gajanayake and Gajanayake, 1993). This view has been reinforced by Thorpe (1988) who sees evaluation as the collection, analysis and interpretation of information about any aspects of a programme of education and training as part of a recognized process of judging its effectiveness. Any value judgement by anybody at all, and on a comparative basis, must have the element of prior experience. Hence, Calder and Panda (2000) succinctly describe evaluation as the process of drawing upon the lessons of one's own experience and the experiences of others.

The synthesis of relevant literature shows that evaluation is a process whereby information is carefully and systematically collected about an institution, a person, an activity, a programme or some of its aspects, with a view to making an informed decision. Such a decision will be about the appropriateness of a programme operation, to improve the *modus operandi* of a programme or its quality or to make the programme more efficient, cost-effective and amenable to the overall needs of the people served by such a programme as well as the organization.

Types of evaluation

We are now in a technological age, characterized by information explosion, thus invalidating the experience of yesteryear as inappropriate to resolving the organizational, social and developmental problems of today (Braimoh, 1999). In essence, apart from the known forms of evaluation as found in the literature, and considering more importantly that life itself is a dynamic process, not only programmes or institutions require a form of assessment using all the different types of evaluation, but also individuals within the institution require introspection. The following types of evaluation process should have the elements of continuity, participation and constructivism:

- 'Formative evaluation', otherwise known as pre-programme evaluation, is a form of needs assessment activity at the inception of a conceived programme, meant to gather data regarding the relevance, feasibility, scope and dimension of the problems to be addressed by the envisaged programme and its objectives which are targeted at a particular group of clientele.
- 'Ongoing or concurrent evaluation' is a continuous monitoring or assessment analysis of the activities, effects and outputs with regard to how it operationally conforms with the set objectives in order to identify any gaps or inhibitions along the line that may be capable of thwarting the achievement of the desired goal. This process will enable the organization to introduce needed corrective measures to its programmes before it is too late.
- 'Summative or terminal evaluation' is designed to have an overall assessment of the programme at the conclusion of the activity. This examines the degree to which the set objectives have been accomplished.
- 'Ex-post evaluation' assesses and monitors the degree of appropriateness of the end products of a programme in terms of relevance and suitability of utilization, particularly after the successful (or otherwise) completion of a project or a programme.

The above evaluation stages must be undertaken by any organization keen to maintain quality.

Institutional and programme evaluation in distance education

McNamara (1998) states that too often service providers, either for-profit or non-profit organizations, rely on their own instincts and passions to conclude what their customers or clients really need and whether the products or services are providing what is needed. Over time, these organizations find themselves doing a lot of guessing about what would be a good product or service, and conducting trial and error about how new products or services could be delivered. Distance education (DE) organizations generally are no different. However, detailed programme and institutional evaluation mechanisms deter deterioration and facilitate progress.

Programme evaluation

Distance education may be offered at single-mode open/distance teaching universities, dual-mode universities and independent virtual universities or as virtual learning programmes. The use of new educational technologies (NETs) facilitates an enhanced geographical coverage while at the same time reaching out to a heterogeneous clientele. The ever-increasing enrolment raises doubts in the public mind about whether quality education is possible while meeting the educational needs of a growing clientele. Therefore, it is pertinent to evaluate the programmes that distance education institutions offer in terms of curriculum design, content organization, delivery mode, design, development and standardization of the study materials, student assessment patterns and assignment turnaround time, including mentoring and counselling of students. Panda (2000: 17) states that, in addition to a deliberate effort to know how well the programme is performing, it is equally pertinent to find out, among other things, the following essential details with regard to the effectiveness or otherwise of a distance education programme:

- how students are learning from the programme;
- the difficulties they encounter at different levels of operations;
- the adequacy and appropriateness of the support services provided to them;
- the necessity of changing or modifying the patterns of continuous and end-of-programme assessment;
- the cost of running the programme and how best to achieve economy of scale;
- whether the programme objectives have been met and the goals achieved.

Calder (1994) has further identified the following objectives for conducting programme evaluation in distance education:

- Monitor progress towards stated organizational goals.
- Support the promotion of the quality of teaching.
- Help monitor and control academic standards.
- Help monitor, control and improve the standards of teaching, student services and student support.

- Support the expansion of the provision without loss of quality.
- Help improve the appropriateness of the provision for students.

As a result of useful, relevant and adequate feedback on the issues identified by Calder (1984) and Panda (2000), and considering the complexity and the enormity of responsibilities associated with the running of any viable and standard distance education programme, it is extremely difficult to completely revise or even provide an alternative programme or put in place new processes of operation. These may include changes in presenting materials, media of delivery, management techniques and assessment procedures, to mention but a few.

Granted that the overall goal of evaluation is to assess the performance of distance education systems in all its ramifications through the collection of useful data that will assist in improving the programme structure and offering, it must be noted that it is difficult to evaluate teaching at a distance (Jegede, 1993). This is because, in distance education, the teacher has little or no direct contact with the students and, therefore, does not present subject content in the way it is done in a physical classroom situation. If the quality of an academic programme is to be ensured, we must evaluate the total delivery system in order to provide or maintain a quality service to students.

We may summarize the benefits that are derivable from programme evaluation as follows:

- Improve delivery mechanisms so as to be more efficient and less costly.
- Verify that we are doing what we had planned. This is because, more often than not, plans about how to deliver services end up changing substantially when those plans are put into action. Therefore, evaluation can verify if the programme is really running as originally planned.
- Facilitate management's deep thought about what their programme is all about, including its goals, how it meets its goals and how it will discern if it has achieved its objectives or not.
- Determine if the programme had the anticipated impact on people or organizations.
- Determine if learners were able to use what they learnt after completing the programme.
- Produce valid comparisons between programmes so as to decide which should be retained or discontinued, particularly in the face of dwindling financial resources or imminent budget cuts.
- Examine effective programmes for possible replication elsewhere.
- Learn to avoid similar mistakes in future projects or programmes.

Institutional evaluation

Institutional evaluation should be a well-designed, articulated and conducted exercise which aims at providing useful information to the funding agency and the public, as well as facilitating informed institutional decision making. As discussed in Chapter 5, a distance teaching institution is a basic living organization with interdependent components. The groups of people involved in this quasi-bureaucratic structure include:

- institutional managers;
- programme planners;
- curriculum developers;
- course designers;
- course writers;
- course editors;
- graphic artists;
- media specialists and educational technologists;
- production crew for print, audio, video and multimedia materials;
- assessors and evaluators;
- support service personnel and counsellors;
- marketers.

At each level of operation, institutional evaluation will include assessment of the staff quality, learning resources available, communication technologies in use, relevance and appropriateness of programmes, and the adequacy of the management information system to assist informed decision making. These are some of the issues to take on board in order to assess or reinvigorate a distance education institution so as to maintain quality control of its operations. The outcome of such institutional evaluation should focus on:

- the worth of the institutional programmes as compared to other similar institutions;
- the quality and efficiency of its personnel;
- the assessment of rational decisions to increase or reduce future funding to the institution;
- the level of appropriateness of the funds already disbursed on some mundane activities having little or no bearing on achieving the goals of the institution;
- the impact of the continued existence of the institution on the larger society, including the adequacy of the utilization of its end products;
- assessment of how well the institution is meeting its mission statements and goals: for example, ability to marry town with gown, to turn out qualified and skilled people, to reduce levels of illiteracy, to work towards the production of job creators in contrast to job seekers and thus reducing unemployment, and to increase workforce productivity and efficiency.

Variables for institutional evaluation

It must be noted that evaluation does not happen as a matter of exigency, chance or coincidence. Rather, it must be a carefully planned activity where necessary provisions should, as a matter of procedure, be made in advance to integrate the evaluation of an institution or programme into the overall activity of an organization's regular strategic plan. To avoid a fire-brigade approach or a management by crisis posture in solving organizational problems, either for improving performance or for maintaining quality or both, adequate provision should be made with regard to human resources, time, money and infrastructural facilities in order to achieve the organizational goals. Vella, Berardinelli and Burrow (1998) stress that evaluation poses some of the greatest challenges to people responsible for planning and implementing effective education and training programmes. To be able to assess correctly the appropriate variables of evaluation, we need to consider many questions. These include:

- What should be the focus of an evaluation exercise?
- Who should carry out an evaluation?
- How should an institution or programme be evaluated?
- When should an evaluation be undertaken?
- What will be the implications of evaluation for maintaining quality assurance?

In the previous section we pointed out some of the important focus areas for an evaluation exercise. There are divergent views among evaluation specialists and educationists regarding the question of 'who' should conduct either an institutional or programme evaluation. For example, Gajanayake and Gajanayake (1993) argue that, frequently, evaluation is perceived as an activity carried out by an expert (quite often an outsider) or a group of experts designated to assess the results generated by a particular project at its completion. To them, this is a common misconception prevailing in most countries. They further stress that it is important that evaluation is carried out as a continuous activity with the participation of all the stakeholders of the project – most importantly, those involved in developing and running the programme as well as the beneficiaries, ie distant learners.

As much as one may tend to agree with this view, bringing in an external evaluator may possibly be the most effective practice in order to avoid bias and subjectivity, and by so doing achieve fairness and reliability of results. Externally designed third-party evaluation can certainly be very effective and useful; however, they are sometimes intimidating to those responsible for implementing the educational programme, especially if the evaluators do not involve, in planning the evaluation, those responsible for implementing the programme. The results may indeed be relevant and rewarding for the funding organization but may not be particularly meaningful and useful to the implementers of the programme or to the learners. Therefore, such evaluation needs to be ingrained in the context in which the programme operates.

Any of the following groups may be considered for evaluation, depending on the orientation, expectation and operation of the organization:

- community/stakeholders' chosen specialist from within;
- target clientele as the end users or consumers of the products;

- sponsoring agency, be it government, an international organization or an individual philanthropist;
- external evaluation specialist, having no affinity with the organization;
- a combination of any of the above categories.

The 'how' part of the evaluation will again depend on the nature and purpose of the information needed. This will include the techniques and tools to be adopted in collecting such data, and what and who will constitute the sources of information and how the data collected should be analysed and utilized.

In a study of the University of Southern Queensland, Jegede (1993) noted that evaluation was carried out on courses in degree programmes offered through on-campus and distance education primarily through the involvement of students. The apparent reason for the choice of students to judge the quality of teaching arose from the belief that those clients with first-hand knowledge of, and contact with, the teacher or study materials were best placed to make valued appraisals. The experiences of Braimoh, Adeola and Lephoto (1999) are, however, at variance with this. More often than not, the process whereby the students who operate the bi-modal educational programme (some face-to-face tuition coupled with distance learning) and who are used to assess the quality of lecturers, adequacy of materials, and teaching effectiveness, leaves much to be desired. This is because such a practice has its own practical negative consequences, which include the following:

- falsification of results so as to please their lecturers for fear of being victimized if they did otherwise;
- lack of interest and time inhibiting thoroughness and objectivity in the analysis of evaluation issues by students;
- geographical distance and lack of regular contacts for mentoring and tutoring, thereby creating communication breakdown and dissonance in the minds of the students;
- inadequacy of the instrument used to adapt to a particular environment even if it were to be empirically tested for reliability and validity at a different setting;
- timing of evaluation by students: for example, whether it is before or after examinations, the result will be tainted, either positively or negatively, depending on the students' views on the examination process and standard.

Collis (1998) states that students need gradually but explicitly to learn that evaluation is a constructive exercise, that self-evaluation requires looking at one's own work and that evaluation needs to be based on criteria that can be used as the frame of reference for evaluative judgement. When lecturers are being evaluated, either by peer review, immediate boss's appraisal or students' assessment, there is always an element of antagonism towards the results, rather than accepting these for future performance improvement.

Implications of evaluation process for maintaining quality assurance

'Quality assurance' is a much talked about concept in academia today, yet because of fear of innovation and the unknown, there is still a lukewarm attitude to embracing this practice. With particular reference to distance education, there are still some aspects of it that are capable of rendering the end product susceptible to the charge of being inferior and substandard. This is why it is essential to conduct regular evaluation activity in order to assess the weaknesses and strengths of the programmes as well as the institution with a view to learn how to do things better so as to satisfy the needs and expectations of the distance learners.

It may be almost impossible to recommend a specific quality assurance strategy that can universally be adopted because the distance education object, the background of the clientele it serves, the extent and levels of programmes offered, the modus operandi and the purpose and scope of the distance education outfit may vary widely from institution to institution and from one country to another. It must, however, be noted that the focus of any quality system must be to satisfy the needs and aspirations of the learners *vis-à-vis* the appropriate delivery of services. There are many factors that may be considered for the improvement of the management strategy of distance education programmes in order to achieve higher quality. Akinpelu (1995) and Braimoh, Adeola and Lephoto (1999) have stated that the major aspects to which good attention should be paid, in a distance education delivery mode, include the following:

- admission requirements and procedures;
- development and production of instructional materials;
- structure and management of the delivery system;
- student assessment procedures;
- quality of materials used for teaching and promotion of learning;
- problem of assessment of the effectiveness of an individual distance education facilitator since distance education has the element of quasi-bureaucratization (teamwork);
- the student support services;
- monitoring, evaluation and feedback systems
- availability of adequate human and material resources for the operation of the programmes.

All these are challenges to effectiveness, and hence to the quality of distance education. This situation has actively engaged the attention of scholars and managers in the field of distance education, as judged by the spate of literature in recent times (Omolewa, 1989; Guri-Rozenblit, 1991; Tait, 1993; Halliday, 1994; Mennuir, 1995; Panda and Jena, 2001). Quality can only be assured if there is a deliberate plan to conduct regular evaluation as one of the most valuable tools for learning. Such experiences gained from the objective results of evaluation will certainly be applied to programme operation to achieve efficiency and maintain standards. However, it must be noted that evaluation can be a highly complex or a fairly straightforward activity, depending, of course, on the institutions involved and their view of the value of evaluation for programme improvement.

Milton aptly summarized the value of evaluation in a philosophical way by saying 'if we know where we are going and how we intend to get there, we can match our expectations against what actually happened. We may then learn how to do it better next time' (1991: 10). No single person has a repository of knowledge, but when we open up to objective criticism from other people even as individuals, we will have a clearer vision of our shortcomings and be able to review our position and learn what we have achieved and what is still left to be done. We need to note that if we are too close to something or somebody, we might not be able to see or recognize the weaknesses of such a thing or person. Therefore, we need some distance to analyse the situation objectively so as to avoid mental and visual hallucination which may result in serious distortion.

Conclusion

From the above analysis, we can conclude that evaluation is an essential component of any human being's process of development as well as for the organization's growth. The purpose of evaluation must be the improvement of what we do. Evaluation also leads to quality maintenance of institutions and programmes, enabling them to produce outputs that will not in any way be inferior or substandard to those produced by conventional tertiary institutions.

The only key to maintaining balance in this regard lies in the effective planning and management of distance education institutions. While we deliberately did not recommend any particular approach as to how institutional or programme evaluation should be done, and when and by whom the evaluation should be done, we have given a wide list to choose from, which should suit any distance education institution. In addition, we have highlighted the quality factors to be scrupulously observed by the management structure of an institution. What is needed in order for distance education institutions to forge ahead with their plans to arrive at a positive goal is the provision of adequate human and material resources with a deliberate focus on their own self-discipline and efficiency in the management of the system.

References

Akinpelu, J A (1995) Upgrading secondary school teachers in Botswana by distance education: The challenge of quality, *Journal of AALAE*, **9** (2), pp 1–14

Braimoh, D (1999) Academics and African academia: A paradox of manufacturers and industries for development, *Higher Education Policy*, **12** (3), pp 253–60

Braimoh, D, Adeola, O A and Lephoto, H M (1999) Evaluation of distance education programmes: The case of the National University of Lesotho, *Staff and Educational Development International*, **3** (2), pp 151–64

Calder, J (1994) *Programme Evaluation and Quality: A comprehensive guide to setting up an evaluation system*, Kogan Page, London

Calder, J and Panda, S (2000) 'Evaluation and quality', in *Basic Education at a Distance*, eds Chris Yates and Jo Bradley, pp 110–21, Routledge, London and New York

Castro, A (1989) 'Tinker, tailor, soldier, spy. . . roles and challenges in evaluative studies of technological innovations', in *Research in Distance Education 1*, ed T Evans, pp 233–40, Deakin University, Australia

Collis, B (1998) Building evaluation of collaborative learning into a www-based course: Pedagogical and technical experiences, *Indian Journal of Open Learning*, **7** (1), pp 67–77

Gajanayake, S and Gajanayake, J (1993) *Community Empowerment: A participatory training manual on community project development*, PACT Publications, pp 124–37, New York

Halliday, J (1994) Quality in education: Meaning and prospects, *Educational Philosophy and Theory*, **26** (2), pp 33–50

Jegede, O (1993) 'Measuring quality in distance education at the University of Southern Queensland', in *Research in Distance Education 3*, eds T Evans and D Murphy, Deakin University, Australia

McNamara, C (1998) *Basic Guide to Program Evaluation*, http://www.mapnp.org/library/evaluatn/ful-eval.htm

Mennuir, J (1995) Quality assurance in the off-campus delivery of professional development opportunities, *Open Learning*, **10** (1), pp 43–46

Milton, D (1991) *Teaching Skills in Further and Adult Education*, The Macmillan Press, London, pp 180–98

Omolewa, M (1989) 'Issues of quality and quantity in external studies programme', paper presented at the workshop for course writers, University of Ibadan, Nigeria (mimeo)

Panda, S (2000) *ES-364: Block 4 - Programme Evaluation in Distance Education*, School of Education, Indira Gandhi National Open University, New Delhi

Panda, S and Jena, T (2001) 'Changing the pattern: Towards flexible learning, learner support and mentoring', in *Innovation in Open, Distance and Flexible Learning*, eds F Lockwood and A Gooley, Kogan Page, London

Tait, A (1993) Systems, values and dissent: Quality assurance for open and distance learning, *Distance Education*, **14** (2), pp 303–14

Thorpe, M (1998) *Evaluating Open and Distance Learning*, Essex, Longman

Vella, J, Berardinelli, P and Burrow, J (1998) *How Do They Know They Know? Evaluating Adult Learning*, San Francisco, Jossey-Bass Publishers, pp 9–15

Chapter 18

External control and internal quality assurance

Mary Thorpe

Introduction

The purpose of this chapter is to explore the issues involved in external control and internal quality assurance, and to comment on the implications for open and flexible learning (OFL) of increased emphasis on quality assurance.

Although external control and internal quality assurance are interconnected in practice, the circumstances within which they have developed are not identical. External control is one aspect of the history of correspondence and distance education, which were initially provided by organizations operating in the private sector and for profit. The desirability of state-regulated commerce in this as in other areas has been less contested because the need to protect the consumer in such circumstances is well recognized. Minimal standards and rights set up by local or national authorities have been welcomed as the minimum safety net for users, and beneficial for providers through their creation of a recognized and respectable framework within which organizations can provide their services.

'Quality assurance' refers to a set of practices which have been introduced into public sector provision, notably in the higher education sector, as part of the changes brought by the expansion of postsecondary provision of education. Quality assurance became important for OFL during the 1980s and 90s, as a result of its use by public sector providers, and also as a result of the growing emphasis on accountability in education generally. Many governments have expanded postsecondary education in order to meet the needs of their economies for more skilled and capable labour. Concepts from business have been introduced into education, as part of this drive to ensure that the increased investment in provision will provide the outputs that governments require. The issue of quality of provision has also been emphasized by the demand for accountability to all the stakeholders involved in an expanded system of higher education in particular, including students as well as employers.

Although the use of media in teaching and learning and of more flexible forms of provision is now widespread, the issue of external control predates these current developments. We need to review something of the history of their precursors, in correspondence and distance education, both of which inhabited a more distinctively separate sector of provision than is the case today. A brief review of this context provides a necessary framework for understanding the two key terms in the title of this chapter.

The historical context – correspondence and distance education

The precursors of OFL are the correspondence education organizations which grew up in the 19th century in the United States and spread elsewhere, and distance education which replaced it in the last 40 years of the 20th century. These forms of provision provided a new potential for profit in the provision of education and training which public sector institutions and states have always been wary of. This wariness is justified, in the sense that the private nature of the transaction may leave the learner open to greater risk than exists where class-based provision by public bodies is provided. Somewhat less justifiably, conventional providers have often viewed such provision with a mixture of disdain and dislike. The charge by public sector institutions such as universities, that correspondence and distance education were inferior, is a theme running throughout their history.

The United States

Distance education for most of its history has had to contend with suspicion among educational authorities about low quality standards or even unethical practices. Pittman describes how William Rainey Harper made correspondence courses an integral part of Chicago University, as its founding president in 1892, and for three decades thereafter, correspondence education grew in both public university extension departments and private colleges (Pittman, 1998). The universities set up a National University Extension Association (NUEA) which sought to exclude all provision 'not of university grade' and in 1924, the NUEA suggested that standards should be based on equal rigour with campus provision, and close supervision by mainstream faculty. Such efforts, however, were insufficient to prevent damaging exposés of the worst of the commercial schools from harming the reputation of university provision and leading to closures and ridicule by conventional faculty.

In spite of efforts led by Wedemeyer at the University of Wisconsin to defend the instructional qualities of distance education, strong leadership on standards setting was never forthcoming from the university sector, and acceptance of the classroom as a valid benchmark for correspondence and distance education remained. While the university providers essentially relied on the reputations of their sponsoring universities, the private colleges had responded to the early criticisms through strong leadership on standards enforcement through the National Home Study Council, which became the Distance Education and Training Council in 1994.

Norway

Ljosa and Rekkedal have also documented the regulation of correspondence and distance education in Norway, noting the same tendency to assume campus-based provision as the norm and benchmark from which to judge distance provision (Ljosa and Rekkedal, 1999). Norway has had the most carefully regulated national system, however, with the passing in 1948 of the Correspondence Schools Act. This established the Correspondence School Council which accredited both courses and correspondence schools on behalf of the Ministry of Education until the early 1990s, by which stage established routines of high quality course provision and institutional management were widely upheld. Accreditation was limited to a three- or five-year period and standards have thus been maintained.

However, even here, the authors outline some familiar problems which have led to a move away from external control. Inspections of courses and institutions were often carried out by conventional academics without experience of distance education and unaware of the importance of the operation of a total system for provision and learner support. The tendency was to overemphasize materials, and sometimes to challenge the validity of distance methods per se. Recommendations for change could actually be detrimental in the eyes of experienced practitioners within the distance education institution (Ljosa and Rekkedal, 1999).

Such difficulties have been compounded latterly by the growth of computer-based media in open distance education (ODE) and the inappropriateness of existing standards for current forms of provision. In 1993, the public regulation of distance education was integrated into the Norwegian Adult Education Act, and responsibility for quality assurance has been devolved to the individually approved institutions. The institutions themselves are strongly represented through the Norwegian Association for Distance Education, which has responded to the new situation by establishing a Standing Committee on Quality (SCQ). The role of the SCQ is to work in consultation with the Ministry of Education and to formulate criteria for quality which create guidelines for the institution's own quality improvement work (Ljosa and Rekkedal, 1991: 1).

In the Norwegian context, these guidelines have both internal and external effects. They set a framework within which each institution needs to define its own implementation of quality, bearing in mind the diversity of purposes and users for which distance education provision has been set up. Externally they create expectations of quality against which all institutions, whether accredited or not, can measure their provision. By ensuring that high quality provision exists within a market lightly regulated by the state, it is hoped that all providers will seek to meet the standards of the best and that consumers will not tolerate low quality.

Such an approach sits well within what is now a mature sector of provision. Norway's 1948 Act concerning correspondence schools was the first of its kind in the world and all courses and institutions have been required since then to be accredited. Until 1992, all courses were evaluated by independent consultants before going onto the market, with accreditation lasting a specified period of three to five years. The Correspondence Schools Council was set up to assist the Ministry of Education and has regulated the providers through regular inspections and monitoring of performance data from the providers themselves. The providers have thus had to embed procedures for regular monitoring and revision of their quality, in order to meet national standards. Both the Norwegian Association for Distance Education (NADE) and the Correspondence School Council (CSC) have worked together to provide staff development and to encourage research and updating of the curriculum provided.

Thus, Norway has been able to use private provision and also to ensure that high standards are in place. The move in 1992 to devolve responsibility to the institutions themselves was feasible because of the good practice already in place. The perceived weakness of the external regulation in the former system was that it tended to prevent providers from taking complete responsibility for their own quality. In satisfying the external body, the risk existed that providers came to rely too strongly on this external approval. In addition, the CSC had to rely on staff from the campus-based sector to make judgements about quality. Such staff were not always aware of the demands appropriate to distance education, and concentrated too much on materials and comparisons with conventional textbooks.

The move away from this situation was thus an expression of confidence in the distance education system as a whole, that its staff were as qualified and professionally committed to their learners' needs as to be able to take responsibility for their own quality standards and monitoring. The guidelines developed by the NADE are thus intended to be used by each institution to establish internal standards and processes appropriate to their own purposes and target groups. Four areas are covered – information and counselling, course development, course delivery, and organization – and within each, there are four aspects to be covered – conditions and constraints, implementation, results and follow-up. These are not intended to be applied mechanistically, but used as a starting point and checklist. Evaluation is stressed in each of the four substantive areas.

The EU

In the European Union, the situation is much more variable. Some states have no regulation other than normal commercial and civil law as it applies to transactions in general. Some regulate courses, others institutions; and there is variety in terms of whether the regulators are state or non-state organizations, with powers of compulsion or not. France and Germany both have state-supervised compulsory controls, but in Germany they apply to the course, whereas in France they apply to the provider (O'Neill, 1998).

In the UK, the situation has another layer of complexity in that provision within the public sector is governed not by the body set up to regulate ODL, but by the quality assurance system relevant to that part of the sector. Since 1969 there has existed a body with responsibility for ensuring the quality of courses offered at a distance. The Council for the Accreditation of Correspondence Colleges was partially funded by government until its privatization in 1982 and it now operates under the name of the Open and Distance Learning Quality Council, as a registered charity. However, it has never had a role with regard to the biggest provider in the UK, the Open University, which is subject to the same quality assessment procedures as all other British universities, as currently developed by the Quality Assurance Agency (QAA).

The QAA's reviews of the quality of subject-based teaching in higher education institutions has set expectations about the areas of provision that will be reviewed, as well as the evidence to be produced in support of the claims made by providers about their quality. The growth of distance education provision by UK higher education has also prompted the development of Guidelines on the Quality Assurance of Distance Learning. These are available from the QAA site (http://www.qaa.ac.uk/) and while not constituting a code of practice in their own right, are intended to become the basis of such a code in the future. The Guidelines specify six aspects where the quality assurance of academic standards is likely to require particular attention when study is by distance learning – system design, programme design, approval and review, monitoring of programme delivery, student development and support, student communication and representation, and student assessment. In general, the introduction of external review of the quality of provision operates on the principle that distance methods should be judged against the same principles as face-to-face or campus-based methods. In the light of the increasing use of computer-based learning environments both on and off campus, this seems the most coherent response. In general, the guidelines and methods of review used by the QAA have stimulated the development of performance indicators and some aspects of evaluation (Thorpe, 1996). In an institution like the OU with already well-developed forms of evaluation, there has been an expansion of activity in response to the expectations set by QAA.

The relationship between external control and quality assurance

The varied history of the different countries touched on above suggests that, as we might expect, national culture plays a strong part in whether or not one approach is preferred over another. There are also tensions for university providers of open and distance learning which are not present for private providers, arising from the negative attitudes often found among conventional academics and conventional institutions. Both the United States and Norway provide evidence of this. And the British Open University took on board the challenge right from the start, in setting about to prove that its teaching was second to none in higher education, and its degrees as good as any other.

While it is dangerous to generalize too far, the Norwegian example is instructive. The current emphasis on internal quality assurance is the culmination of experience with a system of external control which was thoroughgoing and effective. The disadvantages of external control had begun to outweigh the advantages, in the perceived tendency for compliance with the accreditors to take precedence over real commitment to quality practice. The current model, with its stronger emphasis on internal quality assurance, does appear to show that a mature system such as Norway's can move through external control into a more 'hands off' approach, with confidence. The inherent strength and good standards of the institutions give confidence that they both can and will take responsibility for setting their own QA systems, working within the spirit as well as the letter of the NADE guidelines.

The issue of ownership does appear to be central here. The US private colleges in some ways won out over their university-based colleagues, because they were not hampered by having to be judged by university staff and university standards inappropriate to their enterprise. They took responsibility for their own operation in the context of private sector business, and benefited from the strong identity this gave them. Professional bodies which represent the private sector providers can assist in this process. As the case of the NADE demonstrates, they can occupy a midpoint between government and individual institutions which can foster both national standards and independence for providers.

The key question appears to be therefore to ask what is most likely to promote and maintain internal commitment to quality. The existence of civil laws which protect the consumers are essential but not in themselves enough. Where the consumer has choice and is an informed user of the service, it is very possible to reduce external controls and foster professional self-development approaches which place more onus on the institutions themselves. In circumstances where the power of the consumer/learner is obviously less than this, the balance may have to be tipped in favour of a more direct approach to using external controls. Even here, however, it may help to set internal QA as the long-term goal, so that a culture of mere compliance is not the outcome of imposition of external control.

The implications for an effective internal quality assurance system

The linking of both internal and external contexts in the achievement of quality assurance for OFL reflects the fact that each has influenced the other and that there have been different views as to which should have the dominant role. Such differences still exist, and they may be made stronger by approaches to quality more generally. The British Open University, for example, is subject to the same system as all other universities, but it is the campus–based providers that have objected most strongly to the more direct assessment of quality imposed by the Quality Assurance Agency. The QAA's system has brought to the fore all the problems with external measures and controls, which are to do with increased workload and bureaucracy, together with the attendant risks of a compliance culture which undermines 'real' quality.

However, whatever the arguments for or against each national system, it is surely undesirable for 'quality' to be subject to passing changes of emphasis or influence. Quality assurance benefits from continuity and regularity of procedure, so that processes have time to become embedded and refined, and data about the outcomes of provision can be compared reliably over several years at least. The goal to aim for should be practices that meet standards commonly held to be desirable whatever the 'political' fashion of the day. The basic structure for quality must be in place internally, so that external requirements can be met with little extra effort. The main elements of a QA system will be 'in place' because the institution itself values and needs them. The 'proof' for purposes of external audit or checking will take some extra effort, but nothing by comparison with the QA procedures themselves, which are there in any case, because the institution values them.

The reason why such a situation is much to be preferred is that it ensures that the greatest effort goes into establishing internal expectations and practices which the institution believes really do ensure that their primary customers, the learners, have a positive and high quality learning experience. Their efforts will be directed towards ensuring that the quality they think they achieve is actually delivered, and towards taking action where evidence shows that it is not. This is surely preferable to devoting huge effort and expense to trying to prove that the institution has met externally imposed standards of quality, at a particular point in time, such as an external audit or review. Such 'add on' extra activity may divert resources away from actually improving quality for the students (Koumi, 1995). The goal should be to spend the maximum time delivering and monitoring quality assurance internally, with the minimum time proving one's system for external inspection.

The question may be raised as to how feasible it is to set up quality assurance arrangements which will serve the requirements of the day as set by the external regulating body, whatever that may be. Obviously there is bound to be a degree of uncertainty about precisely what the external body may require, notably with regard to the paperwork to be provided. Such requirements will obviously require specific attention when they are known. If the standards and monitoring system are in place, the institution concerned can set up its own internal QA system to ensure that those external requirements are met, and even exceeded in certain circumstances.

However, even where there is no external body or the standards are not clearly in place, OFL providers should still take responsibility for QA and set up a system which they can justify to themselves and to their stakeholders, as ensuring that a quality system is in place. Fortunately there is now a body of practice and standard-setting expectations which can be used to outline the kind of expectations that an internal QA system might typically be expected to meet. The NADE statement on quality standards for distance education would be a good place to begin, and those of the UK QAA are also in the public domain.

Some concluding thoughts

Quality is not a homogenous issue. Protection of consumer rights is important, but so also is the quality of the support to learning as provided by an institution and its courses. Different approaches are required to meet both these needs, but the aim is to create systems that are *mutually reinforcing*. External controls may play a useful role in creating common standards and high expectations. They frequently bring risks alongside benefits, however, and over-zealous and over-detailed controls may stifle rather than encourage commitment to and responsibility for quality, at the level of individual institutions. There is a balance to be struck, in other words, which recognizes the irreducible need for providers to take control of their own quality standards and to make genuine efforts to assure quality.

Internal quality assurance must be both embedded within practice yet also an overt focus for action. It is clearly one function of staff development, for example, to address the ways in which course design or support to learners/students can be made more effective. Regular monitoring of student data should be scheduled into local decision making. Baseline data may show poor performance or negative changes which cannot be addressed without further exploration or information (Calder, 1994). Such needs might occur at the very local level of a particular course or study centre or user group, as well as at the level of the system as a whole (Woodley, 1995). This suggests that some research or investigative capacity ought to exist at both local and system-wide level. Where a specialist unit exists, staff could take on the research issues identified – indeed may themselves identify such needs. There ought also to be capacity among those with the roles of course team or tutors or managers of the system to pursue issues at their own level. Both Thorpe (1993) and Robinson (1995) have argued that practitioners should research the effects of their decision making at local level and thus refine their understanding of user preferences and behaviour and how best to provide for them.

QA systems are never 'finished'. They should evolve and change with the dynamics of the system. Practitioners may fall into the trap of assuming that QA is solely a reflection of their provision and while this stays the same, the QA system can be left similarly static. But this is to ignore the crucial element of the users, who as a body are unlikely to show a constant profile and set of outcomes (Fage and Mayes, 1996). QA systems may, for example, show that a course is now attracting more younger students who are in work. This may indicate needs for change in the kind of assignments set and in the monitoring of tutor marking. Are monitors paying attention to this issue? Are tutors giving enough help to improve the grades of these younger students? A case in point to illustrate is that QA systems should be implemented with the assumption that there will be continuing change and evolution.

One way of fostering an attitude of continuing interest and development is to offer funding to those with good ideas for innovative projects. Staff can be invited to outline their ideas in a bidding process, with a requirement to report back results. Small- and large-scale conferences and seminars to disseminate the results can help spread good practice and keep awareness high. Promotion criteria might even be amended to include good practice in QA implementation. Where individuals make excellent contributions in this area, they should be rewarded as a demonstration of institutional commitment to quality excellence.

Internal QA must be both devolved and given a point of focus. It should operate at all levels of the institution yet also avoid the risk that no one is seen as accountable. This can be remedied by placing quality and standards as the brief of a senior figure or decision-making body (O'Shea, Bearman and Downes, 1996). Through such a means, oversight that the system is working effectively can be carried out. Priorities for action can be set and effects monitored. Those who act as leaders of quality in their own areas can form a committee or advisory body to report the experience and perspectives of their particular areas of operation. Concerns about low performance or lack of attention to problems can thus be identified and powerful backing given to appropriate remedial action.

In conclusion, external controls and internal quality assurance can play complementary roles, and acquire more or less power, depending on the conditions operating in the country concerned. However, experience suggests that the balance between the two is delicate, and can be tipped too far in either direction. This chapter, however, has emphasized that quality in teaching and learning has to be fostered by the active commitment of staff and institutions. Frameworks and positive action to encourage ownership and commitment are more desirable than blueprints and rigid regulation, a view that has also been shared by Shale in the next chapter regarding the development and use of performance indicators.

References

Calder, J (1994) *Programme Evaluation and Quality: A comprehensive guide to setting up an evaluation system*, Kogan Page, London

Fage, J and Mayes, R (1996) 'Monitoring learners' progress', in *Supporting the Learner in Open and Distance Learning*, eds R Mills and A Tait, pp 206–21, Pitman, London

Koumi, J (1995) 'Building good quality in, rather than inspecting bad quality out', in *Open and Distance Learning Today*, ed F Lockwood, pp 335–42, Routledge, London

Ljosa, E and Rekkedal, T (1999) *Quality Standards for Distance Education*, developed by NADE's standing committee on quality (2nd rev edn), Norwegian Association for Distance Education, Oslo

O'Neill, H (1998*) Analysis of Distance Education in the European Union*, Zentrales Institute fur Fernstudienforschung, FernUniversitat, Gesamthochschule, Hagen

O'Shea, T, Bearman, S and Downes, A (1996) 'Quality assurance and assessment in distance learning', in *Supporting the Learner in Open and Distance Learning*, eds R Mills and A Tait, pp 206–21, Pitman, London

Pittman, V V (1998) Low-key leadership: collegiate correspondence study and 'campus equivalence', *American Journal of Distance Education*, **12** (2), pp 36–45

Robinson, B (1995) 'Research and pragmatism in learner support', in *Open and Distance Learning Today*, ed F Lockwood, pp 221–31, Routledge, London

Thorpe, M (1993) *Evaluating Open and Distance Learning* (2nd edn), Longman, Harlow

Thorpe, M (1996) 'Issues of evaluation', in *Supporting the Learner in Open and Distance Learning*, eds R Mills and A Tait, pp 222–34, Pitman, London

Woodley, A (1995) 'A string of pearls? A broader approach to course evaluation', in *Open and Distance Learning Today*, ed F Lockwood, pp 354–60, Routledge, London

Chapter 19

Performance indicators and quality assessment

Douglas Shale

'Don't ask for the meaning, ask for the use.'

(L. Wittgenstein)

Introduction

In 1994 Borden and Bottrill (1994: 11) commented that, 'The term performance indicators may seem straightforward, but even a brief examination of the literature reveals that many shades of meaning have been attached to this concept'. Since then, the literature on this topic has grown considerably – but the matter seems not to have become any more straightforward.

What can be usefully said about performance indicators (PIs) within the constraints of a book chapter given that the literature base is so diverse and mixed? Perhaps we still need a 'definitive' characterization of the concept of PIs. However, I do not believe a definitive explication is possible – and an exploration of this assertion and of Borden and Bottrill's comment provides the framework from which this chapter looks at PIs.

Much of my commentary is based on experience gained from working in a postsecondary system with a government-mandated PI reporting requirement. I realize the potential effect of personal bias might compromise points I wish to make. However, in the many discussions I have been involved with about PIs, I have found it invaluable to offer examples from practice to illustrate or refute abstract argument. One of the points I will make is that argument in the abstract is necessarily inconclusive because the meaning of performance measurement is predominantly determined by context and practice, not definition.

The view I offer of performance measurement is cautionary – often cynical. Unfortunately, the space constraints of this chapter will not allow for a full exposition of and response to views contrary to mine – although they are implied in the arguments I offer. Readers interested in pro-PI positions will find a large literature to draw from. Perhaps the extreme position of advocacy is exemplified by Massy (1999); more moderate views are found in Burke (1999) and Burke and Serban (1998). Critical views are offered by Schmidtlein (1999), Yorke (1995) and Atkinson-Grosjean *et al* (1999).

Proposition 1: You can't deny motherhood and apple pie

What I mean by Proposition 1 is that there is typically so much publicly perceived value in the notion of PIs that, *ipso facto*, performance measurement is a good and necessary thing. Massy (1999), for example, bases his entire article on this supposition. Even if the language used is not that of performance measurement, an almost standard observation is that the more information we have the better things will be. Hence, we have statements like the following:

> The real need, as far as the Commission is concerned, is for measures which indicate how well the university system is meeting the reasonable expectations of its own society and how well a given university is fulfilling its own declared mission (Smith, 1991: 124).

> Taxpayers are unlikely to accept forever the proposition that performance should count in all endeavors except higher education (Burke, Modarresi and Serban, 1999: 23).

> How can we develop measures to evaluate the quality of learning that will encourage universities to improve their educational programs and motivate professors to improve their teaching? (Bok, 1990).

If we look closely at these three statements, we can start to discern some of the 'shades of meaning' alluded to by Borden and Bottrill. For example, the first statement pertains to a societal and system-level assessment of effectiveness. The second statement is about accountability to a taxpaying public. The third has to do with the improvement of curricular and instructional quality.

If we consider what performance measures are appropriate for the purposes embodied in the above comments, we can begin to discern other shades of meaning. For example, the measures that Smith (1991) deems necessary for his purposes (which are accessibility, equitability with respect to admission practices, satisfaction of graduates with their education, and employer satisfaction with the quality of graduates) are arguably related to the accountability issue and not directly related to teaching effectiveness. Even within the specific context addressed by the Smith Commission, we could generate an extensive discussion on whether these are the set of performance measures we should settle on. The Performance Indicators Steering Group set up by the Higher Education Funding Group for England observed that PIs in higher education are 'complicated and often controversial' and 'the interpretation of indicators is generally at least as difficult as their construction' (PISG, 1999: 12). Moreover, the universe of indicators seems indeterminate and large. For example, the Report of the Pan-Canadian Education Indicators Program 1999 (Canadian Education Statistics Council, 2000) lists almost 100 education indicators.

Why should 'the interpretation of indicators' be 'at least as difficult as their construction' and why does the list of possible indicators seem unbounded? Part of the answer, I believe, is to be found in my second proposition.

Proposition 2: Performance measures are not value-free

Any given measure has no inherent meaning in and of itself. Even in the physical sciences a measure has meaning only in reference to an agreed-upon standard. Every measure takes its meaning from a context – and, as Wittgenstein argued many years ago, the context that makes a difference is knowing the use.

As an example, consider time to degree completion – usually defined as the average calendar length of time between when students enrol at an institution and when they graduate. Why is this considered a measure of performance? Because it is presumed that students graduating within the notional time established to complete a given programme is the 'optimal' standard. Underlying this first-level assumption is another level of valuing – which is that a longer time to degree completion is inefficient. Whether or not this assumption is merited seems never to be questioned. However, studies at the University of Calgary, Canada indicate that the nominally slow completers generally do not take appreciably more coursework than required. Nonetheless, time to graduation rate persists as an indicator of performance – with an implicit value placed on 'timely' completion because even perceived inefficiency is evidently not acceptable in the forum of public opinion. Ironically, a longer time to graduation can also be interpreted positively in the context of Smith's (1991) call for genuine accessibility. If students are retarding their rates of study because they have to support themselves with part-time work, which requires them to reduce their course load, then surely this is preferable to forcing them to withdraw altogether.

Where does the implicit valuing of efficiency come from and why is it a dominating concern? A number of writers have noted that public sector reforms over the past two decades or so have induced some fundamental changes 'not only in policies and practices, but also in the culture underlying the public administration of nation-states' (Atkinson-Grosjean *et al*, 1999: 6). This New Public Management paradigm was supported by 'broad accusations of waste, inefficiency, excessive staffing, unreasonable compensations, freeloading and so forth' (Harris, 1998: 137). According to Aucoin (1990) and Power (1995), responses to this sentiment were *inter alia* downsizing, cutbacks, competitiveness and introducing market and quasi-market forces. As a result, 'Criteria of economy and efficiency became dominant' and '"Rational" corporate management techniques – like accounting, auditing accountability, and performance models were installed' (Atkinson-Grosjean *et al*, 1999: 6). So, concerns of efficiency and cost cutting would seem implicitly to represent the dominant social and political values in force. In practical terms, this implies that system-level performance indicators need to be understood, in large measure, from this wider societal context.

If context is the key to conferring meaning on performance indicators, why not just state how a given performance indicator will be used? This leads me to offer a third proposition in the next section. However, I first want to comment on an argument often made that although there are problems with performance measurement we need to participate to ensure it is at least done right (for example, see the 'Preface' to Gaither, Nedwek and Neal, 1994). There is an irony here because this position does hold an element of truth – participating in the exercise can minimize some problems (such as incurring very significant overhead costs for data collection and analysis). However, as Polster and Newson (1998) have noted, proponents of the accommodation strategy tend to focus on technical issues and accounting tools in their efforts to make measures 'more meaningful or less harmful' – rather than consider academically based, normative aspects of performance measurement. And, as Atkinson-Grosjean *et al* (1999: 7) point out, 'Accounting tools are far from unproblematic. While appearing impartial, they selectively construct the world from a complex web of social and economic considerations and negotiations.' Or as Harris succinctly put it, accounting has the power to 'create a new "factual" visibility and discipline performance' (1998: 137).

I have argued that the multi-levels of meaning inherent in the selection and formulation of PIs is one manifestation of creating a new factual visibility and disciplining performance. Another source of confounding arises from the requirement that PIs produce uniform organizational information – particularly at a system-wide level. This standardization inherent in performance measurement is the source of the often-stated complaint that the unique nature of any given institution cannot be properly valued. This is especially problematic for distance education providers, as illustrated in Shale and Gomes' (1998) description of the experiences of Athabasca University (AU) and the Open University of British Columbia (BCOU) within the mandated PI systems in their respective provinces. Some of the system-wide indicators were so inappropriate (eg space utilization) that an exemption was granted. In other instances, the specialized functions of these institutions were not recognized at all – for instance, the methodology of the conventional 'local' economic impact study is not appropriate to a university like AU because AU was created to serve a constituency that is widely dispersed geographically. Although the conventional formulation of economic impact is not appropriate, an institution like AU can legitimately claim that important public economic gains are achieved because students are able to remain in the workforce while studying – thus contributing to the local and provincial tax bases.

In still other instances, much to their disadvantage, AU and the BCOU were required to report on nominally the same indicators as the conventional institutions. However, the context of these is so different that the results are highly misleading. For example, programme completion and number of degrees have traditionally been regarded as important measures of output for postsecondary institutions. However, distance education providers are generally judged to be deficient in this regard because they typically do not produce large numbers of graduates. Moreover, time to graduate for those students generally far exceeds what is considered to be efficient. Special pleading about the specialized mandates of such institutions and the concomitant effect on graduation rates and time to completion have not been effective *post hoc* arguments to temper interpretations of these indicators.

Proposition 3: It may all look rational – but it isn't

How does context get added to give meaning to a performance measure? Every time we compile a set of data we do so with some assumptions in mind about how the data will be used. That is how we determine what data are appropriate and how the data are best arrayed. However, this is only a 'private' level of definition. In most circumstances it must become a negotiated level of understanding arrived at through discussion with whoever requested the data. Seldom is the information requested so straightforward that no adjustment is necessary – and seldom is the requestor ever so clear in the specification of what they want that the process of clarification is unnecessary. Invariably the discussion shifts from the client attempting to explain the meaning to my asking them for the use of the data.

This kind of complexity increases substantially in a larger organizational context – and particularly when one bureaucracy deals with another. The rational 'model' of policy decision making is a very mechanistic view of how authority is distributed in bureaucracies and how decisions are really made. It assumes explicit statements of goals (the fallacy of pre-existent purpose), unanimity of endorsement of the goals (the fallacy of consistency of choice) and concerted, identifiable action to intervene in antecedent behaviours to 'cause' identifiable outcomes (the fallacy of rational choice). Rarely will such certainty exist. Organizations are social and, hence, political entities. This is especially the case where an organization is primarily concerned with process – such as is found in governments and universities. Power relationships are established on all kinds of 'non-rational' grounds (eg affiliations, alliances, kinships). Consensus on values and hence policy positions will generally be compromises of some sort. If the respective points of view are in opposition, then any agreement may well be a trade-off where the agreed action has little relationship to the parties' initial points of view. Given that organizational behaviour is a socially determined phenomenon, it follows that the decision-making process is directly affected by those individuals participating at the time.

This explains why we often see different PI systems from one political jurisdiction to another – and from one occasion to another. The indicators themselves can differ, the system of indicators can differ, the emphasis and use can differ – and certainly the context of their use can differ. Such political vagaries belie the rational model of organizational behaviour and policymaking.

The situation can become even less rational when performance-funding considerations are introduced. Not only do we have the indeterminacies resulting from which indicators are used and how they are defined – we also have more implicit relative valuing introduced because the performance system can accord more points to some indicators than to others and the calculus that produces the aggregated result can vary substantially. Moreover, the associated amounts of funding can vary and can have only an indeterminate relationship to the costs of the behaviours associated with the indicators.

Proposition 4: Maybe it isn't what we think it is

In the first three propositions I have followed the assumption that we should take the matter of performance measurement at face value and believe that the arguments offered in support of PIs are as they appear. However, this can be yet another aspect of the myth of rationality. Atkinson-Grosjean *et al* (1999: 16) offer a similar view when they state that performance models 'can be used to advance state agendas other than those strictly concerned with accountability and performance'. Certainly the expectation that such systems are designed to improve educational systems and institutions has not been reasonably supported by experience (Atkinson-Grosjean *et al*, 1999). What then might these other agendas be?

Atkinson-Grosjean *et al* comment, from their survey of the consequences of PIs, thus: 'we learned that performance indicators as a social technology rarely stand alone. Their consequences – whether good, bad, or indifferent – relate to their role within broader ideological mechanisms characterized as public sector reform, new public management (NPM), or what Neave (1998), in the context of higher education, calls "the evaluative state"' (1994: 4). As government downsizes itself and its supporting bureaucracy we have the appearance of less government regulation – which suits the ideology of the NPM. However, there is an inherent paradox in this apparent reduction of governmental involvement and requirements for public accountability. PIs provide a means for resolving the paradox. PIs need only be mandated and policed. And the values represented by the PIs are under governmental control. The burden of producing the PIs and living with the results falls on the institutions. Moreover, no deep understanding of the specific natures of the educational systems is required. For the purposes of accountability, it is sufficient to be able just to state categorically that the PIs are adequate to ensure institutions perform and that they are seen to be held accountable. In other words, the public appearance of holding them accountable is the issue – not measuring and enhancing performance.

Performance measurement and quality assessment

Performance indicators and quality assessment are terms that are often closely associated in the literature – and they may even be used synonymously on occasion. However, the presumption that the two are necessarily related is arguable. I have already raised issues around the meaningfulness of PIs. The ambiguities inherent in PIs and their application have a sort of mirror image in the concept of quality assessment. For example, there are many definitions of 'quality' and the very act of privileging one definition over another bespeaks an ideological view of what is valued (Boberg and Barnetson, 2000). The deterministic view of PIs as something that exists independent of a 'knower' and only need be discovered is paralleled in the conceptual world of quality assessment. As Dill (1992: 61) points out, 'Quality, insofar as it is an articulated concern, is regarded as a concept to be defined through the procedures of assessment.' Under this view, quality exists independent of the participants needed to create the transaction of adjudging that something has quality (or not). Therefore, an assessment can be made through measurement. And because measurement is a specialized skill, quality improvement often becomes 'the responsibility of highly trained staff experts and sophisticated systems removed from the actual processes of production. Quality improvement was thus pursued through a focus on detection – "assessing in" quality – rather than through the prevention of errors' (Dill, 1992: 62).

Isolating performance measurement and quality assessment through reductionist definitions of indicators, reinforced by implementing them using third-party technocrats 'removed from the actual processes of production', 'disconnects' the intent of these concepts from the means of realizing their objectives. In simple terms, the interpretation of what is measured suffers because it is usually arrived at by individuals and agencies that have little direct knowledge of the processes measured. Prescriptions of how to address perceived problems defined by people not directly involved in the associated activities cannot be effective because it is unclear how to relate the measures back to specific practices. Moreover, prescriptive actions determined externally cannot be useful when you ultimately have to depend on the people actually involved in the activities under review to effect change. As Brown and Duguid (2000: 99) note, 'you can't redesign process effectively if you don't understand practice'. At that, Brown and Duguid note that the transfer from even 'best practices' to process redesign is uncertain and poorly understood – underscoring their theory that information *per se* is not an adequate basis for describing and changing organizational behaviour.

Conclusion

Those who speak positively about performance indicators seem to do so from a presumptive, hortatory point of view. However, PIs *per se* are neither good nor bad. How they are used is the real issue. Of course, if one assumes that they are to be used in a 'good' and meaningful way, something of value could result. However, control of the use of PIs is typically beyond our ability to influence – and often the use can be beyond our knowing. A typical rejoinder to this comment is that we should instruct receivers of the information to use it one way and not another. However, receivers of information are also part of a context and they are actors in a political dynamic that they do not control. Advisory comments fall by the wayside as different groups use PIs for their particular purposes.

In some circumstances one may be able to limit the context of PIs to mitigate ambiguity in the interpretation of performance measures. Often this will be the case in contexts comprised of processes analogous to those found in manufacturing. This would not be the case for much of conventional higher education. However, there are many aspects of distance education operations that are industrial-like, particularly those forms of course production and delivery that are based on printed or electronic materials. At this level of specificity, performance measurement is effectively 'management information' – that is, information specifically intended to address issues of effectiveness in production subsystems. An elaboration of these processes and associated performance measures can be found in Powar, Panda and Bhalla (2000). However, as Brown and Duguid (2000) point out, many organizations have found to their dismay that information about the organization does not necessarily translate into knowledge about how to improve what the organization does.

Paradoxically, PIs at a very general level can be effective in arguing general policy issues. For example, how much money should be invested in higher education is, of itself, an intractable question. However, if we ask how much money does one jurisdiction invest on a per student basis compared to others, we open the door to questions about how to account for observed differences. We also begin to form a platform for arguing for certain levels of investment (that is, setting a policy target) which begins to move the issue from argument to implementation.

Whatever one may think of PIs and their use, in my opinion they will continue to influence governmental and public policy views of higher education, at least in the foreseeable future. The political climate of our times is such that performance measurement plays very well in the public and political arenas – even though there is no body of evidence that supports the sweeping claims made for performance measurement and performance funding.

However, the onus of proof clearly has fallen on the critics of PIs. There is a growing body of literature that critically reviews PIs and their use and a growing body of opinion that all is not as it seems or has been represented in this respect. Nonetheless, I believe we are stuck with them for some time longer because higher education institutions will find they have to play along with the political theme or risk being branded out of touch, if not arrogant (because they refuse to be accountable) and unresponsive (because performance measurement is all about performance and improvement, what does that say about uncooperative institutions?). So, in my experience, for political reasons alone, institutions will endorse government initiatives for performance measurement and performance-based funding. In addition, there will be a segment of senior institutional administrators (who are bureaucrats after all) who will actually believe the rhetoric of performance measurement and who will vocally support the idea.

Whatever view you take, I believe the following pieces of advice are relevant. First, try to keep the number of PIs to a minimum. There will be an inclination to want to show how well your institution does at everything – especially if there is performance-based funding at stake. This will lead to a seemingly never-ending stream of PIs that will become more situation specific and esoteric as the list grows. In my view, the disconnect between actual performance, performance indicators and any flow of associated funding means that, by and large, it does not really matter so much which indicators you settle on – so lobby for those that will show your institution in the best light. Second, keep them simple. Sophistication of methodology is invariably a costly encumbrance in this exercise. Moreover, any resulting refinements in the results likely will not be apparent to most of the intended audience.

Why these recommendations? The administrative overheads required for compiling, verifying, reporting and maintaining a performance measurement system are generally considerable. The more elaborate the system, the less likely that data will be available 'off the shelf' and the more effort will have to be expended to generate what is required.

Finally, always remember to ask what an indicator is to be used for and who will use it. The answers will be interesting and helpful. I think you will find the silences you encounter quite revealing as well.

References

Atkinson-Grosjean, J, Grosjean, G, Fisher, D and Rubenson, K (1999) *Consequences of Performance Models in Higher Education: An international perspective* (study prepared for the Humanities and Social Sciences Federation of Canada), Centre for Policy Studies in Higher Education and Training, University of British Columbia

Aucoin, P (1990) Administrative reform in public management: Paradigms, principles, paradoxes and pendulums, *Governance: An International Journal of Policy and Administration*, **3** (2), pp 115–37

Boberg, A and Barnetson, B (2000) System-wide program assessment with performance indicators: Alberta's performance funding mechanism, *The Canadian Journal of Program Evaluation*, Special Issue, pp 3–23

Bok, D (1990) What's wrong with our universities?, *Harvard Magazine*, May/June, p 59

Borden, V M H and Bottrill, K V (1994) 'Performance indicators: History, defini-
tions and methods', in *Using Performance Indicators to Guide Strategic Decision
Making*, eds V M H Borden and T W Banta, New Directions for Institutional
Research, Number 82, Jossey-Bass, San Francisco

Brown, J S and Duguid, P (2000) *The Social Life of Information*, Harvard Business
School Press, Harvard, MA

Burke, J, Modarresi, S and Serban, A (1999) Performance: Shouldn't it count for
something in state budgeting?, *Change*, **31** (6)

Burke, J C and Serban, A M (eds) (1998) *Performance Funding for Public Higher
Education: Fad or trend?*, New Directions for Institutional Research, Number 97

Burke, J C (1999) 'Arguments about performance funding: Rhetoric and reality',
paper presented at the 39th Annual Association for Institutional Research
Forum, Seattle

Canadian Education Statistics Council (2000) *Education Indicators in Canada: Report
of the Pan-Canadian education indicators program 1999*, Statistics Canada, Catalogue
No. 81-582-XPE

Dill, D D (1992) 'Quality by design: Toward a framework for academic quality
Management', in *Higher Education: Handbook of theory and research*, ed J C Smart,
vol VIII, pp 37–83, Agathon Press, New York

Gaither, G, Nedwek, B P and Neal, J E (1994) *Measuring Up: The promises and pitfalls
of performance indicators in higher education*, ASHE-ERIC Higher Education
Report Number 5, George Washington University, Washington DC

Harris, J (1998) Performance models, *Public Productivity & Management Review*, **22**
(2), pp 135–40

Massy, W (1999) 'Measuring performance: How colleges and universities can set
meaningful goals and be accountable', in *ASHE Reader on Planning and Institutional Research*, ed Marvin W Peterson, Pearson Custom Publishing, Needham
Heights, MA

Neave, G (1998) The evaluative state reconsidered, *European Journal of Education*, **33**
(3), pp 265–85

PISG (1999) *Performance Indicators in Higher Education*, First Report, Performance
Indicators Steering Group, February, Higher Education Funding Council for
England

Polster, C and Newson, J (1998) 'Don't count your blessings: The social accomplishments of performance indicators', in *Universities and Globalization: Critical
perspectives*, eds J Currie and J Newson, pp 173–91, Sage, Thousand Oaks

Powar, K B, Panda, S and Bhalla, V (2000) *Performance Indicators in Distance Higher
Education*, Aravali Books International (P) Ltd, New Delhi

Power, M (1995) *The Audit Society: Rituals of verification*, Oxford University Press,
Oxford

Schmidtlein, F A (1999) 'Assumptions underlying performance-based budgeting',
paper presented at the 39th Annual AIR Forum, Seattle

Shale, D and Gomes, J (1998) Performance indicators and university distance
education providers, *Journal of Distance Education*, **13** (1), pp 1–20

Smith, S (Commissioner) (1991) *Report Commission of Inquiry on Canadian University Education*, Association of Universities and Colleges of Canada, Ottawa, Ontario

Yorke, M (1995) Taking the odds-on chance: Using performance indicators in managing the improvement of quality in higher education, *Tertiary Education and Management*, **1** (1), pp 49–57

Chapter 20

Accreditation in the digital era: preparing for the new distance education landscape

Don Olcott, Jr

Introduction

During the past five years, the unprecedented development of advanced educational technologies has transformed the potential of most colleges and universities to extend their educational programmes to distance learners. Today, however, this rapid transformation is blurring rather than differentiating institutional residential and outreach missions (Duderstadt, 1999; Hall, 1995, 1998). Institutional leaders must now examine the role of instructional technology in all its various contexts rather than adhering to the obsolete axiom – either we adopt educational technology to support all our institutional missions or we wait and see what's on the horizon. As most leaders acknowledge, the *convergence* of campus and outreach missions is here to stay.

At the same time that this institutional blurring of residential and outreach integration of technology has accelerated, major policy questions have arisen at the macro level that can be viewed within the overall accreditation umbrella related to institutional mission, resources, academic quality, assessment, and the general improvement of institutional teaching, research and administrative core functions.

Until recently, most Accrediting Commissions in the United States faced a dilemma of how to assess just where and how distance education fitted into the overall institutional mission. Moreover, most of the agencies tended to impose traditional accreditation criteria on institutional distance learning programmes. In many respects, this traditional approach was appropriate given that many generic components of accreditation (eg outreach mission, faculty, learning resources, facilities, finance, student support services, etc) are critical evaluation questions associated with distance education (North Central Association of Colleges and Schools, Commission on Institutions of Higher Education (NCA), 1997; Western Interstate Commission for Higher Education (WICHE), 1995). As distance learning matured, however, it became increasingly clear that distance delivery raised some basic questions that did not fit precisely into the traditional accrediting structure. The Commissions have recognized the need to focus greater attention on distance and/or electronically delivered programmes.

This chapter examines the current state of accreditation related to distance learning programmes in the United States (mostly delivered electronically), particularly an overview of the accrediting process, major accrediting issues affecting distance learning and the response of accrediting agencies in addressing these issues. The focus will be on institutions where distance learning programmes fall under institutional and programme-specific accreditation. It will not address virtual universities who are seeking full accreditation status as a stand-alone recognized body. In conclusion, the chapter presents key questions for institutional alignment of distance education with the broader institutional and programme-specific accreditation processes.

It may be noted that while the focus of this chapter draws upon accreditation issues facing US institutions, it is not intended to suggest that the varying accreditation and certification processes in the global community necessarily do, or should, adhere to the issues raised here. However, attempt is made to draw upon the crucial issues that pertain to distance education that have generic application for institutions worldwide.

The accrediting agency refocus on distance education

The shift towards a broader view and focus on distance education by accrediting commissions can be attributed to two major developments. First, the ubiquitous assimilation of educational technologies, most notably the World Wide Web/Internet, emerged as a transformational change that was evolutionary rather than temporal. The Internet has transformed every major social institution in society – from education, business and government to medicine, entertainment and the services industries. In sum, educational delivery expanded from local, regional and national venues to global, anytime-anywhere learning.

A second trend that the accrediting commissions recognized was the expanded use and adoption of distance education by more colleges and universities. Clearly, this was not a passing trend and agencies would have to address the implications of this shift. However, the more important question is what caused this accelerated growth? As distance education moved through the 1990s, there were clear signals that institutional faculty and administrators were becoming more receptive to the potential of use of educational technology for residential instruction, research and distance teaching. Moreover, institutions were maturing in the faculty policy arena and recognizing that distance education would have to be addressed in promotion and tenure, faculty teaching assignments and assessment, and professional development and training for faculty.

Equally important has been the continual growth of empirically based research that has consistently shown that distance learning students taught via technology and resident students taught face-to-face had comparable academic performance (Dillon and Walsh, 1992; Duning, Van Kekerix and Zaborowski, 1993).

Additional issues such as faculty release time and course development compensation were becoming 'normative' expectations for faculty engaged in distance teaching (Olcott and Wright, 1995; Wolcott, 1997). Institutional rhetoric emphasized student-centred learning to the emerging technologically literate student and how educational technology could facilitate this process. Technology was changing the roles of faculty as well as the roles of the student in the educational process (Guskin, 1994; Olcott and Schmidt, 2000).

In sum, while these issues have not been resolved across the board or by all institutions, the collective evolution of academic policies, greater faculty experimentation, technologically literate students and market-driven pressures for institutions to serve students anytime-anywhere (on campus, on the job, in the home) have served as a collective impetus for more institutions to enter the distance learning arena. Accrediting Commissions have been astute in recognizing these subtle but critical shifts in academic culture. The winds of change have moved accrediting agencies to assume a greater leadership role in working with institutions that were creating innovative, cost-effective and high-quality distance education programmes.

The accreditation continuum: purpose and scope

The primary purpose of accreditation is to ensure quality assurance and to support continuous improvement of the educational mission of an institution (NCA, 1997). And yet, accreditation is in some respects more than this. Accreditation is analogous to an 'institutional passport/visa' that establishes credibility, integrity, and the status of an institution among its constituents, its peer institutions, government agencies and the broader higher education community. Accreditation is a voluntary, affiliated process and institutions must seek affiliated accreditation status (accredited status or candidacy status) from the appropriate Commission. Moreover, accreditation implicitly acknowledges that while the regional agency provides the stamp of approval and oversight, the continuous improvement and monitoring of quality rests with the institution.

In the United States, for example, accreditation has historically been authorized at the regional level. Institutions seeking initial accreditation typically must meet requirements for candidacy prior to formal accreditation. The Regional Accrediting Commissions grant institutional accreditation as an overall umbrella for an institution's programmes and services. The focus of the Accrediting Commissions has historically been on degree-granting institutions. However, Commissions have the authority to review non-credit training and professional development programmes if they determine that these programmes directly or indirectly impact the quality and improvement of the institution's overall academic credit programmes. In general, however, institutions have much greater autonomy and latitude over their non-credit programmes, whether delivered electronically or face-to-face.

Institutions must also seek specialized accreditation of designated professional programmes. Specialized programme accreditation, particularly in professional graduate programmes, is required by disciplined-based accrediting Associations/ Commissions. This level of accreditation provides institutions with another recognized level of credibility, integrity and programme quality among their constituents, peer institutions, the public, government agencies and the broader higher education community.

Institutional accreditation is initially granted for a five-year period and review must occur every 10 years after initial accreditation. However, the governing accrediting agency can request an institutional review at any time if there is evidence that the institution is not meeting quality and improvement standards established in previous reviews by the Commission. An institution's accreditation status can also be revoked at anytime for not meeting General Institutional Requirements (GIRs) and/or 'patterns of evidence' that demonstrate institutional quality and/or improvement (NCA, 1997). Institutions can appeal any action taken by the Commission. Similar standards and timelines also apply to specialized accreditation by the appropriate discipline-based Commission/Association.

GIRs address institutional mission, authorization, governance, faculty, educational programme, finances and public information (NCA, 1997). Institutions must also provide extensive 'patterns of evidence' that address five criteria for accreditation. The criteria include the following:

- *Criterion 1:* The institution has clear and publicly stated purposes consistent with its mission and appropriate to an institution of higher education.
- *Criterion 2:* The institution has effectively organized the human, financial and physical resources necessary to accomplish its purposes.
- *Criterion 3:* The institution is accomplishing its educational and other purposes.
- *Criterion 4:* The institution can continue to accomplish its purposes and strengthen its educational effectiveness.
- *Criterion 5:* The institution demonstrates integrity in its practices and relationships.

There is a rather paradoxical element in the accreditation process. Institutions are required to prepare a 'self-study' for the formal review by the Commission.

Organizations typically go out of their way for this 'snapshot' external view of performance and all functions of the organization are made to demonstrate the best attributes of the organization. The reality, which we hesitate to state publicly, is that maintaining quality and improving performance rests with the organization. It is the sustainable, continuous commitment to improvement by the organization that results in sustainable performance and improvement.

This perspective is not intended to diminish the role of the Accrediting Commissions. The Commissions provide the standards and criteria by which institutions measure themselves against established performance measures and similar institutions. At the same time, despite the ongoing liaisons between the institutional representative and the Commission during intervening review periods (5 to 10 years), a plausible argument emerges that suggests accreditation is somewhat a 'virtual process', equally difficult to measure as a distance learning programme delivered via the Internet to geographically dispersed students nationally or globally. In sum, the self-regulatory commitment of the institution and/or programme will ultimately contribute to the consistent demonstration of quality and improvement over time.

General guidelines and protocols

In 1997, the Western Cooperative for Educational Telecommunications (WCET), an arm of WICHE, published general guidelines entitled *Principles of Good Practice in Electronically Offered Academic Degree and Certificate Programs*. The purpose of these guidelines was to provide guidance to higher education institutions for developing their distance learning programmes in areas that contribute to the quality and improvement of distance learning delivery. Moreover, the WCET staff clearly aligned their guidelines with generally defined areas that institutions and programmes must address in the accreditation process.

The WCET guidelines have served as the impetus for all the Regional Accrediting Commissions to potentially adopt these guidelines as the starting point for the Commissions to develop a common set of protocols/guidelines for distance learning. NCA adopted WCET's guidelines in March 1997. The original WCET guidelines can be accessed at www.wiche.edu/telecom/.

In September 2000, eight Regional Accrediting Commissions, listed in Appendix 20.1, published a draft document entitled *Guidelines for the Evaluation of Electronically Offered Degree and Certificate Programs*, which is part of a broader document entitled *Statement of the Regional Accrediting Commissions on the Evaluation of Electronically Offered Degree and Certificate Programs*. These documents have been provided as a general resource for the reader. These two most important documents to appear in the United States during the past five years relative to distance learning quality and performance guidelines must be interpreted carefully.

WCET and the Accrediting Commissions have clearly stated that these documents are not to be considered mutually exclusive standards. The term 'standards' carries a very specific meaning to the accrediting community and their member colleges and universities. These documents are simply the first critical steps towards a common set of accreditation *guidelines and protocols* to assist colleges and universities engaged in distance learning, particularly those using electronic media, to establish and maintain high quality programmes. These guideline documents do not supersede general Accrediting Commission institutional and programme requirements. The WCET document addressed the following areas: 1) curriculum and instruction; 2) evaluation and assessment; 3) library and learning resources; 4) student services; and 5) facilities and finance. The Accrediting Commissions' draft document referenced above built upon and expanded WCET's *Principles of Good Practice* in greater detail to include the review areas of: 1) institutional context and commitment; 2) curriculum and instruction; 3) faculty support; 4) student support; and 5) evaluation and assessment.

The following discussion of emerging issues pertaining to distance learning and accreditation are not intended to address every issue that is included in either document. These are practical issues that are currently confronting the higher education and accrediting communities in the digital era.

Accreditation issues in the e-learning environment

Convergence of campus and distance education

Until recently, when distance learning practitioners discussed the definitional attributes of distance education, the one common element they could agree on was the 'separation of instructor and student'. Moreover, while this inferred separation in both time and space, the generally accepted rule was geographical separation defined by significant distances. Today, campus and distance students access the same course via online delivery from 1,000 miles and 1,000 yards. Only the advent of online media capable of delivering anytime-anywhere learning has created our need for new vocabulary such as 'asynchronous' learning, threaded discussions, online student support services and application programme interface (API).

Prior to the online revolution, most distance learning practitioners emphasized the differences between distance learning and traditional face-to-face residential instruction. These differences ranged from new teaching roles, interaction strategies, and assessment to how distance education was financed, the delivery of student support services and general administrative services. This enigmatic response, however, seemed to miss the most important point: the means of educational delivery did not alter the fundamental outcomes of achieving high quality teaching and learning. In other words, even in the pre-online era, our common goals for the educational process did not change. The Accrediting Commissions never forgot this point.

Unsurprisingly, during this period of 'differentiation rhetoric', many practitioners criticized the lack of response by the Accrediting Commissions for not recognizing these differences. The Commissions, certainly with no intent to absolve themselves from the complexities of mediated learning, basically guided institutions to follow traditional institutional criteria for assessing distance learning for accreditation. The paradox is that distance learning practitioners wanted the accrediting agencies to provide leadership in this arena, but to no avail. Today, in the online world, the accrediting agencies have stepped forward to provide leadership on these issues at the same time that institutions (and practitioners) have realized that the convergence of media is drawing campus and distance learning programmes closer together. But, they are also advocating the development of separate accreditation criteria focused on distance learning that may require a convergent, integrated approach.

Is it possible that these divergent shifts by accreditors and distance learning practitioners need to be reassessed from a total educational environment framework, not simply because of the new online media, but rather because the impact these media and advanced technology systems are having on the overall instructional and services functions of an institution? Institutions are now facing mass integration of technology for instruction, administrative services, financial processes and student support services.

There is good news on the horizon. The works of the WCET and the Accrediting Commissions Draft Joint Statement (referenced earlier in this chapter) realize the inherent complexity of formulating new guidelines to govern a moving target in today's digital world. Their general approach is, in the main, an *integrated convergent model* that recognizes similar outcomes for distance education and residential education while also recognizing that traditional and distance instruction may use different means to achieve these outcome goals.

Institutional locus of control for distance education

With the exception of autonomous virtual and corporate universities that are totally distance learning organizations, few colleges and universities in the United States have a centralized, coherent organizational structure for governing distance education. On most campuses, multiple offices have some level of responsibility for distance education, and it is not uncommon for these offices to be engaged in power politics to control distance education.

From an accreditation perspective, this fragmented diffusion of control creates more problems than it solves regarding quality assurance, programme responsibility, and hybrid financing models emanating from multiple budgets. Add the fact that many institutions simultaneously deliver centralized distance education at the same time that individual colleges create their own ventures for distance delivery, and this fragmentation becomes organizationally dysfunctional. Perhaps I should be more direct. Hypothetically, if we applied the joint Accrediting Commissions' *draft* protocols to most distance learning programmes today, it is the opinion of the author that most would fail. This is not aimed at criticizing institutional distance learning programmes. In fact, quite the contrary. Most programmes have not been developed systematically to take into account specific measurement criteria that would be applied by the Commissions.

Regulatory oversight or undersight: the service region dilemma

'I thought that when I brought the Open University to the US I would be dealing with one country. I was mistaken' – this comment by Sir John Daniel, the then Vice Chancellor of the British Open University, addressing the Annual Meeting of the National Governors Association in 1999, sums up the complex regulatory landscape of US higher education. The point that he was making was that education in the United States is a state's right, given to the states under the Tenth Amendment of the US Constitution. This states that those powers not reserved to the federal government shall rest with the states (Goldstein, 2000). Higher education in the US is one of those 'powers reserved to the States'.

Higher education is regulated by the states. Each state typically has a higher education board or commission with regulatory authority over all public institutions within the state. Some boards govern both four-year and two-year institutions while others have separate boards. In addition, each state has the equivalent of a state system of higher education that reports directly to the state board. It is important to note that private institutions have much greater latitude is terms of when, where and how they conduct business and are not governed by the public's state board or state system of higher education.

State boards and state systems of higher education, in concert with other designated state agencies, can impose policies and procedures for distance education delivery on the institutions, specify a geographical service region in which an institution may offer their programmes without prior approval, and specify the requirements by which outside institutions may deliver education programming in their state.

There is considerable variance across the 50 states regarding the requirements, fees and application processes for outside educational institutions to deliver programming within states (Goldstein, 2000; WICHE, 1995). These regulatory constraints are also due to the fact that public institutions are funded with state public dollars that are typically required to support educational initiatives within a particular state.

A critical accreditation issue that arises as institutions explore expanded distance learning delivery is how this affects the institutional mission and whether the change potentially alters the scope of the institution's educational activities, and represents a 'substantive change' that requires prior review and approval by the Regional Accrediting Commission (Lezberg, 1998). State boards and state systems of higher education monitor all changes that may fall under 'substantive change' review and approval. Moreover, most boards and state systems have additional state requirements of what is considered a fundamental change in mission or scope of the institution, hence requiring review and approval by the regional accrediting commission.

Many academic leaders and distance education practitioners argue that this regulatory maze imposes undue constraints upon public institutions to leverage the power of online technologies to deliver higher education programmes anytime-anywhere. They are right. Private institutions and emerging virtual institutions do not face this regulatory maze and have limited restrictions imposed upon them regarding where, when and by what means they deliver higher education.

Critical questions for leveraging anytime-anywhere learning

In summary, these issues, while not all-inclusive, raise many important questions to be considered by institutions, regulatory agencies and Accrediting Commissions regarding distance learning:

- What is the appropriate accrediting protocol/guidelines model for distance learning that reflects the continuing convergence of residential and distance uses of communication technologies? How do these guidelines reflect convergence as well as differences between residential and distance delivery?
- What is the optimum oversight/management model at the institutional level for monitoring distance education for accreditation purposes? Who should be responsible for this monitoring? What criteria will be used to establish recognized 'patterns of evidence' and what 'state-of-the-art distance learning institutions' will be used as the base measure that distance education programmes are meeting these quality assurance measures?
- What criteria do the Accrediting Commissions use for determining whether to approve an institution for programme delivery beyond regional boundaries?
- What policies and regulatory changes at the state level need to occur to leverage the capacity of digital technologies by institutions to deliver programmes anytime-anywhere?
- How do institutions fund distance learning programmes whose primary audience resides outside state boundaries? What percentage of institutional state funding, if any, should be used for educational delivery outside state boundaries? What is the cost–benefit ratio that state boards and state systems of higher education will use to determine that use of state funding for external state programmes either directly or indirectly benefits the state and its citizens?
- How do we bring together the Accrediting Commissions and the regulatory agencies that have overlapping jurisdictions for monitoring institutional, state, regional and national initiatives?
- Should institutional distance education programmes receive separate 'supplementary' accreditation in addition to its institutional accreditation?

These questions are inherently complex. The solutions may be equally complex in arriving at the appropriate balance between regulation and promoting innovation. More importantly, the WCET, the Regional Accrediting Commissions, and state and national regulatory agencies are addressing these questions and discussing these among themselves. These organizations deserve the thanks of the higher education community for leading us forward in exciting and challenging times, and of those students who benefit most from distance education programmes.

Conclusion

Distance education, particularly the use of new anytime-anywhere digital technologies, has provided the impetus for accrediting commissions and regulatory agencies to re-examine the policies, procedures, and criteria for assessing and measuring quality in distance learning programmes. Across higher education, the distribution capacity of delivering learning via these technologies has precipitated institutions to rethink their missions, how they use resources, how they reward and recognize faculty, and most importantly, how these technologies can enhance and improve the teaching–learning process. This chapter has provided an overview of the accreditation process and the major policy initiatives under way, and has raised critical issues that must be resolved to leverage the power of the new technologies without diminishing the quality and integrity of distance delivered programmes. We, in the higher education community, must strive to achieve a delicate balance between regulating distance education without unduly diminishing its teaching and learning potential.

The most important challenge facing higher education is how to balance academic traditions with new innovations. The optimum balance will come from a synthesis of the best of proven academic traditions and the best of the emerging technologies. The best is yet to come – for institutions, for the accrediting and regulatory communities, and most importantly for our faculty and students.

References

Dillon, C and Walsh, S M (1992) Faculty: The neglected resource in distance education, *The American Journal of Distance Education*, **6** (3), pp 5–21

Duderstadt, J J (1999) Can colleges and universities survive the information age?, in *Dancing with the Devil: Information technology and the new competition in higher education*, eds Richard N Katz *et al*, Jossey-Bass, San Francisco

Duning, B S, Van Kekerix, J M and Zaborowski, L M (1993) *Reaching Learners through Telecommunications*, Jossey-Bass, San Francisco

Goldstein, M (2000) '*Regulation of the Web: E-Learning in a nation of states*', paper presented at the Annual Meeting of the Western Cooperative for Educational Telecommunications (WCET), 1–4 November 2000, Albuquerque, New Mexico

Guskin, A E (1994) Restructuring the role of faculty: Part II of reducing student costs and enhancing student learning, *Change* (Sept/Oct), pp 16–25

Hall, J W (1995) The convergence of means: The revolution in electronic technology and the modern university, *Educom Review*, **30** (4), pp 42–45

Hall, J W (1998) Leadership in accreditation and networked learning, *The American Journal of Distance Education*, **12** (2), pp 5–15

Lezberg, A K (1998) Quality control in distance education: The role of regional accreditation, *The American Journal of Distance Education*, **12** (20), pp 26–35

North Central Association of Colleges and Schools, Commission on Institutions of Higher Education (1997) *Handbook of Accreditation* (2nd edn), NCA, Chicago

North Central Association of Colleges and Schools, Commission on Institutions of Higher Education (June 2000) *Statements of Mission, Vision, Core Values, and Strategic Priorities*, NCA, Chicago

Olcott, D J and Wright, S J (1995) An institutional support framework for increasing faculty participation in postsecondary distance education, *The American Journal of Distance Education*, **9** (3), pp 5–17

Olcott, D J and Schmidt, K S (2000) Redefining faculty polices and practices for the knowledge age, in *Higher Education in an Era of Digital Competition: Choices and challenges*, ed Donald Hanna, pp 259–85, Atwood Publishing, Madison, WI

Regional Accrediting Commissions (September 2000) *Draft Statement of the Regional Accrediting Commissions and Draft Guidelines for the Evaluation of Electronically Offered Degree and Certificate Programs*, RAC

Western Cooperative for Educational Telecommunications (1997) *Principles of Good Practice in Electronically Offered Academic Degree and Certificate Programs*, Western Interstate Commission for Higher Education, Boulder, CO

Western Interstate Commission for Higher Education (WICHE) (1995) *When Distance Education Crosses State Boundaries: Western states' policies*, Western Cooperative for Educational Telecommunications, Boulder, CO

Wolcott, L L (1997) Tenure, promotion, and distance education: Examining the culture of faculty rewards, *The American Journal of Distance Education*, **11** (2), pp 3–18

Appendix 20.1

Commission on Higher Education, Middle States Association of Colleges and Schools	info@msache.org
Commission on Institutions of Higher Education, New England Association of Schools and Colleges	cihe@neasc.org
Commission on Technical and Career Institutions, New England Association of Schools and Colleges	rmandeville@neasc.org
Commission on Institutions of Higher Education, North Central Association of Colleges and Schools	info@ncacihe.org
Commission on Colleges, The Northwest Association of Schools and Colleges	pjarnold@cocnasc.org
Commission on Colleges, Southern Association of webmaster@sacscoc.org Colleges and Schools	
Accrediting Commission /Community & Junior Colleges, Western Association of Schools and Colleges	accjc@aol.com
Accrediting Commission/Senior Colleges and Universities, Western Association of Schools and Colleges	wascsr@wascsenior.org

Chapter 21

Networked learning, convergence and accreditation: is it time for global standards?

James W Hall

The world is witnessing an explosion of university-level academic degree programmes that use the techniques of distance learning to communicate with students. As with all explosions, there is much solid content but also a substantial surround of hot gases. The capacity of students – the consumers – to distinguish between solid academic programmes and those that are vaporous is limited. While established practices for programme validation and institutional accreditation continue as regional or national activities (as has been discussed in the preceding chapter), many of the new programmes transcend these traditional geographic and political boundaries. Given the growing capacities of the Internet and World Wide Web, this trend will likely continue unabated in the coming years. Accreditation for these trans-boundary institutions will require new auspices, revised strategies and global standards.

Consideration of three institutional categories helps to explain the speed of success and rapid growth of these new trans-boundary institutions or programmes. The first category includes the largest and most successful of the established distance learning institutions, those that John Daniel has named *mega-universities* (Daniel, 1996). He defines these as having an enrolment greater than 100,000 students (many are much larger) and they are often funded by a sponsor nation. They possess the technical resources and capacity to deliver their already well-crafted courses into the new, worldwide environment. Many, including a number that simply did not exist 35 years ago, are today names instantly recognizable across the world. Examples include: The Open University (United Kingdom); The University of Maryland University College (United States); Fernuniversitat (Germany); Indira Gandhi National Open University (India); The University of South Africa (South Africa); Sukhothai Thammathirat Open University (Thailand); and the smaller but well-known SUNY Empire State College and Regents College (United States). All of these institutions are thriving, continuing to grow in service to large and diverse constituencies.

The second category includes large numbers of new organizations and players whose track record is not yet established, and who are creating highly competitive products for a burgeoning marketplace. For example, within the United States, where distance learning gained currency more slowly than elsewhere, major new organizations, both traditional and for profit, are now active and having an impact. Examples include The Western Governors University, a broadly based but fledgling organization with services initially focused in much of the western United States, and The United States Open University (USOU), sponsored by the leading and still growing UK Open University. The USOU has applied for accreditation under the regional authority (Middle States Association), and Western Governors is seeking accreditation as well from the North Central Association. These are a few of the many new purveyors of distance courses and degree programmes. They continue to show the powerful appeal and educational efficacy of distance learning as an approach to higher learning for many students.

In fact, the perceived appeal is such that this second group is joined by rapidly growing numbers of corporate institutions, old and new, that offer degree courses commercially. They propose to make a profit on the enterprise of higher learning and some appear to be succeeding. Perhaps the best known is The University of Phoenix, currently traded on the New York Stock Exchange as the Apollo Corporation.

The third institutional category is something quite different from the other two. In 1994, I called attention to a growing convergence between distance education and the traditional campus-based education – an historic convergence toward *networked education*. In fact, since the mid-1990s, most of the growth in credit distance learning programmes offered towards a university degree has been in otherwise quite traditional educational institutions. I predicted that this convergence would transform all of higher education, leading to an entirely changed environment. It is in these well-established, traditional institutions where convergence is most visible and where the traditional approaches to learning converge with the new capacities of technology and telecommunications to enable new hybrid networked course offerings to appear rapidly (Hall, 1994). Moreover, the faculties of these institutions are now moving quickly to accept using the new networking techniques. This promotes improved quality control. Many of the earliest pioneers in distance education have not recognized the speed or extent of these new developments within the traditional university. The result is that new programmes emerging from older established universities challenge the near monopoly on distance students once held by the earliest and most successful of those institutions whose sole purpose has been distance learning.

Recent reports reveal an astonishing growth of distance course offerings within traditional institutions. The December 1999 survey conducted by the National Center for Education Statistics of the US Department of Education shows huge increases in the proportion of US institutions that offer such instruction, with some two-thirds of public two-and four-year institutions in the practice. The larger the institution, the more likely that the institution has committed funds to such developments. Moreover, these efforts generate large numbers of student enrolments, creating a super-charged competitive marketplace.

Thus, it is no accident that open, distance and networked learning has grown so rapidly in recent years. While this growth has occurred across many nations, it has been especially vigorous in those which either lack an existing university structure, or where in the past a small number of highly selective institutions served a mostly elite, carefully selected body of students. In all nations, the burgeoning demand for access to a university, or to some acceptable form of tertiary education, is by now routinely expressed through the regional political processes and the global economic requirements. While distance education provides a way to respond to the demand for access, convergence demonstrates a continued blurring of the distinctiveness that once characterized distance learning and campus-based education. We are well along in defining the new, networked higher education of the 21st century.

The pace of convergence will increase, linking the traditional with the networking capabilities of technology. One of the significant benefits of convergence is that those nations which have historically not funded a large institutional infrastructure are now able to use these approaches to higher learning to catch up, even leapfrog to a world standard of higher education. They are able to do this at a much lower investment cost and at a breathtaking pace.

Aided by telecommunications, networked computing and open-learning methodologies, a whole lot of institutions seem to appear almost overnight. They enrol large numbers of students rapidly, and, surprisingly in some cases, do all this at a cost that enables the organization to generate surplus funds. The old manner of designing and building a university campus is thus turned on its head. The hundreds of millions of dollars once required, even for a small university campus of 5,000 students, is no longer a handicap for poorer nations. Large research libraries that once required dozens of years to establish are becoming available from electronic sources. These sources will soon be capable of providing far more comprehensive service in meeting student and scholarly needs than almost all but the largest of the traditional libraries.

For example, although India has many well-established traditional universities and colleges, the demands of the modern economy require vast increases in the number of graduates, especially in areas relative to the new communications and computing technologies. Thus, it is no accident that the rapid growth and success of Indira Gandhi National Open University and Dr B R Ambedkar Open University has occurred in respectively the whole country and beyond, and the Andhra Pradesh State. Moreover, India's potentially high student demand for access (CHE, 2000a) attracts foreign distance universities. And, as convergence occurs in traditional name-brand universities, such as Stanford, NYU and The University of London, a truly global university milieu will become a reality.

While few will argue with the increased student access and opportunities presented by convergence, especially in developing nations, there is a less attractive downside. The relative ease of development also brings into higher education new and sometimes inexperienced providers. Their aims and experience do not always support the characteristic checks and balances that help to ensure a level of academic performance and intellectual rigour critical to university-level education. Thus, while convergence sharply increases the capacity to offer access to a wider range of students, it does not promote the controls and assurances that have, in the past, given the consumer some security regarding quality.

The speed and scope of the growth of open learning institutions, online course offerings and networked instruction has not been matched by a parallel enhancement of accreditation – the organizations and measures that assure the character and quality of these institutions. Accreditation, degree validation, programme evaluation – whatever the description of the process – has been traditionally a responsibility reserved to the state or province, sometimes the nation. More often, it has been a process governed largely by the universities themselves.

Today, however, instruction crosses physical boundaries and former jurisdictions. That renders it impractical to enforce formerly obvious jurisdictional regions. Thus, the emergence of the university of convergence raises a host of new issues for accreditors.

Given this explosive growth and the almost total transformation of the academic structure and organization, how can higher education monitor itself? How can the advanced learning enterprises ensure a high level of accountability to students and others? Can this be done on a global scale, transcending the political boundaries that have traditionally circumscribed the educational marketplace? Who authorizes or charters institutions that operate in a global marketplace? In short, how does academic accreditation function in a worldwide educational market?

Answers to these questions will be difficult to come by. With today's proliferation of institutional providers, many established by for-profit organizations and all increasingly competing for students across the world, regional and national accreditation bodies are unable to keep up with the pace of development. Moreover, their legal jurisdiction no longer covers the geographic span of the programmes provided.

Quality assurance, always difficult, now becomes a significant problem. There are those who will argue, with some credibility, that the marketplace should really be the determinant of quality. Those programmes recognized by the marketplace as providing a high level of quality will compete more effectively in the market and so will prosper. They surmise that those not offering a quality product will soon lose their student appeal and wither in the marketplace.

This is an argument that may work reasonably well in a marketplace of products and goods. But in higher education the consumer is usually not in a position to judge the long-term quality and value of the services provided. Unlike the satisfactions gained by using a product, with an immediate capacity to judge whether the product works well or not, an educational service requires that the consumer, the student, undertake a number of challenging tasks, persevere in performing them, and subject him/herself to an appraisal of success in performing those tasks. Frequently, these tasks are undertaken without a fully developed vision of how the whole will fit together and what the cumulative effect of completion will be. These conditions sharply limit the ability of the market to act as a reliable arbiter of quality.

Moreover, the marketing of educational services often obscures the real issues that determine quality. Emphasis is usually placed upon the degree or certificate that the student will receive. Most purveyors today advertise the ease and speed by which these credentials can be gained. Very few describe the serious academic expectations that attend a truly demanding educational experience. Even fewer offer substantive information regarding the qualifications and experience of the teachers, or the availability of student support services and systems. And none provide a clue as to the fiscal stability and long-term viability of the institution or corporation. The result is an educational marketplace filled with unsubstantiated claims of excellence, offered by a rapidly growing number of organizations that have emerged from an entrepreneurial individual, a powerful idea, or a new issue of stock or debt equity.

Many of these organizations borrow an industrial model for higher learning. That model was perfected in the late 1950s and 1960s in the United States at many of the large universities. It is a model that offers tightly defined courses, with set books and cookie-cutter lessons. They were designed to be taught in a fail-safe structure by graduate assistants, apprentice teachers drawn into the classroom with precious little preparation. The courses could be offered at relatively small cost to the institution, stressing efficiency through replication and mass production. In the 1960s, they were designed to handle the crushing loads of entering students, many with marginal academic interest or capacity. When a significant number of students did not pass the course, those who persisted could be treated more handsomely at advanced levels of study. In this way, the industrial model of course offerings was able to support the greater personnel costs of upper-division advanced level study.

I call this the industrial course model because it emphasizes, as did the assembly line in earlier times, the focus on specific, narrowly defined tasks, the use of a limited range of texts, teaching to a common course syllabus without deviation, and the interchangeability of these courses with all others with the same title. Students who completed these courses gained knowledge and exposure to specific information. What they did not receive was an opportunity to increase their intellectual skills through open exploration, personal interaction with trained and experienced faculty, or individual recognition of their unique strengths and weaknesses.

But the educational reforms of the late 1960s and 1970s discredited this industrial model, showing the intellectual shallowness, the lack of student nurturance and the high rate of student failure or alienation. In the United States, although the university disruptions of this period were triggered by protests against the war in Vietnam, they were sustained by a widely experienced dissatisfaction with a model of industrialized higher education. Students reacted vigorously, often actively, in describing the weaknesses of this approach to university education.

Thus it is ironic that many of the new organizations that have rushed into distance teaching have rediscovered this efficient but inadequate model of instruction. This is the key fact in enabling them to offer courses inexpensively, avoiding the high costs of course development, individual teaching and learning, and thoughtful evaluation. It is a model that has prospered in corporate training programmes, where cost and speed are a fundamental consideration. It has also prospered in the continuing education programmes of traditional universities, programmes that are often required to operate on less than half of the tuition revenue they generate.

To oversimplify, what these purveyors of efficient education do is focus exclusively on the content and the information contained within a course. Not unlike a dry and turgid lecturer, they ask the student to learn or memorize largely factual data, fed to them in bite-sized morsels. They then are 'tested' to determine the amount of information retained. On this basis, students show their 'mastery' and proceed 'successfully' to the next assignment or test. When a sufficient number of such units are completed, students are awarded a degree or credential.

These students are seldom asked or expected to do anything with the information they have thus acquired. There is no curricular design or evolution leading the student to ever-higher intellectual skills. They do not learn to analyse the premises of the information they gain, nor do they compare the relative merits of some information with other information. They are not asked to study the relationships that may exist among ideas, nor are they challenged to test their own reactions, new ideas, or questions. All of these intellectual and social skills, honed within a university setting to strengthen the capacities of individuals whom we call graduates, are found in vestigial form, passing to extinction. They are the stuff around which the faculty, the intellectual coaches of a true university, shape a graduate, given sufficient time and engagement.

The industrial model also requires, as on the assembly line, a high level of standardization. Standardization is admirably suited to the assembly line, for it ensures a high level of product reliability. Yet it can work only in a world of limited choices and homogenous expectations.

But the world we are experiencing today, the environment of global complexity and world-class competence, requires a different graduate. That graduate will be required to respond daily to increasingly diverse needs, widely divergent social and cultural situations, agreements that require creativity and social subtlety, and conflicts that test wisdom and patience. The global village requires the full range of advanced human capacities. All universities, whether traditional, distance, or the emerging institutions of convergence, must reach to those expectations.

By far, most recognized educational institutions do a reasonably good job of monitoring their own academic standards. Their faculties maintain currency with the changing needs of the world. They aim to produce graduates that meet world-class standards. We can foresee already the possibility for international university organizations, perhaps in each of the major language groupings. These institutions will offer globally conceived and managed courses.

But the world marketplace also offers new opportunities for those who see education as simply another commodity to be hawked on the street. These educational operators, like financial institutions chartered and operating from internationally unregulated islands, will use the resources of the Internet to gain easy access to an open and undiscerning market. These organizations, like their more responsible namesakes, will acquire their courses and resources from international providers. They will use the bibliographic and library sources that will be commonly available through electronic means. What will be missing is the professionally empowered faculty who carry the moral responsibility for effective student learning. It is not the new means of delivery that constitute the problem, rather it is the lack of a vision of what constitutes a powerful and effective education.

Is it time, then, for an approach to institutional and programme accreditation that can define, recognize and monitor a world standard for a university degree? We do appear to be groping towards some forms of trans-regional accreditation. In the United States, for example, each regional accreditation organization has worked to redefine the old guidelines, standards and expectations that constitute high quality practice. To an unfortunate extent, their focus has been on 'distance learning', in the narrowest sense, rather than on the product of convergence – networked learning. Nonetheless, the conclusions of these various regional bodies, now widely shared, provide some authentic criteria for evaluating the networked institutions of the 21st century. They are a good starting point.

The key indicators of quality are not difficult to imagine. In the mid-1990s, I chaired a Distance Learning Task Force for the Middle States Association of Colleges and Schools (MSACS, 1997). Responsible for institutional accreditation in the Mid-Atlantic States of the USA, the task force report identifies essential requirements and principles that should be followed. Moreover, its recommendations have a high degree of correlation with similar guidelines prepared by other regional organizations. Such guidelines feature three broad principles that provide a solid framework for consideration: curriculum, student support, and assessment.

Curriculum addresses the expectation that *full* programmes of study leading toward a university credential, not individual courses, define the accredited degree. Such a curriculum fits well within the institution's mission; it sets high intellectual expectations for the instructor and the student; it is solidly supported by the intellectual capacity, usually a committed faculty or faculties and other resources, that give credence to the ability of the institution to deliver the curriculum.

Student support is the second essential to a high quality academic programme. The strongest educational institutions have people and processes in place to provide intellectual and emotional support to help the student succeed. This support includes not only the systems that recruit, enrol and process students, but most especially the capacity to interact with the student, either in person or electronically.

The third key area includes student evaluation and programme assessment. Frankly, these critical processes have not been well developed by institutions in the past and, even today, they do not constitute a long suit. For a decade or longer, accreditation bodies have rightly challenged universities to be more proactive in systematically assessing their academic programmes and, at the same time, to be more careful in evaluating individual and collective student performance.

Today, all of the US regional accreditation associations are reviewing their expected standards for accredited member institutions (CHE, 2000b). Some are exploring ways to accommodate US trans-regional universities, although agreement regarding the shape of such accommodation seems at present to be a political amalgam of all the regionals, rather than a new, consolidated approach. And given the slow pace of this consideration, how will accommodation be made for institutions that are becoming transnational, global in scope?

Is it time for some global basic broad agreements across these three areas? Should we establish some new global body that could recognize those universities that distinguish themselves from non-compliant organizations and purveyors of sub-standard educational programmes?

Many will argue that the complexity of attempting to monitor educational institutions engaged in trans-regional distance teaching on a worldwide playing field defies reason. They will argue that the varying levels of education and educational purpose, or that the differing national or cultural expectations of universities, make establishment of widely accepted and enforceable standards impossible to achieve. I do not agree with these conclusions. Rather, while I assume that the number, the variety, the suitability of purveyors will be daunting, nonetheless, a world standard of educational quality can be established.

Institutions and organizations can, as with current approaches to voluntary accreditation, submit to a review of their own volition. The opportunity for such a review would be open to any organization, without condition as to its size, sponsorship (ie public or private, for-profit or not-for-profit), its national or transnational identity, its current accreditation, etc. For most traditionally accredited institutions, the new world accreditation body could simply acknowledge the validity of the established regional or national accreditation. But for the growing numbers of trans-regional or transnational institutions, a new imprimatur is very much needed.

That imprimatur should come through an organization whose reputation will be widely recognized, whose impartiality can be established beyond question, and whose commitment to quality meets the international standard. Moreover, this body must be apolitical, accepting applications for approval without respect to their point of origin. Nor should this new body be simply another self-anointed specialized accreditation organization, established to address a unique or narrowly defined specialized institution.

My proposal is that the United Nations Education, Scientific and Cultural Organization (UNESCO) should create the new accreditation organization.

Working with the International Association of Universities, the International Council for Open and Distance Education, the Association of Commonwealth Universities and other appropriate bodies, UNESCO seems ideally positioned to offer a new service to future generations of students. In a rapidly evolving educational world, we have little time to lose.

References

Daniel, J S (1996) *Mega-Universities and Knowledge Media: Technology strategies for higher education*, Kogan Page, London

Hall, J W (1994) 'The revolution in electronic technology and the modern university: The convergence of means', in *Studies in Public Higher Education: The challenge of technology to higher education*, No. 6 (November), pp 21–40, State University of New York, Albany, NY

Middle States Association of Colleges and Schools, Commission on Higher Education (1997) *Policy Statement: Distance learning and guidelines for distance learning programs*, Philadelphia, PA

The Chronicle of Higher Education (2000a), 14 July, p A48, Washington, DC

The Chronicle of Higher Education (2000b), 7 July, pp A29–30

Part 6

Internationalization

Chapter 22

Internationalization of open and flexible learning: planning and managing in a global environment

Glen M Farrell

Background

It is tempting to think about the internationalization of education as a recent phenomenon with all the hype about applying information and communication technologies (ICTs) circulating. Actually it is not. Internationalism has been around since the early development of distance education in what was previously known as correspondence education.

The internationalization process started to develop when institutions around the world adopted distance education methods on a large scale. Driven by the need to improve domestic access to educational opportunities at all levels of the system, the use of correspondence and other distance learning methodologies found widespread applicability. Persons involved in these activities wanted to share ideas and discuss mutual problems, which resulted in the formation of international associations. Examples of such associations are the International Council for Open and Distance Education (formerly ICCE) and the Asian Association of Open

Universities. In countries such as Canada, where education is constitutionally within the jurisdiction of the provinces, national associations such as the Canadian Association for Distance Education developed for the same reasons. The inter-actions, networks and information sharing that these organizations fostered, and continue to foster, account in no small measure for the internationalization of the vision and global adoption of open distance education models.

Today, the term internationalization in open and flexible learning conjures up quite a different image than it did 25 years ago. The World Wide Web has become both the means and the metaphor for the provision of educational opportunities without respect for political borders. The notion that the member institutions of the aforementioned international associations, formed in the first instance to share information and support one another, would one day be competing for market share would have been quite foreign to the founders.

The application of ICTs to the processes of teaching and learning has resulted in more than international competition among institutions. It is also bringing about a convergence between the previously discrete activities of distance educa-tion and 'traditional' education, a theme which has been proposed and analysed by Hall in the preceding chapter. Additionally, greater access to learning brings with it an increasing demand for more 'openness' and flexibility of the core business policies of the institutions. This convergence and 'openness' is resulting in an entirely new context within which the planning and management of the enterprise occurs, and is enabling both collaboration and competition among institutions.

Forces of globalization

As with any environment, there are forces that serve to facilitate shifts away from the status quo (push factors), and others that act to keep things as they are (pull factors). This is certainly the case in education where one finds unprecedented change processes under way in most countries. The objectives of these change processes obviously vary; however, generally they are focused on the need to make educational opportunities more widely and equally accessible, enhance quality, and contain or reduce costs. The use of distance, open and flexible learning methods and models features prominently in these change processes. It is against this backdrop that the 'push' forces that encourage the internationalization of open and flexible learning, and the 'pull' forces that constrain it, must be examined. The list that follows is illustrative of these factors. They are generally pervasive in the sense that, to some degree, they are found in all systems; however, they have different impacts depending on the specific context. As well, it is important to understand that the valence of these factors depends on the perspective of the reader. In other words, one may view a push or a pull factor as either positive or negative, depend-ing on one's values, context and vested interests.

Push factors

1. Unquestionably, the most powerful driver of internationalization is the enabling power of ICTs and their applicability to education. The ability for interactive connectivity to occur on a global basis, using appliances that are increasingly 'user friendly', and at costs that are becoming more affordable, all enable educators to 'dream dreams that never were' in terms of:
   - how they might collaborate/partner with colleagues in other countries;
   - how they might share instructional products;
   - how products might be marketed internationally;
   - how to enrol and teach students around the world.
2. The environment of change that pervades many national education systems is another powerful push for internationalization. The perception of change creates an interest on the part of practitioners about what is happening elsewhere. This results in the need to seek and share information about open and distance education on topics that range from training expertise to content resources and instructional materials.
3. Historically, countries in Asia, Africa and South America have relied on institutions in developed countries to provide higher education opportunities, particularly at the graduate level, for their more able young people. In recent years, however, concerns about the cost of continuing to send students to institutions abroad have escalated. Because of this, many countries are now requesting that these institutions assist in reducing costs by providing the educational programmes within the learners' home country, delivered in whole, or in part, by distance and open learning models. The providing institutions are motivated to do this because of a concern to maintain their market share.
4. One of the most significant impacts resulting from the application of ICTs in education is the flexibility that results from being able to 'unbundle' functions that historically have all been managed and carried out within a single institution. The functions of administration, development and distribution of instructional materials, delivery of learning opportunities and related tuition, as well as a number of learner support services can now be managed through value-added partnerships with other institutions and organizations. These partnerships involve both public and private sector organizations and are increasingly international in nature.
5. Another dominant factor pushing the internationalization of open and distance learning is the rapid adoption and application of these strategies by multinational corporations to address their intra-organizational training needs. Many of these organizations have become role models with respect to 'best practices' regarding the application of ICTs. Furthermore, these organizations have become interested in forming partnerships with educational institutions – sometimes for market reasons and sometimes as a means of having their training programmes recognized for credit towards certain academic awards.

6. Another push factor is the fact that the use of these technologies has made it easier for educators to incorporate international content into their curricula at all levels. This, of course, is not a new goal; but it has become easier to achieve. The application of distance and open learning methodologies around the world has resulted in learning materials, institutional linkages, professional networks and resource people being readily accessible. As a result, educators who are interested in incorporating international content into their curricula are taking advantage of these opportunities.

7. A final push factor in this illustrative list is the need to be, and to be seen to be, keeping up with other institutions. This is a very significant factor which is manifest in the growing number of institutions, particularly in North America, who are rushing to establish a 'virtual' delivery capability in response to concerns that, if they do not, student recruitment, donations and grants may decline. More often than not, this development initiative is rationalized by the intent to 'market ourselves globally'.

Pull factors

1. It is ironic that, on one hand, the growing pervasiveness of ICTs serves as a push factor for the internationalization of open and flexible learning, while, in much of the world, the lack of access to these technologies causes it to be a very selective process. The constraint is primarily due to the unavailability of technical infrastructure; and the inability to afford to use the infrastructure, even when it is available. For many of the world's developing economies the consequence is that the process of internationalization is bypassing them totally or, at best, is resulting in their being consumers of the learning products from developed countries rather than being partners in the development process.

2. Marked differences in beliefs about the relationship between pedagogical methods and the quality of the learning experience are also constraining the internationalization process. Those who believe that learning should be structured and directed by teachers are not likely to be attracted to open and flexible learning models that enable a more constructivist or learner-centred approach to education.

3. Another pull factor is the constraining nature of the regulatory environment in many jurisdictions. National and state policymakers around the world are concerned about the impact of the unbridled invasion by 'foreign' providers of education. The concern is particularly acute at elementary and secondary school levels but it exists at the university level as well. It is usually expressed in terms of the need to protect the existing level of educational quality. However, it can also be a facade for other concerns such as a fear of faculty job loss and an inability to compete in the international marketplace. Whatever the reason, most jurisdictions have policies and regulations that require foreign educational providers to be 'accredited' in some manner by national or state licensing bodies before their programmes can be recognized.

4. Policymakers in many parts of the world see internationalization as a double-edged sword. On one hand they need and welcome programmes and courses from providers in other countries, but they also worry about the potential impact on the culture and values in their own society if internationalization becomes too pervasive. The result is that distance and open learning programmes focused on technology, science, business, and non-formal lifelong learning, including continuing professional education, cross international borders most easily. Programmes focused on the arts and humanities are obviously more culturally specific and therefore less amenable to internationalization.

5. The generally cautious attitude that teachers and faculty have towards distance and open learning is another pull factor. Their most commonly stated concern is that these delivery models may erode the quality of education and that this would be exacerbated by allowing out-of-state/country providers to operate within their jurisdictions. However, the issues are usually more complex than this. Fear of job loss, lack of skill in using learning technologies, and fear of teaching in a way that is more public all contribute to this cautious attitude which slows the process of internationalization.

6. International arrangements for the transfer of educational course credits and recognition of learning achievements across institutional boundaries are generally uneven and not well facilitated – even within the same educational jurisdictions. This becomes even more difficult as programmes and courses cross international borders. As a result, learners are wisely cautious about enrolling in the programmes offered internationally because they risk not being able to have their learning recognized in a way that contributes to the achievement of their goals.

7. Related to the previous pull factor are the difficulties encountered in providing support to learners in locations that are far removed from a providing institution's local jurisdiction. Differences of culture, communication difficulties and previous learning experiences all serve to complicate the provision of these essential services to students through a distance and open learning delivery method.

8. Another learner-related factor constraining internationalization of open and distance education is that learners in many parts of the world are simply unaccustomed to learning through these pedagogical models. Many have only been exposed to traditional directed learning. Their lack of familiarity with 'new ways' of learning causes them to be apprehensive about the quality of their education delivered through new pedagogical models.

Current status

The interplay of the above forces makes any attempt to describe the current status of the internationalization of distance and open learning very risky. To say that the scene is dynamic would be a monumental understatement. What follows, therefore, needs to be viewed as a collection of generalizations which, taken together, provide the reader with a snapshot of the developments and an insight into the complexities which face educational policy planners and managers in this dynamic global environment:

1. There is a great deal of confusion as to the exact nature of open and flexible learning. For example, a variety of labels are used to describe it (refer to Chapter 1 for a detailed discussion). Furthermore, the methods used cannot necessarily be determined from the labels. Methods such as print, radio and television broadcasting, audio and video teleconferencing, e-mail and the Web may be used, separately or in combination, within an activity described by any one of the above labels.

2. A casual observer of the educational scene might wrongly assume that, with borderless information and communication technological capacity, and growing expectations about their application to education, the world is rapidly becoming an 'educational free trade zone'. While this may be evolving, many countries have policies and regulations in place which limit the activities of 'foreign' educational providers. This can be, and is being, done through a variety of mechanisms such as: controlling the recognition of learners' credentials and certifications; requiring the accreditation of institutions; and limiting the use of the term 'university'. Exporting institutions also have other regulatory issues to deal with, such as intellectual property rights and quality assurance requirements, and administrators are finding that many of their existing policies and regulations are not applicable in the new internationalized environment.

3. In spite of the pervasive use of the term 'virtual', relatively little is occurring in the internationalization process that can be described as 'pure' virtual learning in which all the functions of administration, materials development and distribution, course delivery and tuition, and learner support services are provided through technology-based strategies.

4. Programmes that are being marketed successfully internationally are focused on niche markets such as technology and business. This makes the marketplace extremely competitive, with the result that local and regional markets for these types of programmes have become fragmented. It is not so easy anymore to generate revenue from these high demand areas and use it to subsidize other programmes. The explosion in the number of MBA programme providers using open and distance methods to market their programmes well beyond their historic jurisdiction is an example.

5. Interest in open and distance learning in traditional institutions of higher education is rampant. Some schools and faculties within these institutions are adopting open and distance learning strategies in the belief that doing so will enable them to profitably market their programmes internationally. As a result we have the anomalous situation where open and distance institutions are developing within traditional ones that have never before had any interest in open and distance education.

6. There are also examples of institutions creating separate entities as wholly owned subsidiaries as vehicles to use for purposes of international 'e-education'. This provides the institution with a way of bypassing cumbersome decision-making processes and enables the subsidiary to operate on a business basis.

7. The impact on established single-mode distance teaching institutions resulting from the adoption of open and distant learning by traditional institutions that have heretofore had no involvement with these models is significant. Their once-exclusive monopoly is disappearing and, out of necessity, they need to reinvent themselves in terms of both their programmes and their delivery methods. To compete internationally, they are driven to convert rapidly from print-based materials to Web-based technology. A strategy being employed by single-mode distance teaching institutions is to form alliances in order to take a collective approach to the protection of market share. An example is the 'Global Virtual Alliance'.

8. The technical/vocational sectors of educational systems are also receiving more attention. Because of the nature of the learning content in the technical sector there is an easier base of partnership with the training divisions of the corporate world. As a result, there are growing examples of joint venture arrangements between technical colleges and institutes and private companies that have been established for the sole purpose of providing a particular programme to a niche market that has been identified.

9. In many ways the elementary and secondary school levels are the parts of educational systems that have, to date, been impacted the least, both by the incorporation of open and distance learning methods within schools, and by the process of internationalization. However, this is about to change. Countries recognize that the competencies developed by schools are critical to overall economic development and they are undertaking major educational reforms to achieve them. The use of open and distance learning strategies will be essential in this process and the international demand for instructional content and teacher training materials and programmes is already escalating. The corporate sector will be a major player in this process as they look to capture a share of this huge international market potential. Some evidence of the emerging development at the schools level can be found in the establishment of various 'Schoolnet' organizations in different parts of the world.

10. While existing educational organizations are changing, new organizational forms are also emerging. This results from the fact that application of technology enables institutional functions to be 'unbundled', providing the opportunity for the emergence of new organizations that are focused and specialized in terms of their core business in order to pursue international market opportunities. For example:
    - Broker-type organizations, which acquire or broker programmes from a variety of institutional providers and then add value through flexible entry and credit transfer policies, are emerging rapidly. Examples include the University of the Highlands and the Islands project in Scotland and the Western Governors University in the United States.

- Information and facility provider-type organizations are developing to the support needs of distance education learners as well as to assist institutions who want to export their programmes. An example is the Sylvan Calibre Learning Network, a private sector organization that operates with partners in a growing number of countries.
- Institutions are emerging that are authorized to award credentials and to provide a variety of additional services such as prior learning assessment, educational planning, and records of learning. They do not provide instruction directly to students; however, their role in helping learners with the selection of appropriate providers to use in carrying out their learning plans will become a critical contribution in a world that abounds with educational providers. Examples of these sorts of institutions include the Regents College in New York State and the Canadian Learning Bank, which is part of the Open Learning Agency of British Columbia.

11. New organizational forms are developing in the private sector as well.
    - Direct providers of instruction, using distance and open methods in whole or in part, usually with a focus and a particular market niche, have become prevalent and profitable. Examples include the University of Phoenix and Jones International University in the United States and the National Institute of Information Technology in India.
    - Corporate training networks that were developed in the first instance to meet internal training needs are now exploiting international marketing opportunities. The most typical examples of these are found in the information and communication technology sector.
    - Specialized service organizations such as the IBM Global Campus and McGraw-Hill Learning Infrastructure have developed to provide consultation, project management, technical support and private tuition on a fee-for-service basis to individuals and institutions.

12. There has been a great deal of rhetoric over the past few years to the effect that dominant worldwide providers will emerge at the postsecondary level and become the 'death stars' of traditional universities. The conventional wisdom was that large telecommunications and media companies would use their global Internet and satellite television capacities to provide higher education in addition to their entertainment programming. However, a 1998 Australian report (Cunningham *et al*, 1998) concluded that there was little evidence of this, and furthermore, that the media companies' interests are in the use of their networks to carry educational content that would come from other providers.

13. The other oft-touted source of looming threat to traditional institutions is that of the 'corporate university'. Some of the corporations, such as Motorola, call their training unit a 'university'. The fear is that they may begin to market their programmes beyond their own staff and, in the process, take enrolments away from the traditional institutions. While this is occurring to some extent, the marketing emphasis of these corporations tends to be on particular niche market specialities rather than on the broad spectrum of content coverage.

14. The perception that huge profits can be made using ICTs to market institutional programmes internationally has enticed many higher educational institutions to 'get into the game'. The results are often disappointing and expensive! Perhaps because of the limitations of what really can be done with the existing technologies, the market opportunities are niche in nature and the environment has become highly fragmented and competitive.

Looking forward

As stated previously, the international context of distance and open learning is extremely dynamic. Nevertheless, while any attempt to describe the future is speculative, it is essential that policy and strategic planners 'look through the windshield' as well as at the 'dashboard' and in the 'rear view mirror'. In the context of internationalization of open and distance learning, there are some developments that are having, or are likely to have, important effects on the process. Some of these will serve to relieve many of the constraints – the 'pull' factors. Others hold the promise of radically altering the manner in which we think of instructional materials and instructional design models. Taken together, they constitute an important set of considerations in the development of strategic plans:

1.   The phenomenon of the 'telecentre' or 'telelearning centre' is rapidly becoming an essential element in using ICTs in education. While it is not new in concept, in its current version it provides community-based access to both technology appliances (eg computer, telephones, television sets etc) and to network connectivity. This development is particularly important in developing countries where access to information and communication infrastructure is so restricted. The internationalization of distance and open learning has therefore been largely among those who do have such access. The development of these centres is well under way in many parts of the world (see Latchem and Walker, 2001) and it will surely expand the size of market opportunity overall as well as broaden the range of open and distance learning products that can be sold, leased, bartered and exchanged internationally.

2.   While the threat to the traditional institutional model from either the mega media corporations or the advent of the 'corporate university' has yet to materialize, there are some impressive consortia developing among some of the world's most prestigious universities that may well pose a threat. For example, EUOPACE 2000 involves 45 institutions plus private companies, research institutes and regional and national agencies. Their aim is to deliver lifelong learning through a virtual campus and distance education network. One would expect that their collective resources, augmented by the collective brand equity, would be attractive to learners around the world and will impact on the traditional educational models.

3.   Along with the development of institutional consortia, and in the vein of growing inter-institutional collaboration, there is growth in the number of

twinning partnerships between institutions of different countries. Sometimes this arrangement serves the purpose of allowing an institution from a developed country to work with an institutional partner in a developing country in order to be able to deliver programmes into that country more effectively. In other instances the purpose is to collaborate on the development of new programmes which will be offered jointly by the partner institutions.

4. The emergence of international 'credit banks' will help learners resolve the current limitations on credit transfer, improve portability of certificates and other credentials, and provide services for the assessment of prior learning. This will make it easier for students to take courses from a variety of international providers.

5. Developments on the technology side are continuing to have profound impacts. One of the current constraints is a lack of bandwidth for the distribution of multimedia learning materials. As a result, the pedagogical applications of the Internet are pretty well limited to text-based materials. Imagine the impact when that constraint is resolved. Imagine also the impact of wireless technology becoming widely available, particularly in developing countries. This promises a quantum leap in terms of the number of people gaining access to learning opportunities, thus broadening the scope of international activity in open and distance learning.

6. Perhaps of greatest significance is the emergence of what is being referred to as 'standards-based learning systems development'. This involves the organization of content into small objects in the form of learning outcomes and associating them with learning resources, activities and assessment strategies. Once developed, these learning objects can be stored in a database using a set of standards that enable the content to be shared among any institutions that use the same standards. Items can be re-aggregated according to the needs of any group of learners and the material reproduced in print, CD-ROM or Web-based delivery formats as appropriate. This work is being led by the Instructional Management Systems Group (IMS) which is a consortium that includes institutions, technology vendors and publishers. Some applications of the model are already under way at the Open Learning Agency of British Columbia (Porter, 2000). The availability of learning materials produced in this manner, based on a common set of standards that enable them to be shared, re-aggregated, and modified according to cultural difference, boggles the mind in terms of the impact on the flexibility and internationalization of learning. It heralds the realization of individualized learning on demand.

An epilogue

As open and flexible learning becomes more pervasive as a component of educational management and planning in the states and nations of the world, it becomes increasingly important, when discussing policies and strategies, to have a clear picture of the context within which they are intended to apply. Hopefully the trends and issues identified and discussed in this chapter will help readers think about the strengths, weaknesses, threats and opportunities that are present in their own context.

References

Cunningham, S et al (1998) *New Media and Borderless Education: A review of the convergence between global media networks and higher education provision*, Commonwealth of Australia, January

Latchem, C and Walker, D (eds) (2001) *Telecentres*, The Commonwealth of Learning, Vancouver

Porter, D (2000) *Learning in a Wired World: Moving beyond the course as the unit of learning*, Product Development and Research Group, Open Learning Agency, BC

Index